# DRIVING UNDER
# THE INFLUENCE
## *of*
# Angels

# DRIVING UNDER THE INFLUENCE
*of*
# Angels

## JAYNE HOWARD FELDMAN

ARE
PRESS

ASSOCIATION FOR
RESEARCH AND
ENLIGHTENMENT

A.R.E. Press • Virginia Beach • Virginia

A.R.E. Press
215 67th Street
Virginia Beach, VA 23451–2061

Feldman, Jayne Howard, 1951–
   Driving under the influence of angels / By Jayne Howard Feldman.
      p.      cm.
   ISBN 0–87604–445–3 (pbk.)
   1. Angels.  I. Title.
   BL477 .F45    2002
   291.2'15–dc21

                                                              2002010116

Cover design by Richard Boyle

# Dedication

*This book is dedicated to St. Joan of Arc,*
*whose inspirational words*
*"Forward with God!"*
*have been a rallying call of service for my life.*

# Contents

# *Foreword*

I was amazed by Jayne Howard Feldman the day I met her. Ten years later, I'm still amazed by her. Jayne lives in an unending flow of grace and inspiration from the angelic kingdom, which she bestows lovingly on everyone around her. Her work, like seeds, produces an incredible field of spiritual flowers wherever she goes. I have long thought that Jayne should record her experiences in a personal book, and I am delighted to see it manifested as *Driving Under the Influence of Angels*, a funny title from a funny and very wise soul.

I met Jayne and her companion, Walt Blatt, now deceased, a decade ago at a lecture I gave in Baltimore. I was a stranger in town, recently relocated after the disintegration of my marriage. I was immediately taken with Jayne's warmth, sparkly energy, enthusiasm, and most of all, her spiritual rapport with angels. Jayne and Walt befriended me, and I can honestly say that they, along with several other new friends, profoundly influenced the course of my life. Jayne helped me through some difficult times, and her friendship was one of the reasons why I decided to stay in Baltimore. Two years later, at another lecture (one I attended and did not give), I met my soulmate, Tom. We were thrilled to have Jayne marry us at a lovely ceremony at her country home.

After Walt's death from cancer, it was our turn to help provide support and friendship to Jayne. Her grief opened ways for her to move her work of service to a new and higher level. In the midst of her own trials, Jayne never stopped giving. Now she is blessed with a joyous marriage to her soulmate, Charles Feldman, who has brought a new stream of light and partnership into Jayne's work in the world.

Jayne tells these and many other engaging stories, along with the lessons and insights they provide, in this wonderful book. It's pure Jayne, one hundred percent gold. Jayne is constantly inspired with fresh and terrific ideas. I've lost track of the times I've said, "That's brilliant!" when she's shared yet another inspiration from the angelic host.

Over the years, I have watched Jayne work with individuals and audiences, and have shared the platform with her on occasion. She has a magic and is able to touch people instantly at a deep level in the heart. What's more, she knows how to make people laugh, and that is often when the real healing begins.

In *Driving Under the Influence of Angels*, Jayne writes that we are moving into the Grace Age. It is time for seekers to become doers. In every chapter, she provides a wealth of practical advice for healing, spiritual growth, and bringing more abundance into life—in short, how we can transform ourselves into "earth angels." She herself is a model to which we can all aspire: she listens to her guidance—and then she acts on it. Her trust in the unwavering and steady hand of God has taken her safely around the world in her service to others. Reading her life's journey, one can only marvel at how seamlessly it all unfolds, how everything—triumph and disappointment—meshes together with purpose.

The same purposeful unfoldment happens to us all when we make the choice to let God take the driver's seat. Jayne writes that angels must love mystery stories, because the guidance they provide is often in the form of clues rather than pat answers. Indeed, life would be much less rewarding if we had everything revealed to us without benefit of self-discovery. We often see just the bit of road in front of us and not the long road way ahead, or the stopping points along the way. Our wisdom comes from experience, and our experiences are the results of our choices. If we keep our spiritual eyes and ears open and trust that God will steer us straight, we receive the guidance that keeps us on the right road and leads us to have experiences that expand and strengthen us as souls.

Life in this body is precious, and short by any measure. Not a moment of it should be wasted. That doesn't mean that we must be constantly "on," but that we savor and appreciate what we do experience, even our times of rest, play, and relaxation, and that we see the presence of the Divine in everything.

I am proud and privileged to know Jayne Howard Feldman. She is an inspiration to me, and I am thankful that she is here to be such a powerful channel of angelic blessings.

—Rosemary Ellen Guiley, Ph.D.
Author, *The Encyclopedia of Angels* and
*Heart and Soul: A Spiritual Course for Meeting Your Perfect Soulmate*

MARYLAND
DUIANGEL

# *Introduction*

*I* *believe we carry within our* hearts a heavenly date book within which are written God's divine appointments in our lives. One of my appointments occurred when I met my first angel at the age of eleven. I was lying in my bed, not yet sleeping. From a corner of the room, a vaporlike energy began to pour in. The energy shape shifted into a being of light.

I began to sense the presence of a large being above my bed, watching over me when I went to sleep. The presence was so big that it first took on the appearance of a large white canopy of light that enveloped the entire ceiling of my bedroom. Initially there was only an awareness between us. I could see the being and I knew the being could see me. Neither of us spoke. After a while, there was no mistaking that it was an angel, because in my child's perception it began to look just like the angels I had seen on Christmas cards.

The message from the apparition was simply "I'm with you." I now know that I was being introduced to my guardian angel and that was to be the first of countless contacts. That divine appointment was not only to introduce me to the angel that God had given the charge of watching over me but also to introduce me to the gift God gave to me to communicate with angels.

The experience was truly an expansion of my consciousness. My guardian angel assured me vibrationally, with a loving energy that enveloped me like wings, not to be afraid of what I was experiencing. Things were never the same after that night. My guardian angel had always been near me and aware of me. What occurred that night was that I became aware of my angel and that my angel was always right beside me.

My childhood introduction to angels led me on what has become a lifelong interest in angels. I embarked on the study of angels and that research led to the writing of a heavenly handbook. It has been ten years since *Commune with the Angels* was first published by A.R.E. Press. I am blessed that it is now in its ninth printing and I give thanks to A.R.E. Press for their commitment to my message.

Since my first experience with my guardian angel, I have continuously interacted with the Angelic Kingdom. I hear angelic whisperings of inspiration, hope, guidance, and most important—love. This did not occur because I am special. It is because I have agreed to serve God alongside of the angels. My first encounter was simply the first step in remembering my service to God.

Everyone has a guardian angel. As I researched the angels and opened my heart fully to the gift from God that they are in our lives, I learned that I am not alone in my awareness of the angels' presence. There are—and have always been—other people who serve alongside the angels. Joan of Arc was one of these people within whose heart the invisible was made visible. Joan of Arc led an army under the influence of angels who were inspired by God.

*Driving Under the Influence of Angels* begins where *Commune with the Angels* ended. It has been an incredible decade filled with amazing "angelic assignments" which I share within these pages—many of which are revealed for the first time publicly.

I have come to know the angels as God's cosmic cheerleaders. They are messengers of God who radiate divine energy. They are streaming light beings. They can take on any form, from a stranger who changes the flat tire of your car to a song you hear on the radio when you need it. One of their missions is to inspire us to raise the quality of our lives through art, music, and literature.

I see the angels in many guises. Sometimes they are light energy that I know with my peripheral vision; sometimes they express themselves in human form; sometimes as a God-thought that is given to me like special delivery mail delivered to the mailbox of my brain.

I believe there is a great evolution of consciousness taking place. Part of this expanded consciousness is the expanded awareness that we are not alone. There truly *are* angels among us.

We are so much more than we ever imagined and God has blessed our lives with messengers who convey to us God's message found in Ephesians 5:1, "Be therefore Godlike, as beloved children."

As I have traveled the byways and highways of the United States, *driving under the influence of angels*, my service with the angels has led me to answering the call of being a blessing to dying people and their families. When I serve God through helping comfort those who are dying, I am truly never alone in the room with the person. On several occasions, those who have been unconscious have sat up and acknowl-edged the presence of angels and loved ones in spirit. One occasion I will never forget. I had been asked to be a part of a family gathering around the hospital bed of a young woman who was dying from can-cer. The family held hands, sang songs of inspiration, read from the Bible, shared prayer, and watched as the woman's breathing went through changes in sound. Following several moments of the woman's gasping for breath, an unmistakable change came over her and all of us in the room. Even though the dying experience was hers, we shared in the peace that permeated the room like the smell of honeysuckle in springtime. As all of us looked at each other and conveyed by our eyes that something was happening that was visible to her and invisible to us, the woman sat up slightly and pointed toward the end of her bed. Her face was aglow with light. Her words are etched in my heart, "Oh, look. The angels are here to walk me home."

It is my prayer that *Driving Under the Influence of Angels* will be a bless-ing to your spirit. God loves you and gives you so many precious gifts. "For he shall give his angels charge over you to keep you in all your ways." Just as God has created angels to be keepers of the stars in the heavens; God has made angels to be keepers of the stars on earth—*you*!

*Cupid's bow delivered a celestial invitation to you*
*Within these pages expose yourself to a heavenly point of view*
*Come learn from angels who navigate outer and inner space*
*Discover your origin as a member of God's Star Race*
*Fine tune your twinkling. Improve your glimmering. Let go and*
*really shine!*
*You're one with the stars and angels. You are truly* Divine!

*Angelic Blessings!*
Jayne Howard Feldman

# CHAPTER 1

# *Be an Angel Day*

On Sunday, August 22, 1993, thousands of people participated in a global heartlink celebrating the first annual Be an Angel Day. But I'm getting ahead of myself.

Following the publication of *Commune with the Angels* in October 1992, I was inspired by the angels with the message, "Do not rest on the laurels of a published book. There is additional service that needs to be done." The message I received from the angels did not identify the service, but rather how I would begin to move toward recognizing what that service would be. The angels must truly love reading mysteries because I have found that the assistance they give to me comes in the form of clues that they drop into my life. The clue I was given was to go to cemeteries to find and photograph angel monuments.

In the Baltimore area, near where I live, I was able to find some very old cemeteries that had angel monuments from the 1890s. Gifted stonecutters have sculpted incredible angelic beings from granite. As I looked into the faces of these granite angelic monuments, it was as if they came to life. I encourage you to seek out the cemeteries in your own community to see if there are similar angelic monuments waiting for you to discover them. The art seen in cemeteries is equal to the mastery found in museums.

I do not in any way consider myself a photographer, but the angels repeatedly encouraged me to go out and take photographs of these monuments. At the time of these inspirations I was dating Walt Blatt, the "angel man" of my first book, and often our dates would center around finding new cemeteries. When we visited the cemeteries we would be joyous over the discovery of angel monuments, which I photographed with black and white film. As I had the photographs developed I continued to inquire of Spirit, "What is this all about? What service are the angels guiding me to do that is mirrored to me in the granite figures?" Oftentimes we want to know the purpose of a particular activity in our life. Sometimes the answer is revealed to us in a holy instant. However, more times than not it is part of the journey and the activity quite simply is preparation for the next step. So here I am in the midst of the activity of photographing angel monuments and wondering, "Why am I doing this? Where am I going with this?" And yet I felt compelled to do it.

One day I received this wonderful imagery from the angels. They said we should view ourselves as gold miners. So, picture yourself having a little pan and everything that you do in your life is a sifting process; you are constantly sifting. Sometimes there's nothing but the sifting of sand taking place. Then one day you look down into your gold miner's pan and you find a nugget right there shining back at you. The gold in the pan is that which has always been inside of you waiting to be discovered. It takes a lot of sifting, and sometimes in our lives we almost throw out our gold with the dirt.

So the sifting in my life was tied in with my taking photographs of angel monuments. I am a person who loves to have focus in her life, so I put myself on Angel Monument Alert—always on the lookout for angel monuments. When I visited friends out of town, I would include them in the assignment and together we would find incredible granite monuments depicting angelic beings.

Now my curiosity grew as I sought information from the angels as to the purpose of the cemetery expeditions. In meditation I asked, "Am I going to create a book around the photographs?" Perhaps it will be called *Angels of the Cemeteries—Guardians of the Grave.* I even found a wonderful quote, "Angels of the Tomb," which I thought would beautifully tie in with this book:

---
❧

*"Immortal Hope dispels the gloom!*
*An angel sits beside the tomb."*

---

This quote by Sarah Flower Adams comes from her hymn "The Mourners Came at the Break of Day." The angels lovingly acknowledged my focus and commitment to the project and said quite simply, "Keep looking for angel monuments. Keep photographing what you find." So I continued my quest. Even in the uncertainty of not knowing why I was photographing angel monuments, I was filled with a certainty that I was doing God's Will.

One day I visited Emmitsburg, Maryland, where the National Shrine of Our Lady of Lourdes is located. I happened to be in Emmitsburg because Mt. St. Mary's College was the site of the yearly retreat of the Mid-Atlantic Region of the Association for Research and Enlightenment, Inc. (A.R.E.). The shrine is only a few miles from the college and includes a beautiful grotto in a wooded area. At the grotto I usually spend time in prayer and meditation. It is truly one of the most peaceful places on earth, and I feel blessed that my home is only forty-five minutes from the grotto. So, I am now able to visit it often. On this particular visit I came out of the grotto and realized that there was a cemetery nearby. I hadn't even noticed the cemetery as I drove into the grotto parking lot. And more important, I hadn't even noticed an incredible pair of angels that graced the entrance of the grotto, standing next to the cemetery. The figures were identical—each depicted a guardian angel with a precious child by its side. The child is looking up to the angel, who is pointing toward heaven. I remember taking the photograph and feeling that as I snapped the shutter I had captured an angelic "Kodak moment." When I picked up the film at the local camera store, I realized I had the missing piece of the puzzle. With this picture—which would become a poster—I was inspired with the thought to establish Be an Angel Day.

What the angels were doing by having me go to cemeteries was preparing me. They were positioning me to be on the lookout for angel monuments. The right one was going to be right in front of me—eventually. I just had to keep looking—and keep snapping. The monument at the grotto in Emmitsburg is symbolic of the inner child in each and every one of us and standing nearby—always—is our Guardian Angel, pointing out for us the direction we should look for support, answers, and strength—Godward.

Additionally I was given the date for the annual celebration of Be an Angel Day—August 22. There is a divine message in the selection of the date. August is the eighth month of the year. In numerology eight is symbolic of success, achievement, and fulfillment. If you take the figure eight and rest it horizontally, it creates the lemiscate—the infinity symbol. The service we send out from our hearts is not only a blessing to others but it comes back to bless us as well. The twenty-second was chosen because twenty-two is a master vibration number. It brings the message of the importance of our serving as an apprentice architect on earth alongside of God, the ultimate Master Architect. We are building a bridge according to God's will and plan. This is a bridge that supports the message of the Lord's Prayer: Thy Kingdom come; Thy Will be done on earth as it is in heaven.

Even though we are inspired by God to be blessings to each other every day of our lives, the annual celebration of Be an Angel Day serves the purpose of raising mass consciousness on earth to the awareness that we, too, are here to serve God—just like the angels. We, too, are ministering spirits to not only the human kingdom to which we belong but to all of God's kingdoms. This celebration is a nondenominational, nonprofit event. The whole purpose of the event is to encourage people to be like the angels—messengers of God's love and peace. There is no right or wrong way to celebrate this event.

While in meditation I was given a motto that was for the first celebration and for all future celebrations of Be an Angel Day: "Be an Angel. Do one small act of service for someone. Be a blessing in someone's life."

In preparation for the first annual Be an Angel Day, I distributed posters, flyers, and bumper stickers around the world during my travels in promoting *Commune with the Angels* and being a spokesperson for the Angelic Kingdom. Following the celebration on August 22, 1993, I received letters from "earth angels" who shared how they had celebrated the event. I counted twenty-two countries from which people had written or called me and described their celebrations, quite an interesting coincidence with twenty-two being the celebration date in August.

The mayors of Baltimore, Maryland, and Santa Cruz, California, issued proclamations, as did the governor of Maryland.

Angel services and parties were held around the world. People sent me church bulletins, press releases, and party invitations that they had produced, promoting the theme of doing one small act of service for someone. Angel food cake was served in abundance.

The *Washington Post* newspaper did a huge article in their religion section the day prior to the first annual Be an Angel Day. The *Herald Standard* in Uniontown, Pennsylvania, included it in their church briefs section on Friday, August 20, with a feature article about the event published a month prior.

Saint Mary's Parish of Rutherford, New Jersey, promoted it in their community by announcing it in their church bulletin. The Spiritual Frontiers Fellowship Buffalo Chapter devoted their entire newsletter to angels and promoted Be an Angel Day. Lower Saucon United Church of Christ in Hellertown, Pennsylvania, chose the theme of angels for their church service on August 22 in conjunction with Be an Angel Day and their service began with the words: "Be still within and without and experience the angelic wonder of God's love for you."

Ann Marie Acacio, Minister of Unity Center for Positive Living in Wilkes-Barre, Pennsylvania, not only promoted the event in the center's publication but also spoke about the event at the Sunday service.

Michelle Stelmach of Dudley, Massachusetts, sent me a photograph of how she got the Polar Corporation, a local bottling company that lists public service messages on their billboard, to promote Be an Angel Day, with a mention of it on that billboard two weeks prior to the event.

Thousands of commuters passed this sign twice a day, five days a week, and saw the message.

Michelle's meditation group got together on the afternoon of Be an Angel Day and had a group meditation. Michelle received a message that there would be a special sign from the angels showing that the angels appreciated all of our efforts in serving God as helpers to each other. Before the afternoon was over, the group saw a rainbow appear in the sky even though it had not rained.

A close friend of mine, Lucky Sweeny, who lived in Columbia, Maryland, organized a picnic to benefit the homeless. An Angel Day Celebration was held at the Westside Neighborhood Center in Santa Barbara, California, with speakers, angel messages, and arts and crafts, and all of the proceeds went to support the Information Press, which spreads God's light.

Jenny D'Angelo in Santa Cruz, California, organized the California Angelic Alliance, which sponsored an afternoon event in which participants were encouraged to come and share in the angels' love and radiant presence.

Sister Elizabeth of the Spiritual Center in Windsor, New York, shared a story with me that clearly illustrates the message of Be an Angel Day. She and another sister were organizing a dinner for some sixty people on August 22. They had cleaned and cooked and were feeling a bit overwhelmed. Just as they started to ask themselves how on earth they were ever going to get everything that needed to be done accomplished, two people drove up and said, "It's Be an Angel Day, and we're here to be your angels. How can we help you? Show us what to do." Sister Liz called me to exclaim, "It works!"

On August 22, I presented a five-hour workshop at the Lily Dale Assembly, a beautiful spiritual community located an hour's drive from Buffalo, New York. More than sixty people attended, some from as far away as Tulsa, Oklahoma. At the end of the day we wrote inspirational messages and affixed them to helium balloons and released them to be delivered by the angels to whoever needed to receive them. I was inspired to organize this activity because of a feature story I had seen on television prior to the first annual Be an Angel Day. It was the story of a young child whose father had been killed in an accident. The little girl's birthday was approaching, and this small child was asking her mother and grandmother if her Daddy in heaven would remember her, perhaps with a gift from heaven, as her Daddy had never forgotten her on her birthday. The adults didn't know how to respond to her question but were inspired to take the little girl to the father's gravesite and have her write a note to her Daddy and affix it to a helium balloon. The little girl sent her love note to her Daddy via the helium balloon and watched it head for heaven. There is no doubt in my mind that the balloon's flight was directed by God's angels. The balloon floated for thousands of miles and came down by a lake where a man was taking a walk. The man read the note and wondered how his own children, who were very close in age to this little girl, would be impacted by his death. He went home and shared the note with his family, and they were inspired to make this birthday special for this little girl. They agreed that the note had been given to them for a reason. They contacted the little girl and her family and stated that since there were no stores in heaven, the little girl's Daddy had guided the balloon to them; they had done the birthday shopping on his behalf. Their plans were to ship the presents to the girl; however, when the media learned of this incredible story of love, the media paid for the families to meet in person.

Kenneth J. Foreman shared the following story in the *Presbyterian Outlook* dated May 9, 1960. "In grandfather's time there used to be a song taught to little children:

---

*"I want to be an angel*
*And with the angels stand;*
*A crown of gold upon my head*
*And a harp within my hand."*

---

Foreman invited readers of his article to imagine standing at heaven's gate with the officer of the day, who is asking why you want to get in. "You might come up with the words of this song 'I Want to Be an Angel.' And then you might have to answer one more question:

What experience have you had?"

How can we be like God's angels? One of the ways is to have the attitude that everything we do we are doing for God and to God. The attitude with which we approach the world determines the kind of world that we are, in fact, going to see and experience in our own lives.

By practicing simple kindnesses toward each other, we are acting as messengers of love. No matter what happens to us in our lives, the angels encourage us to promote kindness, gentleness, tenderness, and compassion. Jesus taught us by example through his kindness to the poor and to the sick, the children, the prostitutes, the tax collectors that when you see with eyes of kindness there is no such thing as selective vision.

I encourage people that as Be an Angel Day approaches each year to look around their community with "Angel Eyes"—eyes filled with God's Light—to see where service is needed and know that God has sent you.

I received a letter from Kena Leek, publicist with the Random Acts of Kindness Foundation. She shared that after learning about Be an Angel Day, she was inspired to write because the Foundation and Be an Angel Day share the same values. She proposed the possibility of the two activities finding ways to join forces and work together for a kinder atmosphere and more participation in Be an Angel Day. I find it so uplifting that the promotion of the God ideals of kindness and service are bringing organizations together. Her letter conveys the message of looking for ways that we could join together to be an even larger blessing to more people.

There's a precious poem entitled "Only Seeds Sold Here," whose author is unknown. It goes as follows:

*In a dream I went into a shop*
*Behind the counter was an angel.*
*I asked: what do you sell here?*
*Everything you want, said the Angel.*
*Oh, I said. Is that so?*
*Then I would like peace on earth,*
*No more oppression, no more hunger,*

*A home for all fugitives . . .*
*Wait a minute, said the Angel,*
*You have misunderstood me:*
*We do not sell fruits here,*
*Only seeds.*

---

The angels provide us with God's "seeds" of inspiration. I was provided the seed for Be an Angel Day. I invite you to take this opportunity to still yourself and envision yourself entering a storefront. There is an angel behind the counter. The angel smiles at you and says, "Yes! It is planting time and the package of Godseeds designated for you is right here." You recognize that, just as for all the Johnny Appleseeds who have gone before you, it is your turn to plant seeds here on earth, so that trees of life may grow abundantly. You will plant the seeds and watch over them as they grow into the fulfillment of the dreams and visions we have for making this world a better place for all of God's Kingdoms. You rush to open the package of Godseeds and are surprised that on every little seed your name is written. You realize that every word you speak, every action you take—all the expressions of you are seeds of energy.

A book I have read and reread is Jean Giono's *The Man Who Planted Trees*. Jean Giono's story is a modern-day parable. I love it so much I even purchased an audio book version. It takes place in France in the twentieth century and is a story of a man who replants desolate areas with trees, one acorn at a time. Its inspirational message reminds us not to underestimate the difference to the planet we can each make.

We are evolving into a community of angels—heavenly and earthly angels existing together and serving God. I honor and acknowledge each of you for your willingness to participate as fully conscious beings. Just imagine yourself as a human computer and you have clicked the "OK," indicating to the Divine Power that it is OK for you to experience all the changes, all the energy, and all the acceleration at 100 percent capacity necessary for growth. And in agreeing to do this, you have joined the divine ranks of those whom angels refer to as Grace Seeds.

St. Thomas Aquinas in writing *Summa Theologica* in 1271 described grace as "nothing else but a certain beginning of glory in us." Even in these times of uncertainty, know with certainty that you are beginning or seeding glory to God. You have planted yourself here on earth to bloom and to "seed" others. Flowers are identified by a genus. Your genus is known as *Amazing Grace.*

As we look around us at all the things on the planet that reflect people's fears, pain, and separation from God, we may sometimes question the reality in believing it is possible for us to evolve into Super Beings—beings who fulfill Jesus' message, "All this and more you shall do." Yet it begins with a seed identity—the consciousness and acceptance of our very beings as seeds of grace. You may be experiencing dirt in every direction you look and even be questioning if you will ever see daylight. None of this changes your identity. You are seeds of the divine.

What does it mean to be Grace Seeds? The word "grace" originates from the Latin "gratia" or favor. A favor is a helpful act or service. As seeds of grace we manifest through our individual selves God's light, love, peace, and inspiration.

As we celebrate Be an Angel Day and its motto "Be an Angel," I encourage you to do one small act of service for someone. Be a blessing (grace seed) to someone. A grace seed is one who serves and in doing so anchors and plants on earth God's helpfulness made manifest in human form. I recently saw a wonderful quote on a greeting card: "How many angels are there? One that transforms your life is enough." You may be that one angel in someone's life. Plant yourself in life!

How can we align ourselves to the energies and vibration of grace in order to be accepting of our identities as Grace Seeds? Using the letters in the word itself, I would like to offer these helpful suggestions on how to embrace our identity as grace seeds and fill our every moment with GRACE.

*Grateful moments.* Whenever I speak to an audience, I encourage audience members to take time to have an attitude of gratitude. Give thanks for all the blessings in your life. Grace is a term for a small prayer or blessing before a meal. I say grace whenever I push my shopping cart down the aisle of a grocery store. We are so blessed with abundance in our country.

People often ask me, "What can I do to be closer to my Guardian Angel?" Your angel is never closer to you than when you are kneeling in prayer giving thanks to God for all the blessings in your life.

If we could shrink the earth's population to a village of one hundred people, keeping the existing human ratios the same, eighty would live in substandard housing; seventy would be unable to read; fifty would suffer malnutrition. If you have food in your refrigerator, clothes to wear, a place to sleep, you are richer than 75 percent of the world.

I also want to encourage readers to consider the vibration of "grace" in the word gratuity. People sometimes get all tied up in determining the amount of money for tipping—is it 15 percent or 20 percent? I encourage you to consider this as a solution: Give more than is expected of you. This is the way the divine operates in our lives. God gives us so much more than we ever expected, and how blessed we are because of God's infinite love.

One morning my husband and I went out for breakfast. Our waitress took our order and then shortly after helping us, she took the order for another table. Some time passed and she brought meals out to those at the other table who had been seated after us. In a few minutes the people at the table called to her attention that, as they started eating, they realized it wasn't their breakfast. The waitress took everything back and shortly returned with their meals. My husband was hungry and wanted to know where his breakfast was. I told him that I felt something was troubling our waitress and was causing her to make mistakes. I told him to give her his patience.

In a few minutes she came to our table and poured her heart out. She shared that her husband was going into the hospital that same day. She was very concerned about him, and she had mistakenly given the other table our breakfast. After they had started eating it, ours had to be redone in the kitchen. We both assured her that we totally understood and whenever the breakfast arrived would be fine with us. God gives all of us His eternal forgiving love. I truly believe we serve God by giving more forgiveness, more understanding, and especially more patience than expected.

*Receptive moments.* Live your life open to receiving all the blessings of grace that God bestows upon us each and every moment. These are truly moments of grace we are receiving and as they form hours and days, weeks and years, we are standing witness to what the angels have identified as the Grace Age. I am reminded of a time when I first was given that term by the angels to help me with an inspiration. I needed a term to replace "New Age" for there needed to be a healing around this terminology to describe this time period on earth. Whenever I was a guest on a radio program, it never failed that someone would call in and attempt to label me "New Age."

This labeling even occurred when I called an angel store located in Pennsylvania, about a half hour from my home. Several friends spoke of the store and mentioned that every other week there was a gathering where people shared angel stories. My friends encouraged me to call the store and offer my service in speaking as they felt I would be a blessing to the gathering. I followed up on their suggestion, and when I spoke to the storeowner, I offered at no charge to come and be a part of their wonderful inspirational gathering. The woman said to me, "We don't want you in our store. You're New Age."

I asked the angels, "Since everything began as a God–thought, and nothing is truly 'new,' how am I to describe this Age?" I asked for a term that I could use and this is the angelic inspiration I received: "Call it the *Grace Age* for it will only be by the grace of God that you get through it."

*Amiable moments.* I would like to divide "amiable" into three words: Am I able? Am I able to see myself as God sees me—full of infinite potential and possibilities. Additionally, amiable means being friendly. Through grace we befriend both ourselves and act as a friend to others. Life is meant to be a user–friendly experience. I've recently noticed that in an attempt to heal road rage, some states are posting signs encouraging people to be Driver Friendly to each other.

*Compassionate moments.* Compassion inspires us to commune or unite with our passion energy. There is a beautiful Sanskrit blessing that I say so often that friends of mine got together and bought me a tee–shirt with this message imprinted: Sat Chit Ananada. Translated it means "Be the fullness of your bliss or joy." Compassion originates from the Latin words "com" meaning together and "pati" meaning to feel. In being compassionate we give ourselves the experience of feeling together— together with the angelic heavenly host, with God, with Jesus, with the sacred inside of each and every one of us. If you have moments in your life when you feel far from being "together," allow yourself to think about what experiences you have had in your life that filled you with joy. What gave you bliss? Make time and devote energy to experiencing your bliss in this life. And make time for togetherness. Spend time together with God, together with nature, together with loved ones.

I have grown to love the word *together*. I feel so blessed to be serving God together with the angels. I feel so blessed to have the togetherness of my sweet husband, Charles Feldman, and the togetherness of family and friends and our two Jack Russells, Benny and Riot. It is a healing word that when used can make miracles happen. When you find yourself involved in a disagreement with someone, try the healing technique of asking, "What can we do together to come to a peaceful resolution of this problem?" Together is a word that heals like a pair of angel's wings as it makes people feel included. In the Book of Revelation, the angel that appears to John admonishes him when John attempts to bow down before the angel. The angel redirects John's worship to God, whom we glorify together and exalt as the angels do.

*Esthetic moments.* Take time to appreciate beauty in art and nature. Every child deserves to experience the arts. Food will sustain us as humans; yet it is art that inspires us to be Divine. When you make time to appreciate art, whether it is expressed as music, dance, poetry, or literature, you make time to appreciate a part of you that is the "muse" or the spirit of beauty and inspiration. You take time to experience the creator essence of yourself. And when you commune with the creator inside of you there is a potential for you to be inspired to create something beautiful in your own life that will be an inspiration to others who witness or are touched by your creativity. We are all artists and the years of our lives are canvases on which we create our realities with words, actions, and deeds. Beginning in 1994, the second year's celebration of Be an Angel Day, the angels have inspired me with a theme message for each particular year in addition to "Do one small act of service for someone. Be a blessing in someone's life." The additional messages were given to me because of the large number of newspapers and radio and television programs that have contacted me, asking how the public can participate in Be an Angel Day. The messages have been as follows:

1994—Lead with Your Light. An Angel Conference was held in Washington, D.C., and as part of that conference a procession of cars originating from Alexandria, Virginia, the site of the conference, drove through downtown Washington, D.C., on a Monday morning in rush hour traffic to the National Cathedral. The advertising slogan for the National Cathedral is: Only the angels have a better view of Washington. Those attending the conference came together in the Chapel of the Resurrection for meditation and prayer, focused upon peace on earth and honoring God's gift to us—a life filled with opportunities to serve. My car was the lead car. The angelic traffic directors arranged for me to lead the twenty-plus cars through Washington, and never once were any of our cars separated because of traffic lights. We drove as a steady procession of God light through our nation's capital with our intent being to lead with light the pathway to peace on earth.

1995—Be of Service to Those Who Are Shut In, Shut Out, Shut Off from Love. The message encouraged the public to visit nursing homes in their communities. I shared the message of opening our hearts and sharing ourselves with those confined to their home or to a hospital or nursing home. As a result of this effort, Be an Angel Day is promoted annually in the National Nursing Home Directory, and I cannot begin to express my heartfelt gratitude to all the activity directors who have created activities around Be an Angel Day. There are those who are confined who would welcome the gift of *you*. Give the gift of your listening ear—your open heart—your loving smile—your warm embrace.

In 1995 QVC promoted Be an Angel Day and sold angelic gift items all day long. In between each segment the program hosts reminded audience members that the message of the day was to "Be an Angel." As a result of the telecast, I received hundreds of phone calls from radio stations wanting to know more about Be an Angel Day.

1996—Blessed Are the Peacemakers. The message encouraged the public to write our servicemen and servicewomen around the world who are keeping peace. I distributed the APO addresses for the armed forces in Bosnia and encouraged people to send letters to these precious souls as their "angels," thanking them for keeping peace on earth.

1997—Have a Tree-mendous Be an Angel Day. The trees are the lungs of the earth. The trees do not exist because of us. We exist because God gave us trees. I encouraged the public to plant trees wherever children were, as a symbolic gesture of supporting the children on the earth and our desire to leave the earth in better condition than we found it. Additionally, I encouraged the public to plant a tree in memory of a loved one in heaven. Life is eternal! As trees are planted for the children of the earth and in memory of children in heaven, we are accepting that the circle of life is never broken. My service has expanded to include serving those who have children who now play in heaven with the angels, and I share this story in the chapter about Joshua's Lighthouse Angels.

In 1997 a national airlines promoted Be an Angel Day throughout its company as well.

1998—Your Life Is a Canvas: Paint a Beautiful World for the Children. I encouraged everyone to introduce children to art—through art classes, field trips to art museums, and hands-on art experiences. The theme of this year was accentuated by the appearance of Angels of the Vatican: The Invisible Made Visible—a ninety-eight-piece exhibit of art from the Vatican that visited five cities in the United States. My own beloved Walters Art Gallery of Baltimore, Maryland, hosted the exhibit during the holiday season in 1998. I take this opportunity to express my heartfelt gratitude to Art Services International of Alexandria, Virginia, for making this exhibit a reality and, in particular, Joseph W. Saunders, chief executive officer of Art Services International. It was the best Christmas present I could have ever received. I organized a trip for the Angel Heights Angel Collectors Club members to visit the exhibit while it was in Baltimore. Additionally, I would personally spend every Wednesday evening at the museum just being with the art. The art show allowed me the opportunity to more easily and openly communicate with the angels. The ease of communication was supported by the high vibrational frequencies brought under one roof by this powerful gathering of angelic art, much of which was painted with gold. I enjoyed seeing which of the paintings attracted the most attention. Without question the painting most enjoyed was *Saint Matthew and the Angel*, by Guido Reni. The painting of an angel assisting St. Matthew in the writing of the gospel held people's attention the longest. It conveyed the inspirational exchange that exists between humans and angels. The painting shows St. Matthew writing, yet his eyes are not focusing on the paper—but rather on God's inspiration in the expression of the angel. I love teaching a class entitled "Writing with Spirit," and this painting by Guido Reni expresses divinely inspired creativity beautifully!

I also encouraged every individual to consider "commissioning" one of today's artists to create something beautiful and then to gift it to oneself. We would not have the great works of art from the masters of former times were it not for people of that age who believed in the artists and commissioned them. It is important to invest in our personal life and at the same time support beginning artists by commissioning them. You may be supporting someone who in generations to come will be looked upon as the Raphael of our lifetime.

1999—Make a Joyful Sound in the Key of You. In *Commune with the Angels* I shared the message that when something is right, when something is true, your whole body chimes in the *key of you*. The message urged the public to make a joyful sound on the earth—by filling one's life with joy and letting that joy overflow through sound. The sound could be words of love, chants of inspiration, songs of hope, childlike giggles of delight, or joyous laughter. Additionally, the sound of harp music was an important message for this year's celebration. I asked the public to open their hearts and spirit to the sound of the harp. I will share more details of the blessing energy of the sound of harps and the healing role of harps in the chapter "A Sound Choice."

2000—What Will *Your* Verse Be? The theme came from Tom Schulman's *Dead Poets Society*. I share Schulman's words expressed by one of the movie's characters, John Keating: "We don't read and write poetry because it's cute. We read and write poetry because we are members of the human race." And the human race is filled with passion—poetry, beauty, romance, love; it is for these that we are alive. To quote from Whitman: "O me! O life! Of the questions of these recurring; of the endless trains of the faithless—of cities filled with the foolish, what good amid these, O me, O life?" Answer: "That you are here—that life exists—that the powerful play goes on and you may contribute a verse. What will your verse be?"

The message "What will *your* verse be?" was beautifully enhanced by the service of Robert Pinsky, American's Poet Laureate. At Centennial Hall, Augustana College, in Rock Island, Illinois, Robert Pinsky shared in a lecture, "The medium for a poem is not words, not lines. It is the reader's body, a column of breath shaking the reader's organs. Your breath becomes the poet's medium. So it is highly individual. We crave that, and that is why poetry is on the rise. Poetry is a vocal art."

Pinsky encourages "Favorite Poem Readings" in communities across America, offering the public an opportunity to read a favorite poem and share why it's a favorite. He created the Favorite Poem Project (www.favoritepoem.org) and from this project was birthed the book *American's Favorite Poems—The Favorite Poem Project Anthology*. I believe that remembering favorite poems opens a door to self-discovery

of our soul's verse. Robert Frost's "Stopping by Woods on a
Snowy Evening" is a "Jayne-favorite" poem. In traveling the
byways and highways of America with the angels, I have
many times said to myself, "The woods are lovely, dark and
deep. But I have promises to keep. And miles to go before I
sleep, And miles to go before I sleep."

Erica Jong said that the poet is caretaker of the soul. So
tap into your inner poet. Think about poems you remember from childhood, poems you had to memorize and re-
cite while in school. Give yourself permission to express
your divine verse and in doing so you are caring for your
soul and the soul of the earth.

2001—Sacred Shapes in Sacred Space. The message was
connected to a quote by poet John Neihardt in Black Elk
Speaks. "A prophetic boyhood vision is recounted of an old
Sioux medicine man, Keeper of the Sacred Pipe of his
people, who at one point declared that in imagination he
had seen himself standing on the central mountain of the
world . . . and while there, 'I was seeing in a sacred manner,'
he said, 'the shapes of all things in the spirit, and the shape
of all things as they must live together, like one being. And
I saw that the sacred hoop of my people was one of many
hoops that made one circle, wide as daylight and as star-
light, and in the center grew one mighty flowering tree to
shelter all the children of one mother and one father.'"

In 2001 the angels were inspiring us to see in a "sacred
manner" the "shape of all things as they must live together,
like one being." The message for Be an Angel Day 2001 was
to look for ways that many hoops could come together to
make one circle.

We are living in times of great openings. The angels serve
God as guardians of these glorious thresholds of discoveries. These are discoveries being made in both inner and
outer space. We have the choice to open our minds and
hearts and spirits to the reality of oneness or to remain
close-minded, following the paths of the dogma of bigotry,

intolerance, and hatred. Through opening ourselves up to unlimited expansive realities, such as sharing sacred space with the Angelic Kingdom, we allow ourselves sacred space in which to see more, sense more, feel more of the infinite around us and within each of us. As we open ourselves to that which we initially perceived as outside of us—or outer space—we simultaneously open more deeply and profoundly the sacred inner space within us.

When I was hosting a Be an Angel Day celebration on August 22, 2001, I shared the message that when things change their shape on the earth, remember that one shape that is eternal is the circle. The circle is the symbol of God, and when we come together in a circle of love, we are letting God guide us through whatever changes we are experiencing. Little did I know how prophetic my words were until reflecting upon them after the horrific tragedy of September 11.

Up until then, I was also unaware of a certain legion of angels in our midst. I have always believed the words of Hebrews 13:2, "Be not forgetful to entertain strangers: for thereby some have entertained angels unawares." Yet on September 11 I would witness them en masse as would all of America. These angels weren't wearing wings but rather the uniforms of the New York City fire and police departments. On September 11, 2001, I watched firemen and policemen answer the ultimate call of service—laying down their lives to rescue as many lives as possible. I was humbled by the greatness of their service when I saw a video of firemen going into the South Tower of the World Trade Center. As I watched this video several months after, I knew these brave individuals had been photographed going into "the valley of the shadow of death." These brave souls did not fear death for they eternally embody the light of service. I believe even though they closed their eyes to earth and opened them to heaven, they in some way continue to serve. Service was in their blood here on earth;

service is in their spirit in heaven.

In looking at the anagrams from the world *America*, I observed the words *I am race*. I asked myself, "What race of beings would define the diversity of our population into one nation?" After September 11, I answered my own question from what I learned from the firemen and policemen who died helping others. I am an American. I am a member of the Grace Race. God's grace was shed upon our nation. It wasn't delivered by a member of the heavenly host from a celestial realm. God's grace was shed upon us by the firemen and policemen who shed lives for others. God bless them and the members of their brotherhood across America—a brotherhood whose members continue to serve as earthangels. After that day, no one need ask if there are angels among us. I encourage everyone to say a prayer of thanks to God every day for these precious earthangels in uniform.

Thursday, August 22, 2002, marked the tenth annual Be an Angel Day. As I promoted the celebration of a decade of angelic inspiration, I shared that within the number "10" we have "1"—the symbol of individuality; and "0"—the symbol of God—the infinite. The two numbers together create a message of the "1" moving forward with God right beside us.

The theme for the tenth annual Be an Angel Day was revealed to me while reading Robert J. Morgan's *The Red Sea Rules*. Robert Morgan shares ten inspirational "rules" that we can learn from Moses' and the Israelites' experience of being caught between "the devil and the deep Red Sea."

One of the ten "Rules" is to "Envision God's enveloping presence." So when life is overwhelming you and you feel caught between the rock and the hard place, or in the case of the Israelites, trapped between the armies of the Pharaoh and a Red Sea that looks uncrossable, think of yourself as a "10." You are the "1" who is facing the illness, the problem, the divorce, the challenge. However, you are not facing it alone. Right beside you is God. Let yourself feel God's enveloping presence come over you. God's enveloping presence is a peace that is calming, soothing, and comforting. It is a peace that fortifies you and enables you to face whatever you are facing in your life. God is with you.

The message Spirit asked me to convey in promoting the tenth annual celebration was to convey to friends and family—people who are facing challenges, dangers, and strife in their lives—that we are right beside them enveloping them with our love. Our love can be an enveloping presence in the lives of others just as God's love is an enveloping presence in all of our lives.

I know if my own life when I have had to do something for the first time, it was comforting when someone else was there. Sometimes it was a stranger who was going to have the same medical procedure that I had to go through. As I think back over these incidents in my life, I wonder if it wasn't one of God's angels in disguise, reassuring me that God was with me and His presence was enveloping me.

Think about those around you who might have recently learned they are being laid off from work; someone who is in the midst of a divorce; someone who has recently been diagnosed with cancer; someone who has recently lost a loved one. Think of how they might feel they are all alone. Now let God inspire you as to how you can be God's angelic messenger to this person. Think of how you can convey to this individual that God is with them every step of the way.

Open yourself to ways to *Be an Angel*. Do a small act of service. Be a blessing in someone's life. Donate blood. Work in a soup kitchen. Grocery shop for a shut-in. Write someone in prison. Organize a food drive. Scrub graffiti off a building. Plant a garden in an abandoned lot. Become a volunteer firefighter. Drop off old clothes, blankets to a homeless shelter. Give toys to a children's hospital. Staff a suicide prevention hotline. Teach an adult to read. Be a Big

Brother or Big Sister to a child. Be a mentor. Recycle. Work
at a battered women's shelter or rape crisis clinic. Become
involved in Meals on Wheels. Play with the dogs and cats
at the local animal shelter. Become involved in tree-plant-
ing programs in your community. Encourage restaurants to
save leftovers for organizations such as Share Our Strength.
When you go card shopping, think of someone who might
need a message of hope and encouragement.

Diodicus in *Spiritual Perfection* (fifth century) wrote, "Usually grace begins by illuminating the soul with a deep
awareness with its own light." Create time and sacred space
to discover, explore, and get to know your own inner light.
And once you do, let it shine! I believe the angels are messengers of God's grace. They illuminate our souls through
healing, inspiration, and love so we become aware of our
own light.

In aspiring to serve God in cooperation with the angels,
it's important not only to think about the good we can do,
but also to make certain that we do no harm to others.

One day I received a phone call from an acquaintance. I
was not home, so the woman left me the following message, "Hi, Jayne, this is Maxine. I had a dream about you
last night. You are going to discover you have a lump on
your breast; it's going to be cancerous. I just want you to
know that I am here for you." This is a perfect example of a
what I call a drive-by psychic shooting. Needless to say I
was stunned by her message. Even though I am one who
supports Carl Jung's teachings that all characters in our
dreams mirror parts of ourselves, and as such the dream
had symbolic meaning for Maxine and not me, I still was
unnerved. I thank God for knowing this was going to happen before I knew it. I had been inspired to set up a breast
examination that was scheduled for that week. From the
examination I was found to be in picture perfect health. As
people open to their intuitive gifts, it is sometimes tempt-
ing to give people messages to demonstrate psychic prow-

ess. However, it is important that the person receiving the messages really wants them. Always ask before blurting a message out. Additionally, do not give any message that could be harmful. Scaring a person to death is harmful.

In my travels as a public speaker, I meet many people whose service is healing. Following one of my lectures, I received a kind letter from a healer who shared that he had been inspired by my talk. In closing, the person shared he did healing and prayer work and he would feel blessed if I ever needed his support. At the time of receiving this letter, I had Walt on everybody's prayer list because he had been diagnosed with inoperable cancer and I believe prayer can move mountains. So I wrote this individual and asked if he would place Walt on his prayer list. I share this story because it is another example of only giving people what they ask for. I had written and asked for prayer support.

I got a letter back from the individual saying that he could not offer prayer for Walt's healing because he had checked with the doctors in spirit that he worked with and had been told that Walt was going to die. The person then proceeded to give me a day that was going to be the day Walt died. Can you imagine opening your mail and getting a letter that reads, "I'm sorry but I can't help pray for Walt because he's going to die and this is the date he is going to die."

The shock of the letter threw me into a tailspin. It truly tested my faith. I could feel the fear energy rising inside of me. I had to get a grip on myself. I didn't want to energize the fear. I was inspired by the angels to take down a picture of Jesus, by artist Nanette Crist, that I have hanging where I can look right into the eyes of Christ—His incredible blue eyes. I got the picture and sat on the sofa in my home, and I sobbed and sobbed and sobbed before Jesus. The more I looked into His eyes the more I became aware that His energy was pouring into my heart. It was comforting. It was peaceful. It was Jesus to the rescue.

Then He spoke these words to me: Who are you loving Walt for? Are you loving him for yourself or are you loving him for God?

Very quickly and honestly I replied to Jesus: I'm loving him for myself. And I don't want him going anywhere!

Jesus said: Really, Jayne?

There was a silence as Jesus gave me sacred space to contemplate my words. This was long before the television show *Do You Want to Be a Millionaire*. However, I know Jesus was asking me, "Jayne, is that your final answer?"

I then replied: No. I know I am loving Walt for God. I know we are stewards. We do not own people, and we cannot hold onto people when it is for their highest good to go home to God. All that I do, I do for God. I am being God's messenger of love to Walt at this time in his life.

Jesus then smiled at me and said: Then, Jayne, let God be God. Don't give your power to someone else.

That's what I had done. By energizing fear I was saying that the person who wrote the letter to me knew more than God. In all the healing acts we do in service to God, we must always ask ourselves: Are we harming anyone? Is anything that we are doing in any way going to be a harmful act or hurtful act?

Every year there will be new inspirations around the celebration of Be an Angel Day. However, the core message of this divinely inspired event is service. Be an Angel Day is a day to serve God together with the angels by looking for ways to be a blessing in someone's life. When someone you know is experiencing the "dark night of the soul," remember the light you have that has been given to you by God is for helping to turn any darkness here on earth into light. Shine light upon someone's path to help them find their way. Give others a track of light—just like the angels do for us. I once read the following church inscription:

*I will not wish thee riches*
*Nor the glow of greatness,*
*But that wherever you go . . .*
*Your path shall be a track of light,*
*Like angels' footsteps passing through the night.*

Pour forth your light. Shine brightly in all that you do.
Be an angel to someone today. Do one small act of service
for someone. Be a blessing in someone's life.

# CHAPTER 2

# Bend in This Wind

*A*ngel Man, Walt Blatt, who I met on March 1, 1990, and I shared many angelic adventures together, including exploring cemeteries in search of angel monuments as I shared earlier. Throughout our relationship, we faced together the challenge of Walt having had both of his kidneys removed because of cancer and the continuous growth of the cancer cells. Walt was an incredible blessing in my life. The greatest gift he gave to me was the gift of being witness to his dying.

On March 1, 1995, at 1:11 a.m. at Angel Heights, precious Walt closed his eyes to earth and opened them to heaven. Walt came to my home Friday, February 24, because that is where he wanted to die. On Monday, February 27, we were visited by a hospice nurse and as she looked around at the hundreds of angels in my collection, she said to Walt, "When it is time, this is where I want to come, too! What an incredible place!" Walt smiled and said, "That is why I am here." The nurse went on to tell Walt that she, too, collected angels. Walt smiled and said, "Why am I not surprised?"

Several days before his death, during the early morning hours, Walt awoke from dreaming. I was by his side, and he looked at me and said, "You are going to be invaluable to the hospice program." I reached for his hand and said, "Only because you allowed me to walk this final sacred walk with you. You have given me the gift of sharing this experience with you." He smiled and said, "Don't forget to use music in your work. The music is important." I agreed and asked, "Will you inspire me from heaven as to the music to use?" He nodded and drifted into a dream. I am convinced that Walt was instrumental in introducing me to the harp in the months following his death.

The day before his death the angels told me that a wind would soon be blowing through the house. It would be a wind that would take Walt home to God. They told me that I would need to be like a willow and bend in the wind. I could not hold onto Walt but needed to let him go home to God. At the conclusion of the conversation with the angels, I wrote this poem to help give me the courage to deal with what was rapidly approaching.

### Bend in This Wind

*The angels are coming; they'll soon be here.*
*'Swing lo sweet chariot' for my Walt Man, so dear.*
*I can feel approaching the gentle winds of love*
*That will carry my darling Walt safely to his home above.*
*The winds will lift him up and take him away from me,*
*And heaven will instantly heal him in the name of the Trinity.*
*But I must bend like a willow when these Angelic winds blow through*
*And surrender to God's Will; accepting my beliefs as true*
*That life IS eternal and Walt's with the Angels on Heaven's side,*
*And one sweet day in spirit together we will abide.*

Walt and I were blessed to have had time to say everything we wanted to say to each other and to reminisce about the five incredible years we spent together. We did that on Sunday, February 26. On Monday I told him how much I would miss him, and he replied, " I cannot talk about it anymore." I was not happy about that, as I wanted to talk about it up until his last breath. The angels comforted me in telling me that Walt could no longer focus on that which would keep him here. His sights were set forward—God-ward—heavenward. He had to focus on going home and I needed to recognize my role was now to help him do that.

The angels made that even clearer to me in another reflection they gave to me. I had gathered together all the photographs that Walt and I had taken of our many angelic adventures together over the past five years. I had dropped them off at a video company and a video was in the works. I realized that the video would not be finished in time for Walt to see it. I said to the angels, "Oh no! The video won't be ready in time! Walt won't get to see it!" They replied, "He could not watch that video. It would rip his heart out. He has to be free to go home. The video is for you. It will be a healing for you when you watch it."

My service in being beside Walt was not one that I performed alone. Of course, the angels were there, too. Additionally something had happened two weeks prior to his death that made me aware of those waiting to greet Walt in heaven. I had taken Walt to the Greater Baltimore Medical Center in Towson, Maryland, to receive a radiation treatment for a brain tumor. Walt was resting in a wheelchair and he was facing me. I looked up and saw in spirit a woman that I knew without a shadow of doubt was Walt's mother. I knew this even though I had never met his mother, as she was deceased. I didn't speak out loud as I didn't want to shock Walt. Speaking through inner thought, I asked, "Have you come for Walt?" I thought his mother was present because Walt was going to make his transition in the hospital. She replied, "Not now. I am here to make you aware that we are all waiting for Walt. Take him as far as you can and we will do the rest." Her words were so comforting and they brought to mind a wonderful rainbow bridge. I would walk Walt to the middle of the bridge and say goodbye and his mother would meet him with open arms and walk him over the bridge to "the other side." I am known for pushing the envelope, for wanting more information than necessary; so I asked Walt's mom, "Can you tell me when he will die?"

She lovingly replied, "It is not for you to know." At that moment I heard my Angel Team chime in, "Good try, Jayne!"

As I thought back over all the things I observed Walt doing the five years we spent together, I realized that here was a beautiful man whose everyday actions spoke the words: "God, you can count on me to get things done on earth!" Walt was truly a mover and a shaker. And on March 1, 1995, at 1:11 a.m., his daughter Gibby and I heard God whisper back, "And you, my beloved child, can count on me!"

I was so thankful that Walt allowed me, with his daughter, Gibson Bell, to be a part of his dying experience. As I shared earlier, Walt came to my home, Angel Heights, the last Friday in February 1995 to live his last days. Tuesday evening he asked Gibson to stay the night with us. As Gibby had come to visit with her daughter, Nikki, I asked him if she had time to take Walt's young granddaughter home. He said that she did. So Gibby went home to take care of the family and then returned to Angel Heights around 8:30 p.m. While she was gone I said to Walt, "It's to-night, isn't it?" He replied matter-of-factly, "Yes." I said, "It's not going to be until after midnight." He nodded yes. When the clock moved past midnight the day would become March 1, which was the day five years prior in 1990 that Walt and I began our relationship together. Somehow, five years earlier, when I learned of the seriousness of his cancer I knew I would be by his side when he died. I was just keeping a divine appointment that Walt and I had etched in our date books somewhere in time.

At a Thanksgiving celebration at Walt's vacation home, Leaf Lake Lodge, in the beautiful hills of West Virginia, Walt sat at the head of the table surrounded by oodles of family and friends who all adored him. When we went around the table and gave thanks for the blessings in our lives, Walt paused and looked at me on his right and Gibby on his left and said, "I am grateful for being here with the two women I love by my side." He would choose those two same women to be by his side when he died.

At around 12:30 a.m. Wednesday morning, Walt's breath became ac-celerated. He was fully aware and conscious during his transition. Gibby and I held his hands and up until the final twenty minutes he had asked that each of us be massaging a foot. For those of you who know

reflexology you can understand the assistance this brought him in relaxing his body. Gibby and I took the role of breathing coaches—much
as husbands provide wives at childbirth. We were telling him, "You can
do it." We prayed with him. We comforted him at this time of transition
and uncertainty. We encouraged him to go to the light, to go to God. At
1:11 a.m. he released my hand; he released Gibby's hand and took his
final breath; and in that holy instant he was with God. Interestingly
enough, just after he released our hands and prior to his final breath, he
crossed his arms across his chest. I never knew what that meant until
years later while speaking at a conference on stage with someone who
translated with sign language. There I discovered that *love* is communicated with arms crossed across the chest. At the holy moment of Walt's
death the room was filled with an incredible energy of love, peace, and
stillness. Gibby and I looked into each other's eyes and in unison rejoiced, "He did it!" Walt died the same way he had lived—fully alive!
Gibby and I both knew without a shadow of a doubt that he was safe in
the arms of God—fully healed from cancer and filled with enthusiasm
for his new life.

I also wish to share that prior to Walt's dying experience, Gibby and
I had the television set on and were watching TV with Walt resting
peacefully. At around midnight the angels told me to turn off the TV
and put on music that would assist Walt. A few weeks earlier I had
presented a workshop hosted by Marta Robinson in Centreville, Virginia. Marta told me about a new tape entitled, "Ascension Harmonics."
When I heard the tape, I knew I was going to need it for something. I
bought a copy of the tape and had not listened to it until that evening
when I knew I had purchased it for Walt's transition. This tape is seventy minutes on each side, and it played from 12 midnight to 1:11 a.m.
The tape ended exactly when Walt closed his eyes to this world and
opened them to the next. As Walt had shared with me several days
prior to his death: "Don't forget the music. The music is important."

Music is so very important in the dying experience. I will discuss the
role the harp plays in a future chapter; however, take your cue from the
person who is dying. I remember reading an obituary, which mentioned
that a Catholic priest had died with the Alleluia Chorus playing in the
background. I have a feeling he heard it playing not only on this side

but on the other side as well.

About six months prior to Walt's death, he and I went to visit Rev. Reed Brown, pastor of the Arlington Metaphysical Chapel in Arlington, Virginia. Reed is a truly gifted medium and inspiring pastor. It is my belief that mediums are born with this gift, and Reed is someone whom God has blessed with this ability. There are many wonderful mediums who have gained public recognition through television programs. Rev. Reed Brown was one of the pioneers who blazed the trail with Spirit that allowed others to follow, and he began blazing that trail at a young age. God has given Rev. Brown a "private line" to heaven and because of this I have guided people to him. The messages Rev. Brown "retrieves" from heavenside are a gift of healing to those who make an appointment with him.

When Walt was a young child he unfortunately was the first person to discover that his grandfather had committed suicide. It was something that impacted him tremendously. He adored his grandfather and treasured the love and fun times the two of them shared. He never understood why his grandfather had made this choice to end his life. I knew that in order for Walt to have a smooth transition it was important for him to have closure on this concern. I also knew I was not the person who could do it. I talked to Walt about Rev. Brown and indicated that if and when he wanted to have an appointment, I would make the arrangements. In the early summer of 1994 Walt expressed a desire to meet with Rev. Brown. Following the session, Walt asked that I listen to the taped reading, as he was quite frankly speechless.

When you visit Rev. Brown you are given a piece of paper that is called a billet. You write on that piece of paper up to three names of people you love and care about in heaven, and you also are able to write one question that you sincerely want God's insight on for your life. Walt wrote simply his grandfather's name, Carl Blatt. He also asked for insight about his courageous battle with cancer. You then are ushered into Rev. Brown's office. He places the billet in your hand—never opening the piece of paper—it always remains folded and closed. Rev. Brown says a prayer of honor to God and asks to do God's will and service in the session. Rev. Brown immediately expressed that there was someone named Carl standing in spirit right behind Walt. He then identified two other people that Walt knew and said that the three of them had something in common. Walt knew immediately the common denominator. These three people's lives had ended by suicide. Grandfather Blatt then spoke personally to Walt and expressed his sadness that Walt was the one who had found his body. He asked for forgiveness for that happening and then went on to indicate that there had been a severe chemical imbalance within his body that had created within him a feeling that there was no other way to heal himself except through taking his physical life. He emphasized that he had received healing on heaven's side. And then Grandfather Blatt addressed Walt's illness. He said, "Walt, you are going to live longer than the doctors think and longer than you think. And when it is your time to die you will die the same way you have been living your life on earth—graciously." That statement became Walt's greatest source of inspiration. Even though he was uncertain about the dying experience, he was certain how he was going to do it—with grace! Walt blessed me with the gift of witnessing a man who lived and died consciously—and who lived and died with grace.

The day after Walt's death, Sister Paula Matthew, csj, of the Spiritual Center in Windsor, New York, received a phone call from our mutual friend, Lucky Sweeny, that Walt had died early in the morning at Angel Heights. Sister Paula felt the angels wanted to give her a message of comfort to deliver to me. Instead of words, an incredible computer painting came through. I refer to the painting as an expression of evolutionary angel art. The painting clearly depicts Walt heaven bound, as it shows Walt's spirit leaving the earth. By his side are two angels, representing Gibby, his daughter, and me. Sister Paula had no knowledge of who was with Walt at the time he died. The painting shows the two angels with an electrified energy. Gibby and I both felt a powerful surge of electrical energy go right through our bodies at the moment Walt took his last breath. This painting clearly captured the feeling we experienced. I especially rejoiced when I saw the angel art, as Walt's lungs are totally white—healthy and clear—free of all cancer. And Sister Paula didn't know why, but the angels had guided her to draw little threes in the kidney area of his body. I knew what it meant. As the angels had told me just days before Walt's death, Walt was instantly healed in the name of the Trinity and the healing went straight to the original source of the cancer—which was in the kidneys. The background of the paint- ing is comprised of glorious colors and images that I know in some way gave all of us a sneak peek at what Walt saw as he crossed over the rainbow bridge into God's arms.

I want to emphasize one of the most important lessons I learned from Walt and the angels during Walt's time of dying. Dying is a per- sonal experience and when it is possible, let the person who is dying tell you what they want or don't want you to do as a witness. It is their experience.

As I mentioned earlier, Walt and I had an opportunity to not only look back over our time together but also to review Walt's entire life. After Walt's death, I met a lovely woman who is a teacher of a healing technique. Her name is Dorothy Daniel and her technique, known as Tunneling, assists the dying person with detaching from the physical identity in order to birth the light identity. Dorothy is truly an earth angel and has given her blessing that I share the following information about tunneling. At the back of this book is contact information for this precious woman. As Dorothy describes tunneling, it is a gift that you bring to your loved ones. When you work with individuals in tunnel- ing, each color of their tunnel represents a different stage of their life. In so many near-death reports, people who have had the experience talk of going through the tunnel. The tunnel is the key component in Dorothy's technique. As people connect with each color or stage of their life they are freeing themselves of attachment to anything that would keep them from going home to God.

Dorothy encourages those who use the tunneling technique by leav- ing the tape for them at night so that they may add to it if they feel inspired to do so. When the actual dying or transition time comes, you can repeat everything to the person that they have told you and have recorded on the tape. Tunneling gives you the most sacred role of hon- oring the person and their life experience and assisting them as an Angel of Freedom. You help them come out of the cocoon of earth to spread wings of light in heaven.

When you have a conversation with the dying during the tunneling exercises, ask who they want to be waiting for them on the other side.

And if they are conscious during their dying experience, bring forth this name as someone who is waiting to greet them.

Once the person has passed, give the tapes to whomever they wanted to receive the tapes after their death. If they want the tapes to be buried with them, follow their instructions. If they request they be destroyed, destroy them.

The colors of the sections of the tunnel coincide with the chakra colors. The chakras are energy centers in our body. The colors are red, orange, yellow, green, blue, indigo, and amethyst. The white energy is that which is experienced by the dying person at the holy instant of transition.

Your role is to create conversation and dialogue around each of the stages to help the individual experience completeness with the life experience.

---

**Red Stage**—*When Mother carried them; this is one state that does not last long; ask about how Mother felt about their birth. How was the delivery, and so on.*

**Orange Stage**—*When they first realized they were here on earth; this stage can last a little longer. When they first started to walk and talk. What were their favorite games. Who were their first friends. Early childhood memories.*

**Yellow Stage**—*School years. Teachers they remember, subjects they took in school, schoolmates. Family members. This is one of the longer stages of the tunneling experience. Did they follow their dreams? Was this a good time for them?*

**Green Stage**—*This is the stage filled with memories of firsts. First job, love, career, car, marriage, or relationship, first pet. This is much longer and can blend into the blue stage of their tunnel.*

**Blue Stage**—*Attitude right before illness struck. Thoughts on life and family and friends. Thoughts about their experiences on earth. Work. Self. Have they had an attitude change in their life? What information would they like to share with family, friends, and co-workers?*

Indigo Stage—*How do they feel about the current illness? How has the illness affected them physically, mentally, emotionally, spiritually? Ask about any other memories they would like to share. Any special messages they would like to be put onto the tape and desire to have shared with others—if so—whom are they to be shared with and when?*

Amethyst Stage—*Who do they want at the back of the tunnel and why? Arrange what they want to have at their funeral. Are there any requests they want to make certain are fulfilled?*

---

I was fortunate enough to have the opportunity to attend a tunneling workshop led by Dorothy Daniel. During the workshop we each teamed up with someone we didn't know and took one another through the tunneling experience. It is a wonderful healing experience that is beneficial at any time during one's life—not just prior to making one's transition.

Someone else's work that I believe to be an outright blessing on the earth is *Hello from Heaven!* by Bill and Judy Guggenheim. I recommend this book to people who have experienced the loss of a loved one, as Bill and Judy share the many, many ways our loved ones make contact with us from the other side.

When Gibby and I were at the funeral home standing in front of Walt's casket, I made the comment to her, "I don't understand why I haven't heard from Walt. I'm surprised he hasn't 'called me' to let me know he arrived safely." I made that remark because Walt and I had an agreement. I traveled so much in my angelic assignments, and it gave him peace of mind to know when I arrived at my point of destination safely. He was emphatic about my calling him to tell him "I've arrived!" I hadn't finished telling Gibby my thought when the funeral director motioned that he needed to talk to Gibby. Gibby went out of the room and came back shortly. "Well, Jayne, Walt just called us. The funeral director just told me that the alarm was at that moment set off at Walt's condo." When Gibby and I went to turn off the alarm, we discovered that there was no earthly cause for the alarm to have gone off. We both knew Walt was ringing us up to let us know he had arrived safely.

Two weeks after his death I experienced a horrible night in which I couldn't stop my tears. I couldn't sleep. I couldn't stop crying. I was angry that Walt was in heaven and I was here. I was anything but angelic in my mood. I remember thinking of Matthew 7:7—Ask and ye shall receive. So I sat up in bed and said the following to Walt: "Walt, I know you are in heaven and you are having a joyous time being reunited with your family and friends. However, I've got to be very honest. I feel really forgotten. I know that sounds terrible, but I feel forgotten and left behind. I need a sign from you, Walt, that you can hear me. I know that in heaven St. Theresa is wonderful with the way she uses roses for signs. So I am going to ask that you track her down and ask her how she does it. And if possible, by tomorrow morning when I open my mailbox, I ask that I see some sort of rose image as a sign from you that you can hear me. I need your help, Walt. I need to know you can hear me."

Strange as it seems, I felt better. It was as if I had released it over to Walt and the angels, and I was able to go to sleep on a pillow that had been drenched with my tears.

The next morning I drove myself as usual to the Upperco Post Office and opened Box 95 as I always do to pick up my mail. I remember seeing three envelopes. One was a big brown envelope with a book inside. I tore open the envelope and was stunned to be looking at a book written by world-famous medium George Anderson. The title of the book was: *You Are Not Forgotten.* I shuddered as I remembered my words from the night before, "I feel forgotten." I knew Walt was setting the record straight.

The second envelope was a sympathy card sent to me by my sister-in-law and brother, Bonnie and Jim Howard. The card is one that many people will recognize. It features a poem that is entitled, "The Rose that Grows on the Garden Wall." It tells of a rose that is blooming on one side of the wall, and one day finds a crack in the wall and chooses to bloom on the other side.

I could feel the energy mounting as I opened the third and final envelope. There was a cassette tape with a recording of a song. The song on that tape was Bette Midler singing "The Rose."

I thanked God, Walt, and the angels for answering my prayer. I knew that the gifts I received were not just for me but were to be shared. In seminars that I would lead, as healing experiences for people dealing with grief, I would tell the story of my needful requests to Walt and the angels and then I would encourage everyone in the audience to think of someone they love and who loves them—someone who is watching over them from heaven. I then would say, "They are sending *you* this song." When you are driving in your car and from your car radio you hear "The Rose" being played, remember my story and remember that not only was it a gift for me but a gift for you, too. So many blessings have been given to me in my life, not just to help me through difficult times, but additionally because God and the angels know that I will take from each experience what I need and then pass it on to others to be a healing to others as well. The name Rose means "giver of love." Know that when you hear the song someone in heaven is sending a bouquet of love to you! We've all got friends in high places!

Here is a meditation that the angels gave to me as a healing meditation for those who have loved ones in spirit. Make yourself comfortable. Make certain the phone won't disturb you while you do this meditation. Close your eyes. Take a few relaxing breaths. Allow yourself to detach from any demands or concerns of the day. Within your mind's eye imagine you are experiencing a beautiful day of bright sunshine in an exquisite garden. The temperature is just the way you like it. You are feeling totally comfortable in the environment. You look above you and you see a vast blue sky with white puffy clouds. The angels shape shift the clouds in images to delight you—the shapes of hearts, flowers, and angels. Your attention is drawn to the garden itself. You see a grove of trees and you feel the strength radiated to you by the trees. There are trees of all varieties, but one tree draws your attention. What type of tree is it? Perhaps you know the name of the tree or perhaps you experience it by its shape, color, or leaves.

Feel your connectedness to the trees of the earth. In the trees and also flying about in the garden are birds—so many beautiful birds. One particular bird draws your attention. What type of bird is it? Experience the color of the bird; the movement of the bird. Feel your connection to the birds of the earth. There are flowers in abundance in the garden.

Wild flowers! Garden flowers! Flowers of all shapes, sizes, and fragrances. It is probably difficult to choose one flower but somehow one flower draws your attention. What flower is it? Admire the beauty of the flower. Feel your connection to the flowers of the earth.

There are animals scampering about in the garden. You delight in their presence. One particular animal pauses and makes eye contact with you. What type of animal sees you? Feel your connectedness with the animals of the earth. You hear the sound of water flowing and you follow the sound. It brings you to a brook that flows through the center of the garden. It reminds you of the Twenty-third Psalm. You have been led by God to the still waters. You feel your soul renewed and comforted. There is an oriental bridge that allows you to cross over the brook. You start across the bridge and pause in the center of the bridge. You look down over the bridge and observe a sacred pool of water that has gathered beneath the bridge. It serves as a mirror to give you a divine reflection of yourself. As you look into the sacred pool, you see yourself as God sees you. You may see yourself as the precious self that looks back at you from your bathroom mirror each morning or you may see another image of yourself. How do you see yourself with God's eyes? Take this image into your heart. Let it warm you and comfort you and bring you peace. You now continue over the bridge to the other side of the garden. You see a marble bench that is placed near the brook. It is in the shape of a crescent moon. You rest on the bench. You inhale all of the beauty of this garden of love. You exhale a gratefulness and peacefulness, knowing that you are connected with all life. The sound of the brook reminds you that life flows eternally. There is room on the bench for you to be joined by someone in spirit. A family member, a friend who has closed his or her eyes to earth and opened them to heaven. Think of someone who loves you very, very much and watches over you from heaven. Who is the first person to come to mind? By thinking of them and honoring their spirit you are able to image them seated beside you on the bench in the garden of love and life eternal. You may imagine them as you remember them when here on earth, or they may be donning a light body just like the angels. Imagine them now beside you. Feel your connectedness to them. Love never ends. It flows forever. Imagine talking to this person. Let them know any feelings you have in your heart that you would like to express and then open yourself to receiving a blessing from them. Let them tell you whatever they wish to inspire you with at this time. We can always visit with our loved ones when we remember them in the garden of our hearts.

Sense yourself wishing them well as they do the same for you. Bring your attention back into the precious present remaining connected with our kingdoms and all of God's infinite dimensions. You are connected by love.

Just as I shared the imagery of a brook flowing through the garden of love, God's enveloping presence is always streaming through our lives. There have been so many times in my life that God's plan is flowing without my even knowing!

I have been contracted for a number of years by the Southeastern Conference to be a presenter at their yearly summer conference in Greensboro, North Carolina. It is one of my favorite conferences because of the family energy that is shared between everyone who attends. They are all a bunch of "love puppies" and that is a Jayne high compliment.

Shortly after the book *Simple Abundance* was published, Margaret Mohr, who serves as the conference's master of ceremonies, shared with the attendees on opening night that a quote appeared in the book that had been given by me. The quote I had given was this: "Call it a clan, call it a network, call it a tribe, call it a family. Whatever you call it, whoever you are, you need one." I had totally forgotten about having been approached for a quote and so I felt amazement and happiness.

A year or so later I would be employed by Gardiner's Furniture and my supervisor, Liz Roberts, was devoted to *Simple Abundance*. She reads it faithfully every day. During my initial interview for employment with them, I commented that there was a quote by me in the book. I remember Liz looking at me and remarking that she didn't remember reading it. My immediate thought was, "Way to go, Jayne. This nice lady thinks you are making up stories. I'll never get hired now." Well, I did get hired, and Liz and I would become dear friends, and the Gardiner's experience was a wonderful blessing in my life. Some months would pass and one day at work Liz stood in front of my desk. She stated that she loves *Simple Abundance* so much that when one year ends, she starts reading the book all over again. It continues to inspire her with new information and insight. (I might interject here that Oprah is a big fan of *Simple Abundance*. She promotes the Gratitude Journal suggestions in this book, and now Oprah has opened America to being grateful every day.) Liz indicated that this particular day was her mother's birthday and when she read *Simple Abundance*'s message on this special day, she was amazed to read: "November 20—Blessed Be the Ties That Bind—'Call it a clan, call it a network, call it a tribe, call it a family. Whatever you call it, whoever you are, you need one.'—Jane Howard." I wouldn't be telling the truth if I didn't say I felt a little validation. But the validation was quickly replaced by awe in the way we are all connected. As Chief Seattle puts it, "We are each one strand of the great web of life." As I shared, God's plan is always flowing without our even knowing!

That quote would be a blessing one additional day in my life. It would occur in November 1999. One of my best angel buddies—whom I call an angel sister, is Sharon Shreve. Sharon telephoned me and told me that her daughter, Melissa, who lived and worked in Atlanta, Georgia, was missing. Sharon is not only a friend but a member of a tape subscription group that I founded called the HA HA Group. The angels inspired me with the name—HA HA—representing Human Angelus: People who strive to shine as God lights in their lives. Sharon was asking for prayer support, angelic support, anything that I could offer. I immediately contacted all HA HA members and indicated that though Melissa was missing in our eyes, she was not missing in God's eyes. I asked everyone to visualize God's light around Melissa and that she be found as quickly as possible.

On Saturday, November 20, I went to Sharon's home as she had prearranged for me to be there to present a seminar for a group of her friends. I repeatedly called Sharon the week before and stated that if she wanted to cancel, I totally understood, as Melissa was still missing. Sharon said she needed me to come to her house. When I was in Sharon's beautiful home preparing for the seminar, I noticed *Simple Abundance*. I commented about how so many people love this book, and Sharon added that with all that had been going on she had not been able to read it at all that week. She thought it would be nice if, as a way of opening the gathering, I would read that day's message. I agreed and opened the book to the message for November 20. I had forgotten that was my message day. I looked at the words on the page before me: Blessed Be the Ties that Bind.

In the following week Sharon and her family would learn from the Atlanta police that Melissa's body had been found. This beautiful young woman had been murdered.

I was asked by Sharon and the family to lead the memorial service to honor Melissa's eternal life and light. There weren't enough tissues in the room for the tears when Melissa's adorable son, Shane, stepped up to the podium and honored his mom. Sharon would later tell me that even though she didn't want the news she received from the police, she was grateful that there was closure, not only for her and her husband, but for Shane, too. At the memorial service Melissa's cousin honored her life with the song "In the Arms of an Angel" from the movie *City of Angels.* She has an incredible voice that touched every soul in the room. We knew Melissa was truly in the arms of an angel at the moment of her transition. Following the memorial service, my husband, Charles, and I had to catch a plane to Las Vegas to be in attendance for Chuck's son's wedding. It was a weekend of overwhelming emotion. Chuck and I were to stay at the Luxor Hotel and arrived at the hotel close to midnight. Neither of us could sleep because of the emotion-filled memorial service that had taken place earlier in the day; so we walked through the halls of the Luxor. We came to one point in the hotel where the ceilings seem to be right up next to heaven. There was a vast open space above us. There were very few people moving about, and just then the silence was broken by the sound of a song. It was Sarah McLaughlin singing, "In the Arms of an Angel." Chuck and I looked at each other and smiled, and both said at the exact same time, "Hi, Melissa!"

# CHAPTER 3

# *Joshua's Lighthouse Angels*

*F*ollowing *Walt's death, I was* inspired by Spirit to include as part of my service to God in cooperation with the angels, opening the *Baltimore Sun* each morning to the obituary section and reading all the names of those who have died. As I am reading the names and stories of the lives of these individuals who have died, I surround them with God's light and offer up prayers for a smooth transition from the earth reality into the heavenly reality. I was taught a technique called the "halo" technique by the angelic kingdom. When I say prayers for anyone, whether they are deceased or dying, in the midst of any other type of transition or change, or missing, such as a missing child, I surround the individual with light forming the shape of a halo. In every direction light surrounds the individual. It is a symbolic exercise that expresses a prayer that is similar to the words of Isaiah 42:16—I will make darkness light before them.

I have been inspired by God to perform this service because the darkness represents the unknown. As we move through all the changes of our lives there is always a darkness of the unknown. My service is to pray for God to make darkness into light before the individual for whom I am praying. This is a wonderful prayer to say for yourself every morning. Ask God to make the darkness light before you.

In January 1997 I was reading the Baltimore obituaries and doing my prayer service when I read of a young man, Joshua Dansicker, who had been killed in an automobile accident. The obituary featured a picture of Joshua. He was an extremely handsome twenty-one-year-old who was a senior at St. Mary's College in St. Mary's, Maryland.

As I read the article, I heard the angels say to me, "God wants you to be of service to this family." I replied, "So be it."

When responding to God's assignments, I often use the response, "So be it." Bet is the first letter of the Hebrew text of Genesis. The name of the letter Bet is spelled Bet–Yod–Tov in Hebrew.

Letter–by–letter, the spelling of the word is Bet, meaning in/with; Yod meaning hand; and Tov meaning sign. Thus Bet, or "be it" means "in a hand sign" or "with a hand sign" of blessing. Just as the Bible began with a blessing from the hand of God as God brought forth creation, when I say the words "So be it," I am energizing with my words and thoughts that whatever the hand of God wants created will be achieved through me as God wills it to be done.

Joshua Dansicker is the elder of two sons of Mary and Arnie Dansicker. The younger brother is Scott, called Skeets by friends and family members. The entire family was devastated by the death of Joshua. It was as if their energies were frozen in time—frozen at the moment that they learned of Joshua's death. Numerous friends recommended to the Dansickers that they come visit the Angel Lady of Upperco. They heard the remark enough that they thought to themselves, in the midst of their pain, sadness, loss, "What do we have to lose?" And so they called me. I invited them to come visit me at Angel Heights.

I remember the first time I met them. I shared a little bit about my service and myself. I asked them what activities Joshua was doing before his death. They shared that he worked part time at Piney Point Lighthouse. I indicated that when we are in our physical bodies, it could be compared to our being a ceiling paddle fan. In the physical body it is similar to when the fan is turned off. You can easily see the blades. When we die, our energies become a faster, finer vibration than when in physical expression. It is similar to the switch being turned on and the paddle fan moving. You can no longer see the blades, however they are there. Joshua's vibration was now a faster, finer vibration that cannot be seen by human eyes. Joshua from heaven would be sending them messages to give them strength that he is OK and he wants his family to carry on, to rejoin the world, and to enjoy what life offers them. Joshua was carrying on; he was rejoining the world of the angels; and he, too, would be enjoying what life offered him. It's all about remembering that Joshua lives and forgetting that he died.

I encouraged them to be on the lookout for messages Joshua would send them. I told them that a new language would be created between them and Joshua. The messages would be sent in the expression of lighthouses. Whenever they saw a lighthouse, it was Joshua's way of saying, "Hi, Mom and Dad. I'm OK. I love you."

A week or so later Mary Dansicker called. She asked if I had time to meet her for lunch. Just talking to me made her feel better. I was happy to be of service to her. I met her at a local shopping center parking lot. When we arrived at the same time we pulled into parking spaces that were near to each other but left an open space between our two vehicles. As we stood by our cars, a large van pulled in between us. Written on both sides of the van was: Dorman's Lighthouse. I looked at Mary and winked, "Joshua says *Hi, Mom!*"

Lighthouses came to Arnie and Mary in all directions. I do not want to convey that Mary and Arnie and Skeets stopped hurting. There's a beautiful quote from C.S. Lewis's *Shadowlands* expressing that for as much as you love someone, when they are gone, that is how much you are going to hurt. However, you wouldn't give up the love to avoid the hurt. Their hurting was an honor to the love they shared for Joshua.

I would continue to talk to the Dansickers. I shared over and over with them, that they should go gently forward. To accept that their energy was reduced. Their fuses were short. Not to expect too much of themselves. Their focus was blurred not only by tears but also by this tremendous loss. I encouraged them to recognize that grief is exhausting—mentally and physically. I also recommended that with regard to holidays and traditions, they might consider doing things differently, consider making changes—even if only for the first year. And that they might consider changes that included celebrating the life of Joshua.

Ann Landers wrote, "You cannot change the past. You can, however, take care of the present. Total recovery may never come. But what you kindle from the ashes of the tragedy is up to you."

With God's help, and Joshua and the angels' inspiration, what Mary kindled from the ashes was a vision for a store to be called "Joshua's Lighthouse Angels." The mission statement of the store would be to celebrate Joshua's life and everyone's life. Mary was inspired to have a Memorial Room. This is a room where the public is invited to bring a picture of their loved one in heaven, to post it on the wall with a love note that they write. The love notes are on pastel colored paper in the shape of angels and lighthouses.

Mary asked if I would write a poem about the story of Joshua's Lighthouse Angels.

---

### Joshua and His Lighthouse Angels

*Angels are ministering spirits bringing blessings to our lives from God above.*

*And as God's messengers, they take on many shapes and expressions of love.*

*Sometimes they are invisible beaming God's love like sunshine rays of early morn;*

*Sometimes they take on an earthly presence as was true with Mary and Arnie Dansicker's first born.*

*Joshua Dansicker was a typical boy doing all the things that earthly children did.*

*Those around him were never conscious of the pair of golden wings he hid.*

*He grew in character as he grew in height;*

*And then at the age of 21 he spread his wings and his soul took flight.*

*Joshua answered the call from the company of Lighthouse Angels to serve from afar.*

*On a fateful evening he would leave his earthly body in the crash of a car.*

*Joshua had worked on earth as a Keeper of Light.*

*While a senior at St. Mary's College, he worked part time keeping Piney Point Lighthouse shining bright.*

*His service would continue when on January 12, 1997, Joshua joined the heavenly host.*

*As a keeper of a heavenly lighthouse he would fill a divine post.*

*For in heaven there are lighthouses that shine upon us when we feel alone in the dark;*

*Lighthouses that guide our path when we feel forsaken and the presence of hope seems stark.*

*Now this store is a result of Joshua and his Lighthouse's beam from above.*

*For after Joshua's death his parents started receiving reassurance of his presence and love.*

*Whenever his family was feeling as if their grief-stricken hearts would break,*

*Lo and behold there would be a sign of a lighthouse that they couldn't mistake.*

*Though they no longer saw Joshua as the son or brother they knew,*

*There was always a lighthouse on a truck or a license plate or in a magazine right in their view.*

*And through the lighthouses they heard Joshua ask them not to stand by his grave and weep,*

*"For I am serving God and I have a Lighthouse to Keep."*

*In honor of Joshua and his Lighthouse Angels, this store to God's Will we dedicate.*

*May you find peace and comfort here and may God's Light help you through dark times and life's choppy waters navigate.*

---

The signs and signals from Joshua continued to bless Arnie, Mary, and Skeets. One day Arnie's watch stopped at 11:18. November 18 is Joshua's earthly birthday.

They would experience his presence in their dreams, and I would in my dreams, too.

In November 1999 I had learned from Sharon Shreve that her beautiful daughter, Melissa, had been found murdered. When I went to sleep that evening I was greatly troubled over the news. When I am troubled, I grind my teeth in my sleep and sometimes my mouth feels pretty sore in the morning.

In the middle of the night I was awakened, realizing I had just seen a woman standing in front of me. I knew it was Sharon Shreve's mother telling me she was there for Melissa's arrival in heaven. I remembered that Sharon's mother had died suddenly in August in her home in Florida. As I rested in bed thinking about Melissa, I realized that my jaw was hurting because of grinding my teeth in my sleep.

I went back to sleep and as I fell asleep I called upon God's light to come into me. I love saying a decree that goes: "God's light, descend, descend, descend. God's light, defend, defend, defend. God's light, expand, expand, expand. God's light, command, command, command. God's light I am, God's light I am, God's light I am."

In my dreams I saw a college campus with handsome, beautiful young adults having a wonderful time together. Peacefulness and happiness permeated throughout the heavenly campus. Joshua Dansicker came up to me. He was so extremely handsome that it was "breathtaking" to see him. He came up to me and handed me his guitar. It was not the guitar he owned here on earth but a heavenly guitar. It was quite big. He laughed and laughed at me as he saw how awkward it was for me to hold the big guitar. He told me to play with it until he got back.

The scene in my dream was an absolute hoot. Here I was with this oversized guitar on my lap. I started strumming. On my first attempt to play the guitar I broke one of the strings. I was horrified. I broke a string on Joshua's heavenly guitar. Josh came back immediately and laughed and laughed even more. He then showed me that the strings were not like earthly guitar strings. These strings cannot be broken and they merely reconnect with little latches. I kept apologizing and Josh reassured me that it was no big deal. He then told me to always remember in everything I do in my life to use a *light touch*. He said to live life with a light touch. Then he touched my jaw with his finger. He touched the place in my jaw that was hurting from my grinding my teeth. Instantly the pain went away. When I awoke in the morning I realized my jaw didn't hurt.

I never experienced pain from grinding my teeth after my healing experience with Josh. I thanked Josh for being a dream messenger to me. I felt the guitar was symbolic of the heart. When we are heavy in our hearts, the heartstrings appear to break and Josh was showing me how we can heal our lives with a light touch.

Joshua's Lighthouse Angels is a little shop of miracles. People who are in need of comfort and support find themselves guided to the shop. A friend may tell them about the store or they may be walking down the sidewalks of Reisterstown and a feeling draws them inside the store.

I've learned of other mothers who, like Mary Dansicker, have lost a child and have been inspired by God to heal themselves and others in ways that they never would have believed possible if someone had told them this prior to the death occurring. I have met these courageous women through Mary and the beautiful God service she provides at Joshua's Lighthouse Angels.

Lisa is one of these people. Her son Michael was killed in an automobile accident in the spring of 1999. She now spearheads an organization called CARD—Citizens Against Reckless Driving.

She shared the following message with us after the trial of the reckless driver who killed Michael. The driver, James, was sixteen years of age.

---

*"Mary, I think you and the angels were with me today. James is a nice kid. I felt sorry for him. I could see that he was hurting from the beginning of the trial. It lasted almost one and a half hours. The judge found him guilty of negligent driving, failure to control speed to avoid a collision, driving on a median strip, and driving on the wrong side of the road. He put him on twelve months probation and assigned him fifty hours of community service along with driving instruction in a course of collision avoidance. His dad and mom both made very emotional apologies at the end of the hearing to all in the courtroom. James' lawyer read a letter written by him. It was also mentioned that he has been and is under a psychiatrist's care for the emotional trauma.*

"At the end of this very emotional experience, I went over to him. I hugged him. I told him that I knew he had not purposefully caused all of this. I told him that I forgave him and that he needed to forgive himself, to move on with his life and do good things with it. He was very grateful and humble and sincerely sorrowful, as were his mom and dad. I felt better afterward. Nothing will bring my baby back, but why should this kid suffer so. I certainly didn't want to hear that he had put a gun to his head a year down the road. Depression is a serious thing, as we well know and very, very difficult for teenagers. My gut told me that this young man was in serious pain.

"I think Mike would have wanted me to react as I did. I hope so. And as hard as it is, I really do believe that our boys—my son, Mike, and your son, Joshua—were called home because the Lord wanted them, needed them, they were a gift to us for the time that they were here. I know we will join them again.

"On the way to the trial, I passed the scene of the collision for the first time. It struck me as so improbable for it to have happened how and when it did. The road is flat, the median strip wide, and the lanes are long and straight. It was hard, but now I feel I have two barriers behind me—passing the place my baby crossed over and this trial. I am drained. I should sleep tonight. I know what you mean about not being able to sleep. Some nights it just doesn't seem that anything will bring peace. Thanks for always lending a gentle ear and a kind heart, Mary. It has meant and does mean more to me than you can know. XXX Lisa."

---

Joshua's Lighthouse Angels is a place for hope and healing. Mary is a messenger to other families who have lost children to let the joy of your child's life replace the hurt and pain caused by the death. What are some of the signs that you are healing through the loss? I asked people I know who have experienced loss to help me create a list:

*You find yourself laughing and you do not feel guilty.*

*You may—for just a moment—feel "better" and you do not feel guilty.*

*You sleep through the night.*

*You don't hurt as much when you go into the grocery store and see the child's favorite foods.*

*You're aware of others' hurts in addition to your own.*

*You notice the beauty of the world around you and don't cry because the loved one is in heaven, not here to view it with you.*

*You're able to do things without breaking down into tears.*

*You can plan for the future.*

*You accept there are going to be days you just feel like wallowing.*

Even though it is part of my service to inspire people in the midst of transition, I have been so blessed by the inspiration given to me by the courage with which these people live their lives.

Charlene is such a person. Charlene is someone who has always believed there are angels. It wasn't until her mother died that Charlene realized that they could communicate with you here on earth. Charlene's mom died of cancer after four long years of struggling. It was very painful for the family to watch her die in the hospital. Charlene shared with me that the doctor had told her that her mother was in a coma and wasn't feeling any pain. The last night of her mother's earthly life, Charlene doubted the doctor's words. Charlene stated that her mother looked and acted just like an animal that had been hit by a car. Her mother's dying had not been a peaceful experience. The mental image haunted Charlene for several years after her death. She had such violent nightmares that she couldn't sleep. Charlene felt she should have helped her mom in some way.

Three months after her mother's death Charlene was awakened by a bright light coming through the living room toward her bedroom door.

There in the doorway was Charlene's mom. A beautiful glowing light surrounded her. She was dressed in a white gown and was absolutely radiant. She called Charlene's name and then told her to stop worrying about her. The doctor did not lie; she wasn't in any pain. What she had seen were just the result of involuntary reactions. She told Charlene how beautiful it was in heaven and that everything was so much better for her now. She was feeling better than she had ever felt in her life. She named all the friends and relatives who were there with her. Charlene's mom was having a wonderful time in heaven.

Charlene was thinking to herself that she had to be dreaming. It couldn't be real. Charlene started getting out of bed, walking toward her mother, when her mother said, "I have to go now. Stop worrying. I'm fine and I will always love you." Then she added, "Oh, by the way, the vegetables up here are out of this world. Especially the carrots." Then she started to laugh, a belly laugh that only Charlene's mother could have. Charlene realized it was real. Her mother had come to her. Charlene stood in the empty doorway and watched her mother's light disappear. She was shaking so hard that her knees felt weak.

Charlene woke her husband to tell him what had just happened in their bedroom. Charlene shared that she was happy and sad at the same time; happy that her mother was not in pain as she had thought. She looked so beautiful, so joyous. But Charlene was sad because she still missed her and wished she could have hugged her one more time. Charlene's husband didn't believe it was real. He thought it was just a dream. Charlene knows it wasn't a dream. She knows her mother came to comfort her and after that night the nightmares were gone for good.

In November 1997 an even worse thing happened to Charlene. Her oldest son, Michael, committed suicide. It was such a shock. Charlene shared that she couldn't even begin to convey how she felt. It was bad enough to find her child dead, but the fact that he took his own life was almost more than she could handle. Michael left a note but not one that explained why he had taken his life. Charlene was beside herself. She blamed herself endlessly for not realizing how depressed he was and for not helping him.

Charlene later realized that there was absolutely nothing she could have done. Michael was thirty years old. He had his own home and had always been independent. He did things his own way in his own time. After Michael's death the holidays were unbearable for Charlene. She and her husband decided to get away for a few days.

They left for Ocean City, Maryland, on New Year's Day. The ocean had always been a calming presence for Charlene. One night she went out on the balcony of their hotel room and started to pray to God. She asked God for help. She wanted to find out the reason Mike had done this. She needed to know. She shared with God that she was at the end of her rope. She couldn't sleep and felt that living was a nightmare. Her heart had been broken. It felt like it had been ripped out of her chest. It hurt to breathe. She was crying so hard in her prayer to God that Charlene woke her husband and he came out to comfort her. Later she found out that she had scared her husband because he awoke to see her on the balcony and feared she was going to jump.

When they got back home Charlene felt inspired to go upstairs to a spare bedroom where they were storing Mike's personal belongings. There was a file cabinet drawer that had all of his paperwork in it. She looked through the papers hoping to find something but not knowing what she was hoping to find. Another day would go by and again she would feel drawn to the file cabinet drawer. She would look through the contents a second, third, and finally a fourth time. Charlene said out loud to God, "OK, I'll go through it one more time." This time it took two and a half hours and finally, she put the last folder back in. She was distraught. She had spent hours and had found nothing. Then she saw it. A small green slip of paper on the bottom of the file drawer.

Charlene reached down and picked it up. It was a note Mike had written after having spoken to his doctor. The findings were that Mike had cancer. He had a tumor taken off and it had tested positive. He needed some other tests run and there was an appointment date. In the center of the word tumor was a cigarette burn. Mike had made it clear how he was feeling. Angry. Upset.

Charlene was shaking as she held the piece of paper. Then a very strange sense of peace came over her. God had answered her prayers. God had told her why her son had killed himself.

Charlene was saddened that Mike had chosen to keep it to himself. He suffered in silence all those months. She talked with his doctors and found that the tumor had in fact spread. The tumor was on his neck, and there was nothing that the doctors could have done. It had not been detected early enough to save him. Charlene also remembered that when her mother died with cancer, Mike had commented that if he ever got cancer he was not going to take treatments. He would rather have quality of life than quantity of life. So once again, Charlene had been given an answer. Mike didn't tell her because he knew his family would try to talk him into treatment of some sort.

There was one additional prayer Charlene asked. She needed to know if Mike was OK now. She wanted him to come to her the way her mother had appeared, but Mike hadn't done that yet. She had received many signs and signals but she needed to see him. While visiting Joshua's Lighthouse Angels, Charlene met Mary, who suggested that she visit with the Angel Lady of Upperco.

During our meeting I encouraged Charlene to stop expecting Mike to come to her, as she was obsessing over the idea. Mike was indeed sending her many signs. Charlene needed to relax to be able to receive them. I explained to her that the telephone ringing with no one on the other end, and the caller ID reading "out of the area," was a sign from Michael. Charlene then shared that Mike had called her often the last six months of his life. In fact he called three or four times a day. So I pointed out that he was still calling her. The lights blinking in her home for no apparent reason were signatures that Mike was there. He was sending her messages through songs that he loved. I indicated that the sky would be a heavenly message board with messages to her from Mike. I encouraged her to relax and look up to God for inspiration.

I then played my harp for Charlene and sang a blessing to her. She shared that she felt so much better after our time together. As she was leaving I gave her a hug and said, "If you thought that your mother coming to you was something special, wait until Michael comes to you. It's going to be like the Fourth of July—spectacular. He is going to do it his way. He'll send a message through another person. You won't believe it. It will be like nothing you have ever imagined. Just relax. Stop expecting it. It will happen when you relax and when you least expect it."

Charlene would later tell me how right the message had been. She and her husband went with another couple on a cruise to St. Thomas. Charlene awoke at 5 a.m. on Sunday morning. She got dressed, grabbed her camera, and went up to the top deck. There was no one else there. She couldn't believe that she was the only person who was up to see the sunrise.

Charlene walked to the front of the ship and was amazed by the beautiful clouds and how calm the ocean was that morning. It was so peaceful and quiet. She noticed that she was feeling peaceful and relaxed. She looked out at the clouds and started to notice shapes in the clouds. There was a little cherub with a tear running down his cheek; a cloud that looked like the "north wind blowing" as an angel. As she stood looking at the clouds, it was as if cloud art was being unveiled just for her. Suddenly she realized Mike was sending her a message in the clouds. She remembered my words, to watch the clouds. Mike was an artist who loved to paint. I had told her that the sky would become his canvas now and he would send her messages of comfort through drawings in the clouds.

Charlene continued to relax and observe the messages given through the cloud shapes and images. She realized that no one else was out on the deck because it was a private time between her and Mike. She felt so happy that she started to really enjoy herself on the cruise. She found herself laughing without feeling guilty, something she had not done since Mike's death.

On Tuesday the cruise docked at St. Thomas. The cruise director told everyone that they could get a great picture of the ship if they rode a sky lift to the top of the mountain. Charlene wanted to go on the sky lift. Her husband didn't like to ride on lifts and neither did Nancy, her friend. So Charlene and Don, Nancy's husband, decided they would go up.

Charlene commented that she wasn't sure they had made the right choice because the sky lift car was very hot. They couldn't wait to get off at the top. When they did reach the top the view was breathtaking. They took pictures of the ship. Because it was a hot afternoon they looked for a place to get a drink. They found a place at the end of a row of shops.

There was a lady washing glasses when they sat down. She told them the bartender would be right with them. In a few moments he came around the corner and Charlene nearly fell off the barstool. He looked just like her son, Mike. His hair was more dirty blonde than strawberry blonde, like Mike's, but it was long just like his. It was pulled back and twisted into a little knot or bun held by two sticks. Her heart started pounding harder because that's exactly what Mike did with his hair when he didn't have an elastic band. He would twist it and get two little sticks out of the yard to hold it. He had even done that one of the last times he was at Charlene's home to clean flowerbeds for her. The bartender was the same height and build as Mike. He was wearing tan shorts and a tee shirt, work boots and socks. The outfit was almost identical to what Mike had on the last time he came to do the yard work.

Charlene's heart was racing. She was breaking out in a sweat. Her hands and knees were shaking. She thought for certain she was seeing things, hallucinating because of the heat. She struggled to calm herself. The bartender asked what they wanted to drink. Don asked for a beer and Charlene managed to ask for a diet soda. The bartender laughed and said, "Oh, a teetotaler, huh?" Mike used to call Charlene that all the time because she would hardly ever drink liquor. Don saw how upset Charlene was becoming. He looked right at her and said, "Are you OK?" She tried to say she was but Don took her hand and said, "I can't imagine how you feel. I wasn't around Mike that much, but our bartender looks exactly like him. It's eerie." Charlene replied, "You see it, too. I'm not imagining that he really does look like Mike." Don continued to express his agreement that the bartender was a double for Mike.

He came back with the drinks and Charlene really looked at him. He had the same high cheekbones and same fair skin. His eyes were green just like Mike's. Suddenly she felt a warmth come over her. Her heart stopped racing and a peaceful feeling embraced her. When the bartender spoke, she heard Mike's voice, not the bartender's. He even walked like Mike as he left to wait on a group of guys at the end of the bar. The guys were asking him if he was new there because they hadn't seen him before today. He told them he had been drifting at sea for about three months and was drawn to the island and thought he'd stay there awhile. Then the bartender turned around and walked back to

Charlene. At the same time Led Zeppelin's "Stairway to Heaven" came over the radio. He started to sing, dance around, and pretend he was playing the guitar in the band. Charlene had to leave at this point. Mike had done this same thing to the same song while he was working in the yard.

Don and Charlene caught the sky lift down. They met up with Steve and Nancy and the foursome went to an outdoor café for dinner. Charlene immediately started telling them what had happened. Steve didn't believe Charlene until Don spoke up and said it was eerie how much the bartender looked like Mike. Nancy said, "It was your sign from Mike."

Charlene needed to use the restroom. Nancy pointed out that it was outside of the café. She warned Charlene that it was hot, without windows or air-conditioning. Charlene left the table and went up the steps to the bathrooms. Both were occupied. It was so hot that she walked over to the railing and leaned over in the hope that maybe a breeze would come up the stairway. As she stood there the bartender from the top of the mountain walked through the doorway, paused at the bottom of the stairs, smiled at Charlene and walked away. Charlene said to herself, "It's Mike!" She ran down the stairs and there was no one in the room at the bottom of the stairs. There was no other door to the outside except the one he came through and the other wall had windows. Then she noticed a door back in a hallway. She went down the hallway, which led to the kitchen. She asked if a blonde-haired young man with tan shorts and a green tee shirt had just come in. They said no and told her no one was allowed in the kitchen. She had to leave. It was as if he had vanished into thin air.

Charlene couldn't stop thinking about the experience. Then it hit her! I had shared the inspiration that Mike would come when she least expected it. It would be spectacular like the Fourth of July. It was July 7 when she had seen Mike. The cruise had left port on July 4. It all made sense to Charlene. It was better than fireworks. She thought back to the conversation at the bar when he told the guys he had been drifting at sea for three months. It was Mike's wish that his ashes be scattered at sea in the ocean in April, three months ago. Charlene doesn't believe any of this is coincidence. She feels it was Mike's way of showing her he was fine and he had taken the stairway to heaven.

When she got home Charlene listened to the tape of our session together. I had said to her that he would send a sign through another person. That's exactly what he did. He morphed his energy through the bartender. Mike knew she would be in St. Thomas the Fourth of July. Charlene knows firsthand that God answered her prayer. God's peace came to her when she relaxed and let God make the miracles happen.

Sometimes I'm the messenger who delivers angelic clues, and sometimes I am inspired to suggest someone else whose service can help the family move through the grief. I recommended for Mary Dansicker a private consultation with Rev. Reed Brown. As I shared previously in chapter 2, when you have a session with Rev. Brown, you write the names of up to three people in heaven you wish to know about, and the question you would like God's help in answering. Mary later shared with me that she wrote on the billet in the three spaces: Josh. Josh. Josh. Her question was this, "Did you suffer or feel any pain when the car hit the tree?" Mary couldn't get out of her mind the thought that Josh may have felt pain the last minutes of his life on earth.

Rev. Brown took the billet in his hand, and spoke a beautiful prayer honoring God for the opportunity to be of service. He then said to Mary, "Josh, Josh, Josh. I didn't feel a thing, Mom. And that's your answer." Even though Mary had booked a half hour appointment with Rev. Brown, she had in the first two minutes been given the answer she sought. Rev. Brown's God-inspired messages caused the door of Mary's heart to open and God's peace to bless her in a way that passes beyond understanding. It's the peace that passes all understanding.

# CHAPTER 4

## *Come to Me Free in Spirit*

I n *March of 1994* in Calgary, Canada, a Conclave of Michael was held. It was an event that brought together people who felt called by God to serve alongside Archangel Michael. I was a presenter at the Conclave offering: I AM the Sword of God. The message of that presentation had been given to me by Archangel Michael during a profound experience at my home, Angel Heights.

In *Commune with the Angels*, I share the story of a wooden statue of Archangel Michael that I purchased while I was in Mexico and how important that statue became in my life. It was that statue that seemed almost to come to life when Walt Blatt came to my home for a private consultation. Prior to Walt's visit the angels had inspired me with a message that a new love was coming into my life and they would point him out to me. At the conclusion of the reading I did for Walt at Angel Heights I asked Walt if he had any further questions. He inquired whether or not he would have a love life again. He was a widower and wanted a relationship. At that very moment the statue came to life and pointed to Walt, indicating that he was the one the angels were pointing out to me. I shared with Walt to just have faith and trust that the angels would be sending someone to him soon, and the subsequent week we did in fact go out on our first date on March 1, 1991, and were together until his death March 1, 1995.

A second experience would occur with the statue where it served in giving me an important message. My cat, Baron Maurice, a beautiful pure white Persian, became ill. He was losing weight. He wasn't eating. He didn't seem to have an appetite. I took him to the vet and was told from the examination that it appeared the problem was tartar on his teeth, which perhaps was causing an irritation, resulting in his not want-ing to eat. If it became worse, the vet felt it would need to be addressed. Baron Maurice was tested for feline leukemia and was found not to have this disease. But for me, the diagnosis of tartar build–up just didn't seem to ring true. Every morning I would open up more than one can of cat food trying to find something that would please him. He was becoming more and more finicky. He just would not eat for several days at a time. He wanted to rest and sleep more than usual for a cat. One day while I was in my office, Baron Maurice came in and seeing the statue of Archangel Michael placed up on the table, jumped from the floor to the level of the statue and literally knocked it to the ground with his paw. Now here was a cat who had been acting listless and without energy, knocking a large wooden statue to the floor with one swipe of his paw. When the statue hit the floor one of Michael's wings broke off. As I looked in disbelief at what had happened my first thought was not of anger at Baron for breaking the statue but rather, "Oh dear Baron, what am I not seeing that you want me to see?" He wanted my attention and I knew in that instant that I had to take him to another vet and get a second opinion. I had to find out what was the problem. I took him immediately to another vet. In testing his blood it was discov-ered that he had feline AIDS. They told me that there was nothing that could be done for him and that the merciful thing to do would be to have him put to sleep. I went home with Baron and through prayer and meditation, gained from God the strength to fulfill my role in helping Baron find peace. Once again the Archangel Michael statue had helped point out my path of service.

Shortly after Baron's transition I was holding workshops in my home as well as seeing private clients. The only part of Michael's statue that was moveable was a sword, a very small wooden sword that you could move from his hand. One day I happened to walk past the statue of Archangel Michael and realized that he no longer had his sword. I couldn't imagine how the sword had disappeared. As I looked at Archangel Michael, now with one broken wing and his sword missing, I expressed an inner hope that in no way was this a reflection upon what was going on in my life. I remarked to myself that Archangel Michael needed a healing. And a healing is exactly what he got, but it would not occur for almost two years.

At one of my in-home gatherings a man sat in the circle and during the class he was whittling a small animal figurine out of a block of wood. As I saw that he was beginning to learn this craft, I commented that I had just been to a country craft show and had purchased a small wooden angel. I told him that he might want to look at this wooden angel as it might be something that he could follow as a pattern in making Christmas gifts. This wooden angel was no more than four inches in height and was patterned after a simple design. I forgot about the earlier conversation until after the workshop was over. The man came up to me and said, "May I see your wooden angel?" Well, the angels of healing must have cast a veil over my thinking because with his words I thought of the wooden statue of Archangel Michael. I said to the man, "Follow me." I took him up the steps to my office and there I showed him the quite large and impressive figure of Archangel Michael with broken wing and missing sword. Even with these imperfections, Michael stood strong, crushing the demonic force that was beneath his feet. The man looked at me in total disbelief and said, "You think that I can whittle that?" When hearing his words I realized my mistake. I laughed, "Oh, when you said you wanted to see my wooden angel, I don't know why, I just immediately thought of this statue of Michael." He looked closer at the wing and said that he knew a master craftsman, in fact, the man who was teaching him to whittle in wood. He asked if I would be willing for him to take Michael and his broken wing to this craftsman to see if he could repair it for me. With angelic blessings I sent Michael on his way to be healed.

Six months would pass by before Michael would return to Angel

Heights. He returned the third week of September 1993. I clearly remember the events that surrounded Michael's return. I was in the midst
of transition. I had a sense that I was going through a major transformation in my life. It was as if I was walking through a tunnel and the
woman that had walked in through one end would not be the same
woman who came out the other end. There wasn't anything in particular that I could identify that had changed, just a feeling in general that
I knew I was changing and transforming my life. I didn't have a clue
who the new me was going to be.

To assist me through this dark night of the soul, the angels inspired
me to take everything off my altar and just leave one object on the altar
that reflected what I aspired to be when I came out of the tunnel. I had
found a wonderful clear crystal. It was very small in size but it had a
point. When I looked at it I saw several things. It was a flame. It was the
point of a sword. I especially liked this crystal because when you looked
closer there was a smaller crystal affixed to its side and it was in the
same shape. So I was seeing a larger sword with a smaller sword inside
of it—or a larger flame with a smaller flame by its side. I liked the inspirational message the crystal gave me. It was saying to me, "God's will be
done. Not my will, God, but Thy will." The crystal sat on my altar for
about three weeks. As I passed by the altar or did prayer service at the
altar I would pause and wonder about the new me—the new me that
God was molding and creating, a new person more aligned to God's
will. In fact, I was feeling quite peaceful about the entire transition as I
knew God was in the driver's seat. I was "little sword/little flame," going
along for the ride.

I encourage those of you who are going through a similar time of
change and uncertainty as to where you will be led and what your new
experiences will be, to place one object on your altar which reflects, for
you, a quality that you hope to express in this vision that is being held
by the Master Potter—God. Well, the third week of September came
around and that particular weekend I was initiated into an order where
I was given a sword as part of the initiation ceremony. It was quite a
large sword, I might add. When I came home I placed the sword on my
altar. There residing on my altar was the symbolic crystal and now the
sword of a holy order.

A few days later I hosted an angelic gathering and the man who was a novice whittler returned. When he came to my house, unknown to me, he was bringing Archangel Michael with him, and so presented to me a mended Michael. I was elated over the healing that Michael received, and I placed Michael on the altar. A trinity blessing was created—the statue of Michael, the sword of the holy order, and the crystal sword. I remember sitting by my altar, viewing the objects of inspiration. My heart immediately went to the statue of Michael. Even though the master craftsman had healed Michael's broken wing, Michael was still missing a sword. I thought to myself that maybe I should go to a local toy store and search out a sword that would make Michael complete. At the very moment, as I was holding that thought, a presence came into the room. I knew immediately it was Archangel Michael's energy and radiance. Michael spoke to me and said that it was not necessary for him to have the sword. The sword was now made manifest through the heart's conviction of all who served God on earth. All the wonderful people who were responding with their life and with love were now the swords of God. He then went on to say that as the Swords of God we are being called to Speak our God truth, Write our God truth, Own our God truth, Radiate our God truth, and Dedicate our lives to God's truth—to wield our S–W–O–R–D.

In November of 1993 Michael came forth into my life again with a communication. I will never forget the moment for I heard his words so crystal clear. When the presence of Michael appears I can only equate it to the energy of rolling thunder. It always causes me to stand at attention. Michael's words were as follows: "The antichrist is upon the earth now." I shuddered hearing his words. I can remember thinking to myself, "Oh no! Michael is saying the antichrist is here now." Michael spoke a second time, "The antichrist is upon the earth now and its name is . . . " Michael stopped just short of telling me the name. In that split second my heart stopped. Did I want to hear this? Did I want to know the name of the antichrist? I filled up with total fear. If I knew the antichrist's name, would the antichrist come after me? I was almost paralyzed with fear until I got a grip on myself and said, "Wait a minute, with God I have nothing to fear." I asked Michael to reveal the name. Michael spoke to me a third time, "The antichrist is upon the earth and its name is

HOPE!

hopelessness." When something is right, when something is true, your whole body chimes in the key of you! I was chiming with God's truth. The truth of Michael's words rang through me as I realized that no one man or no one woman would bring about the destruction of this earth. That no one individual could take our power into his or her control but rather it would be up to us whether or not we would hand it over freely to hopelessness. The message was given to me to share in my lectures and in my writing as we are God's messengers of hope eternal. When we give up on God, we give up on hope. This is why the Bible inspires us to take refuge in God, because with God all things are possible.

As you are reading my words, think of yourself as an earth angel of hope. You may find yourself in what appears to be a hopeless situation. It is never hopeless if you let God inspire you as the messenger of hope you are in this situation. It may be that someone in your family is trying to find a job. This person may have sent out resume after resume with no response. They may be at the point of giving up hope. You are there to uplift them and encourage them that they only need one job to open up for them. The same is true when people feel hopeless in finding a love relationship in their life. We sometimes allow statistics to set us off on a path of hopelessness. If you are looking for that someone special, just remember that it is just "one" someone special that you need to find.

The summer of 1993 I spoke at Kutztown University as part of Life Spectrum's week-long conference. I presented a five-day workshop about the angelic kingdom. I worked with a class of thirty people every morning for about two hours. On Friday when I concluded my class I went around the room and said to my students, "Don't confuse the messenger with the message. What I am saying is not to be confused by what my service is. Think about it right now. What is it that you want to do in your own life? How do you want to incorporate the message of the angels and service to God in your own personal life? How do you want to use everything that has been shared this week with you by the angelic kingdom to make your life better and the world a better place? What can you do in service with the angels?"

I went around the room and one after another, each student indicated how he or she was going to work with the angelic kingdom. One woman in particular had a whole new outlook on her job. She works for a blood laboratory and has the role of seeing thousands of samples of blood pass before her every day as she processes them. She indicated that she was going to work with the angels in blessing each one of these samples. She was going to pray that the information that came from the blood work would assist them for their highest good and would provide a healing in their life. She had never seen her role through the eyes of empowerment, but the angels have given her that opportunity to see herself as a servant to God. She went away from the workshop realizing she was going to touch the lives of thousands and thousands of people and would be fulfilling a service to God in doing so. She was quite excited about going back to work on Monday morning.

Again, I continued around the room asking how the angels had inspired the class members to serve God in their lives. It was apparent that the angels had blessed each life and each person in turn was going to be a blessing to their family and their community.

One woman named Irina, who was visiting the United States from Moscow, stood up before the class and announced with conviction, "I'm going to take the hope of the angels to my people in Russia, too. I am going to inspire them with hope in these challenging times of transition, and I am planning to take Jayne to Russia, too, to bring her message to my people." Needless to say I was as amazed as the rest of the class to hear these words. I was honored by her invitation. Irina was the editor of *Urania* magazine, a beautiful spiritual publication that had been in existence for approximately three years and was published in both English and Russian.

Irina came up to me after the class and shared her enthusiasm over her service with the angels as an editor and in her life in Russia. She then invited me to participate as a workshop presenter at a conference to be held in November 1993 in Moscow. Hearing her words brought back into my awareness an incident that had foretold this happening. It had been a few years prior and it occurred on Sunday, December 31. Every December 31 I participate in promoting and being a part of the World Healing Meditation. I wrote about this event and included the actual meditation in *Commune with the Angels*. On this particular December 31, which fell on a Sunday, I came home from a group meditation and turned on one of my favorite television programs, Dr. Schuller's *Hour of Power*. That particular Sunday was an extraordinary Sunday because Dr. Schuller had just returned from Russia. He was the first western hemisphere minister to be allowed by the Russian government to give a series of sermons over the Russian television network. He had been instructed that he could not have a sermon that promoted Christianity, but rather, it had to be a general inspirational sermon to uplift the people and give them hope. I remember that Armand Hammer had arranged for the Russian telecast to be broadcast to the people who were tuned into the *Hour of Power* in America. I was one of the people who witnessed this history-making sermon being given by Dr. Schuller. I stood in front of my television almost frozen, knowing that walls were being brought down by every word Dr. Schuller spoke. We were transcending time zones. We were transcending past fears. We were transcending cold wars. The message of hope was being delivered to all of God's people on the earth. He shared the words from Jeremiah 29:11, "For I know the thoughts that I think toward you, says the Lord, thoughts of peace and not of evil, to give you a future and a hope." As I stood riveted to the television set, I heard the angels say, "And you, too, will be a messenger of hope to the Russian people." That was the first time I had ever thought about the possibility of my going to Russia. I knew in that moment that sometime in my life I would be visiting Russia as a courier of hope carrying with me God's message. That became a reality on Monday, November 1, 1993, when I flew from Dulles International Airport to Heathrow in London, England, and then flew on to Moscow. As part of a week-long conference I gave my workshop with the assistance of a translator and, of course, the assistance of the angels. The theme of the conference was "Sophia Returns." Sophia is a term for the Wisdom of God.

While I was in Moscow the organizers of the conference took a group of us to a local flea market. At the flea market I came across a painting of Archangel Michael holding a sword that was not a sword of steel but rather of fire. I loved the symbolism of the fire because so often God is depicted in the Bible as fire. One such example is Moses' experience with the burning bush. The painting was of Michael cutting through all darkness with the power of God's energy. The painting was on a piece of wood. After I purchased the painting, one of my hosts commented that I might have a problem getting it through customs, as Russia's customs agency was funny about artwork leaving the country. When it came time for me to leave Russia, I went through customs with the painting of Michael out in full view. When the customs officer asked what I had to declare, I showed him Archangel Michael. He asked if it was old. I told him I didn't know, that I had bought it at a flea market in Moscow and had paid $50 for it. I was totally stunned by what he did next. He took out a pocketknife and cut the edge of the painting to see what was underneath. I heard the angels inspire me with the words, "Detach! Detach! Detach!" I knew what I had to do. I said to the officer, "Look, I am really homesick and want to go home. If you need to keep the picture, keep it." The officer's attention was drawn to the eyes of Archangel Michael. He never looked at me again. With his eyes affixed upon Michael, he handed back the painting and said, "You take it with you." It was as if he couldn't give it back to me fast enough. I have been so blessed in my worldwide travels to be guided by the angels to awesome works of art depicting Archangel Michael: the wooden Michael I found in Mexico; the painting of Michael with a sword of fire in Russia.

At the beginning of this chapter I shared with you the opportunity I had to speak at the Conclave of Michael. Many of us serve alongside Archangel Michael. Michael's name in Hebrew means "He who is like God." So if you have made changes in your life recently that are inspiring you to commit yourself to live your life in fulfillment of God's vision of you, chances are you are hearing Michael's calling.

Calgary, Canada, has been written about as an established location of Michael's energy on earth, and when I saw the magnificent Canadian Rockies for the first time, I commented, "Michael, this is so you."

The week before I left for Calgary I felt Michael's promptings to release my job of twenty-plus years with an advertising agency. I heard Michael's calling: "Come to me free in spirit. Come to me without your job." I was panicked by the very thought of leaving my job. How would I survive? I was scared. I was a woman alone and paying the bills was totally up to me. I could feel the vibration of truth in Michael's words but my fears were too great. I just couldn't do it. Michael did not judge me. The angels never judge us. They merely stand back and let us "chew" on their wisdom. They are in our lives to inspire us, not to live our lives for us. The decision would be up to me.

While in Calgary on one particular morning during a lecture, the presence of Michael came to me again. I heard him speak as clearly as the speaker on the podium. Again he said to me, "It is time to be free in spirit. It is time to leave your work and take your place serving God with the company of angels." My dear friend, Paula Kyle, who was seated next to me, felt something going on. She looked at me and said, "You just got a message, didn't you?" I shared with her what Michael had said and she asked, "Did he give you a date to leave?" I replied, "We're negotiating on that." There was really no negotiating except in my mind. I knew Michael was right. It was time and it was to be accomplished on May 5, 1994. On this date there would be a trinity or three-times blessing of the vibration of the five, which is the energy of change, expansion, growth, moving forward. I was inspired by the angels to look up the message for two times five, or the master number 55 because the energy of 55 was also included in May 5, 1994. Master numbers are numbers that emphasize the quality of the single number and raise its vibration to a higher level of intensity or consciousness because of its being doubled; therefore 55 is a higher consciousness of the number 5 and 555 is a higher consciousness of 55. I used *Numerology and Your Future* for my research. It is written by Dusty Bunker, whom I consider to be a master numerologist. Dusty shares the possibilities that there are Masters who physically walk the earth or hover above it, and each of these Masters guides watches over a different department of life. Under "55" Dusty wrote: "Master Agents 55 are assigned to the department of communications and investigation. They must separate the true from the false . . . The Ace of Swords in the Tarot would be a good card to reflect upon." Could Dusty be describing Archangel Michael as the Master Agent of 55 who is inspiring us to the Swordbearers of the Truth for God? Since that time I have come to know without a shadow of a doubt that Archangel Michael reveals himself thorough the numerical vibration of 555. Interestingly enough, years later I would catch a public radio broadcast with a scientist who spoke of the geometric symmetry in a flower known as the Michaelmas that has some sort of 555 configuration. His words were over my head but not over my heart.

When I came home and went back to work I was rationalizing as I sat at my desk at the advertising agency that what had happened maybe didn't happen, but in my heart I knew it had. It was all so scary and rationalizing was an easier path than taking the plunge. As I played mind games with myself I questioned, "Was it really Michael?" Almost like a Memorex commercial. Was it real or was it Memorex? I didn't have to play the game for long. A beautiful necklace of Austrian crystal beads that I was wearing around my neck just exploded and the beads flew in every direction of the office. I heard the angels lovingly whisper, "Jayne, you know it is time. You are out of here."

Later that day when I got ready to leave the office and reached inside my purse for my keys, which were attached to a key chain with my name spelled out in big letters, I realized that my name had separated from the key chain. I knew I was being given signs and signals that it was time to separate myself from my old identity.

There was no doubt I had to resign. I knew it. The angels knew it. And my boss was going to know soon, too. I was certain about my leaving but was still dragging my feet on the date. Was 5-5-5 the date for sure? That evening the confirmation came through loud and clear. As I finished a telephone reading, I turned on television and saw the final scene of a program. A woman falsely accused of being a witch in Salem was sentenced by the judge. His words to her were, "You have been sentenced to die on May 5." I knew May 5, 1994, was the death of my old identity at the advertising agency.

The very next day I gave notice. My boss, though somewhat surprised, stated, "I knew it was coming. I just didn't know it would be this soon." I shared with him that it was now because now was the time.

My boss asked me whom I was going to work for. I stated, "God and the company of angels." After I had this conversation, I went to the post office as I did each work morning to pick up the office mail and at the same time picked up my own personal mail. There in my mailbox was a large package. When I looked inside I saw copies of a newspaper article. I had forgotten that three weeks earlier a reporter had visited my home and had written an article about my service with the angels. I opened the article and saw the headline the reporter had chosen for her article: The Company of Angels Is Her Employer. So it was official—

in black and white print—I was working for God and the Company of Angels.

I share with you the following personal ceremony to rededicate your life to serving God and fulfilling your role as an earthly member of the legion of Archangel Michael.

---

*Light a blue candle upon your altar. It is symbolic of the Blue Ray of Michael and represents the Will of God—the Power of God—the Protection of God.*

*Say these words or put the thought into your own personal expression:*

*Michael, I kneel before you in humility and dedicate my life to the fulfillment of God's plan for earth. I have answered your call to serve alongside you glorifying and exalting God in all my choices, my actions, words, and deeds. I AM THAT I AM.*

*Mastering my life and its experiences.*

*Intuitively responding to life with my inner God-inspired wisdom.*

*Caring for all that I am given stewardship and guardianship over.*

*Healing and helping others to heal.*

*Abundantly embracing with joy my identity as a beloved child of God.*

*Energizing my life with love.*

*Living in the eternal now.*

---

Stretch out your arm and visualize your arm as a sword. It is not a sword that serves as a weapon. It is a sword that cuts you free from all that is less than God's will in your life. Your whole body is activated with the Blue Ray vibration.

Hear Michael inspire you with the message: You are God's swordbearers on earth. Speak your God truth. Write your God truth. Own your God truth as your identity. Radiate your God truth. Dedicate your life to your God truth. Remember, you can use the sword to cut yourself free from all the illusions in your life. Cut yourself free from any bonds to the past that prevent you from fully embracing your highest good. Cut yourself free from anything that is no longer useful or purposeful in your life. You are the Sword of God's Truth—and the truth will set you free

Accept this dedication as fulfilled. May God be glorified and exalted by this ceremony and may you be blessed for you are truly a blessing on the earth.

As a closing for this chapter I wish to share the following prayer sent to me by Shelley MacDonald of South Attleboro, Massachusetts. She shared with me that by saying this prayer she is given strength and courage, especially during the times when she feels anxious or discouraged. Shelley is the host of an inspirational radio program and truly is a member of the legion of Michael. She is a blessing of God's light upon all those who meet her.

> *Come, come, O Michael, dear.*
> *By thy faith my way is clear.*
> *Sword of blue*
> *Flashing through*
> *Give me faith and protection, too!*
> *Shine within me, all about me.*
> *With Michael's faith will none doubt me.*
> *Guard my way, right now, today*
> *Casting all my fears away.*
> *Within, without I see your flame.*
> *Go forth in God's own name.*

# CHAPTER 5

# Vision of Mary—
# Vision of Love

W hile attending the Michael Conclave in Calgary, Canada, in March 1994, I was inspired by Spirit that I needed to attend a conference that was being held in Egypt in December 1994. The purpose of the trip was to gather people together on the twelfth day of December—the twelfth month—for a ceremony of rededicating ourselves and the earth to God's will. Spirit was calling us to be messengers from God to choose love instead of hatred, understanding instead of judgment and peace instead of war. The place the ceremony was to be held was the Great Pyramid of Giza.

Even though I clearly heard the message, the part of me that likes to mimic Bill Cosby's Noah, "You want me to build what?" asked for confirmation through what I call the Trinity blessing. Give me a message three times and I know it has God's stamp on it. I considered the inspiration at Calgary as sign number one. As I shared in chapter 2, prior to Walt's death I drove him to Arlington, Virginia, for an appointment with Rev. Reed Brown, pastor of the Arlington Metaphysical Chapel. I also scheduled a reading from Rev. Brown. I expected to receive mes-

sages from loved ones in spirit just as Walt had. God had other plans for
my session. As Rev. Brown opened to God's inspiration, he indicated
that there was a large animal being shown to him. He described its big
nose and humps on its back. He proclaimed that there was a camel
being shown to him. Rev. Brown explained that the camel wanted to
give me a big friendly lick and that the camel was a messenger from
God that I was to go to Egypt and that while I was there I would receive
a message in a sacred place similar to a "holy of holies." Now understand Rev. Brown knew nothing of my plans to go to Egypt. I knew that
Rev. Brown had delivered sign number two.

About a week later my cousin Marty called me from Las Cruces, New
Mexico. Marty was so excited she could hardly get the words out. Marty
had just begun to learn to meditate. During one of her meditation sessions, she clearly heard God's voice say to her, "Go visit Mrs. Brown, she
has something to share with you." This was all new to Marty and so
there was a part of her rational self that was questioning an inspiration
that wanted her to go next door to Mrs. Brown's house and inquire
what Mrs. Brown had for her. Marty decided "nothing ventured, nothing gained," so she went next door and knocked on the front door of her
eighty-five-year-old neighbor. Marty explained to Mrs. Brown that what
she was going to ask might sound crazy; however, she was meditating
and felt she had clearly heard God's voice tell her to visit Mrs. Brown
because Mrs. Brown had something to share with her. Mrs. Brown
smiled at my cousin and replied, "Come inside, dear, I've been expecting you." As it turns out, Mrs. Brown was a long-time student of spiritual development and religions. Mrs. Brown and Marty chatted the
evening away. As Marty rose to go home Mrs. Brown remarked, "And by
the way, please tell your cousin that God is calling her to go to Egypt."

Marty dashed home and called me and shared the message. Just like
Rev. Brown, Marty did not know I was considering going to Egypt. After
she shared Mrs. Brown's message, Marty asked, "What does it mean?" I
replied, "It means tomorrow I am sending in my deposit for the trip to
Egypt."

There would be several more messengers who would come forward
prior to my trip to Egypt. One was Michelle Anderson. God has blessed
Michelle as the guardian of an incredible healing technique known as

the Master Alignment. Prior to my going to Egypt, Michelle gave me a message that while in Egypt I would change my name. I have to admit that when she told me that my first thought was, "Oh great, I am going to come back thinking I'm the Queen of Sheba." My thoughts were very flippant when she shared her message.

During my trip to Egypt both Rev. Brown and Michelle's messages would come true. While I was visiting an ancient Egyptian temple, I toured a part of the temple known as the Holy of Holies. While standing in the energy of this sacred space, I felt the presence of God come over me and give to me the following message: Change the spelling of your name from Jane to *Jayne*. When people ask you, "Why did you change your name, tell them the 'Y' stands for YAHWEH and you are serving as a messenger to inspire people to put God in the center of their lives." From that moment forward my name has been Jayne. I love the letter "Y" in the center of my name. "Y" inspires me with the image of myself with my arms held up to God.

During my trip to Egypt I had the opportunity to be in the Queen's Chamber of the Great Pyramid. While in the Queen's Chamber I had a vision of Mary and the Christ Child in her arms. I knew I was to share this vision with others and was guided to Marty Betz, a truly gifted artist, whom I commissioned on behalf of the angels to create in physical form what I saw on December 12, 1994. Interestingly enough, I picked up the completed artwork from Marty on September 29, 1995—Michaelmas Day.

As I experienced the vision in Egypt, I saw Archangel Michael standing in front of Mary and the Christ Child. I felt he was a protector of her energy and that was why he was in front of her. It would later be revealed to me that Michael was standing in front of Mary as a veil to an energy that I was not yet ready to experience or witness.

On Mother's Day weekend of 1995 while co-leading a women's spiritual retreat with Lucky Sweeny, the veil was lifted, and I encountered Archangel Raphael and began learning of my co-service with Raphael in creating a Star of David grid energy pattern as an angelic assignment. When Michael stepped away from the front of the vision, which first began in the Great Pyramid on December 12, 1994, and was completed on Mother's Day 1995, I saw Raphael holding a Grail Cup with the world on the front of the cup.

The Holy Grail has fascinated the minds and captivated the hearts of many of us. I can remember as a young child being enchanted with the legend of the heroic King Arthur, his glorious knights, and his inspirational Round Table. That enchantment grew into my quest to learn more.

I became a Grail Seeker, one who began her journey in pursuit of information about the Holy Grail, and in time realized that I was on a journey of self-discovery. That which I sought outside of myself was leading to that which was within me waiting to be found.

The Grail shows up in many cultures and traditions.

One tradition teaches that the Grail came to the earth during the mighty battle for good and evil waged in heaven. While some angels sided with Satan and some with God, a third group of neutral angels brought down a "loving cup" and placed it on earth. This act was to be a reminder to humanity that through communion with the Christ energy, those lost in hell could find their way back to heaven.

A similar interpretation describes the sacred chalice as originating as a stone, an emerald from the crown of Lucifer. Michael, with his flaming sword, struck the jewel from Lucifer's crown. The stone fell to earth and out of this gem the Holy Grail was created.

According to Christian legend, it was the same cup used by Jesus at the Last Supper. It was believed that Joseph of Arimathaea, a disciple of Jesus, brought the Grail to the place of Jesus' crucifixion. The cup is said to have caught the blood pouring from the body of Jesus.

Years later, Joseph captained a ship and crew and took the sacred relics in his possession, the bloody spear used by the Roman soldiers to pierce the side of Jesus and the Holy Grail cup, to England to a place now known as Glastonbury. It has been inferred that the oarsmen on that ship were later incarnated as the Knights of the Round Table. This same group would gather again as the founders of the United States of America.

At the Round Table, symbolic of unity with God, was a mysterious empty seat, called the Siege Perilous, where none might sit except he who was successful in questing after the Holy Grail. It represented the perfect individual, or the "Christed One." Sir Galahad, son of Sir Lancelot, attained this high honor because of his spiritual purity.

In lore, the Grail has been described as a greatly sought-after object. While the search for the Grail is depicted as long, hard, and demanding, it is deemed as an exceedingly worthy pursuit. This is because the search is symbolic of seeking balance in one's own life. In all the stories, the knights went out beyond themselves, sacrificing much along the way. Vigilantly walking the path between the opposites of good and evil, between fear and courage, they were inspired with the realization of their highest spiritual potential.

In James Russell Lowell's "Vision of Sir Launfal" the arrogant knight rode forth in search of the Holy Grail and threw a gold piece to a leper who rejected it. After years of unsuccessfully searching for the Holy Grail, the knight returned home and encountered the same leper. This time Sir Launfal shared with the leper his last piece of bread and offered him a drink from his cup. The leper revealed himself to be Christ and the cup transformed into the long-sought-after Holy Grail cup. This is a lesson that Christ taught: What you do for others you do for Christ.

As I witnessed Raphael holding the Holy Grail cup I asked myself, "What significance does the Holy Grail hold for us now?"

The cup itself is symbolic of the heart. Christ's command "Drink from it, all of you" is an offering of the Christ energy to all who commune and drink of the cup of the love of Jesus for humanity.

The Holy Grail is the embodiment of love from God's heart to ours. It is the outpouring of God's love, which fills each of our lives as we search for truth. Gaining God's truth will unlock the mysteries of life and death, by revealing to us our own eternal being through Christ.

We are all knights. We are all seekers of that which is our own internal truth. However, like Sir Launfal, we discover the Grail only when we come back home or to the center point of our life. Sometimes it is when there is a loss of something, or it feels as if we've hit rock bottom, that we discover that which has always been within us waiting to be uncovered. Every one of us has within us the potential for this spiritual awakening. The moment that occurs is when we realize that instead of seeking a cup outside ourselves we are able to proclaim, "Aha! I am the cup I seek." Each one of us is a sacred vessel of God's life and light. We are a vessel of God's love, one breath, one heartbeat, one body, one energy, one consciousness through which pours God's illumination.

In the vision Raphael inspires us to discover the cup within us and lift our cup, our life, upward in glorification of God through service. Spirit inspired me with the message that through service to God—drinking of the cup of service—God's will for earth will be achieved. Raphael represents God's healing hands lifting us up in consciousness, frequency, vibration, awareness, and understanding. God lifts us up from the ashes of our lives.

At the same time I was communing with Raphael on Mother's Day weekend, a woman named Allison Carter who lives in Berkeley Springs, West Virginia, was in meditation. During that meditation she looked out of her home, which overlooks Cacapon Mountain. She saw a huge angel appear and the angel said to her, "Please invite Jayne Howard to your home and ask her to come spend time with me here." Allison later shared with me that she felt she was "angel ignorant" at that time in her life and so she asked the angel, "Who do I tell Jayne invites her?" The angel replied, "Archangel Raphael." Allison thought I would think she was crazy, as she didn't know who Raphael was, but did what was requested of her. When she told me the name Raphael, I immediately asked, "When can I come?"

As we looked at our schedules I realized the importance of the meeting and chose the Fourth of July as the date to make the trip. As our country celebrated the energy of freedom, I was enveloped with the energy of God's desire for us to freely embrace the "God–thoughts" that we are.

While in meditation with Raphael at Allison's home I received further instruction with regard to my angelic assignment to create an energy Star of David across the United States. At the conclusion of my meditation, Allison asked me if I had ever visited Cacapon Mountain. It was one of those moments when a cosmic connection is made. One of those times that you sense the bigger light bulb going on inside of your head. I replied that I had in fact been there twenty–four years prior—on my honeymoon. I had returned to participate in a mystical marriage to God's Will for my life. Allison was also blessed by the angelic energies sent by God that weekend. Her own life became a life of service to God in cooperation with the angels.

The painting of Mary holding the Christ Child and Raphael holding the cup of service started on its own traveling tour. I was guided by the angels to take the painting into homes where people were establishing healing practices, and to leave the painting there as a blessing upon their service. For several years the painting moved from home to home. Finally it came to a permanent place of service. The painting, entitled "Vision of Mary—Vision of Love," can be seen at Joshua's Lighthouse Angels in Reisterstown, Maryland. Joshua's Lighthouse Angels is a place where people who have lost children come to find solace and comfort. How perfect that when they walk through the door, there is waiting to greet them a painting of the Blessed Mother holding baby Jesus, her son. So many people have shared that as they gaze upon the painting, the true painter's voice—the voice of God—speaks to them personally. I was asked to commission this painting not as validation of my vision but rather as validation of God's eternal love for us and desire for us to experience divine healing. God blesses us to be a blessing to others.

The art that I have been led to purchase or the visions I have been given and have commissioned others to create in tangible form are blessings I am to share with others. I always laughed that I get to do the art shopping for the angels. I get to buy the art or commission the artist to create the art that God wants people to see. Later in my book, I will share how the placement of the painting of the Blessed Mother was not only a blessing for visitors of Joshua's but was also holding sacred space for another plan that would be a gift to inspire our hearts that God had in the works.

# CHAPTER 6

MARYLAND
DUIANGEL

# *Driving Miss Mary*

*T*he *vision of Mary that I* experienced in the Great Pyramid was in actuality an invitation to serve God alongside Mary and Archangel Raphael. Through divine inspirations I was asked to participate in the creation of an energy grid in the shape of a six-pointed star, known as the Creator's Star and Star of David by weaving energy at six points chosen by God.

The six-pointed star has many symbolic meanings. The upward pointing triangle of fire and masculine energy meets the downward pointing triangle of water and feminine energy, the two merging in perfect harmony. Because the blending of the two triangles creates divine emergent energy, six is known as the perfect number.

The base of each triangle bisects the other under the apex, forming the symbols for air and earth. The star portrays the four elements, which are combined with the vibration of the number three (the triangle) to produce the sacred number seven. The star itself has only six points, the seventh point is said to be invisible and represents the spiritual element of divine transformation.

In Freemasonry the six-pointed star represents totality. The Star of David was worn on the Shield of King David. It has also been called Solomon's Seal because Solomon, son of David and Bathsheba, summoned angels with it until his death in 903 B.C. The Seal of Solomon appears in holy writings and has strong associations with Hebrew mysticism.

This symbol has also been called The Creator's Star and the six points of the star have been known as representations of God's power, wisdom, love, majesty, justice, and mercy. It is believed that the concept of the six-pointed star representing the Star of Creation originated from the last verse in the first chapter of Genesis: "Then God saw everything that He had made, and indeed it was very good. So the evening and the morning were the sixth day." At the completion of the sixth day God had completed both heaven and earth. In my research of the Creator's Star I was intrigued when guided to the biblical reference because the verse is Genesis 1:31. January 31—or 1:31—is my birth date.

The star has also come to represent the temple of Jerusalem, an elaborate sacred space where heaven and earth, spirit and soul conjoin. In alchemical teachings "conjunction" or sacred marriage took place in the Holy of Holies—the heart of the temple.

The function of my weaving a Creator's Star/Star of David energy grid was to serve in providing sacred space, conjoining angels of heaven with people of earth in service to God. When Raphael first inspired me with God's assignment, I was simply asked if I would be willing to serve with the angels in the creation of a six-pointed star grid that would be a blessing to children coming to earth. I was not initially told where the points would be. Each location would be revealed just prior to the time when God wanted me to go to that location. To Raphael's question as to whether or not I was willing to answer this call of service, I simply replied, "When do we start? I'm ready."

The first point of the star was Portland, Oregon. I was asked to spend twenty-one days in Portland in November 1995. This is where the weaving began.

The angels shared with me that the Creator's Star would serve as a guiding light for children coming to earth. I met in my travels incredible men and women who in their marriages were experiencing difficulties in pregnancies. The angels sent special blessings to these people. To some souls on earth life has no value or meaning. We have witnessed the tragedy of a man blowing up a building with many lives lost, including the lives of innocent children in a daycare center. There are, however, precious people on the planet who are dedicating time, energy, and resources to welcoming a baby into their lives. The angels referred to the next generation of children as "Angel babies."

In addition to my Creator's Star weaving experience, in several of the locations I was asked by the angels to give a workshop as a fundraiser and all monies from the workshop went directly to the families of a baby who was experiencing major health afflictions. For example, the weaving tour energy began in Baltimore, Maryland, with a "kickoff" fund-raiser at Heavens to Betsy Angel Store in Ellicott City, Maryland. Betsy McMahan, the storeowner, hosted my workshop and the monies raised benefited a Maryland child who was in need of surgery for a collapsed lung. Not only had I been made aware of this child by the angels, but the angels inspired many others, as over $50,000 was raised by people responding to a photograph and article about this child, which appeared on the front page of the *Baltimore Sun* on September 29, 1995—Michaelmas Day. This was just one example of the angels revealing to us that we are making a difference in each other's lives. We do not have to feel that we have to do it all. We just have to do our part.

At the end of October 1995, I was asked by the angels to prepare to go to Portland, Oregon. As I truly do operate on a wing and a prayer, I asked for inspiration on where I could stay for the twenty-one days in Portland. I heard the name, "Hilda Kemp." Hilda Kemp was a woman who had contacted me for a one-hour spiritual consultation over the phone. She and I had never met in person. She knew of me through my book. I knew it was quite possible that when I called Hilda and asked if I could stay at her home for twenty-one days, she would quickly say goodbye to me. Yet I knew this was who God wanted me to call. When I called Hilda, I outlined why I was being called to Oregon. Hilda paused for a moment and then shared that she was a widow and had a spare bedroom and for me to proceed with my plans to come to Portland.

Hilda was eighty years of age but, because of a diet of natural supplements, looked liked she was in her sixties. I am quite certain I was placed in Hilda's home as an attempt by Spirit to clean up my un-healthy eating habits. Hilda was like the grandmother I never had. We watched *Anne of Green Gables* together. We talked spirituality into the wee hours of the morning. Hilda was called home to God a few years ago. I know there was a joyous reunion between her and her husband. I truly miss her.

I was placed in Hilda's home not only because of the blessing Hilda was to be, but additionally because I was one block away from the Grotto in Portland. The Grotto, as it is commonly called, is the National Sanctuary of Our Sorrowful Mother, a beautiful sixty-two-acre Catholic Shrine and botanical garden located in Portland, Oregon. The Friars of the Order of Servants of Mary administer it. Each morning for twenty-one days I would go to the Grotto for prayer and meditation time.

While in Portland I was asked by the angels to meet them at Mt. St. Helens. I remembered that, as I dashed out the door of my home in Upperco, Maryland, on my way to the airport to fly to Portland, Or-egon, I had reached into a heart-shaped basket in which I keep holy cards honoring saints. As I shared earlier, I believe the saints are truly universal messengers of God just as the angels are. I asked for a blessing from the saint that would be traveling with me and the card I drew was St. Helen. St. Helen had a church built over the Holy Sepulcher in Jerusa-lem and over the cave where Jesus was born in Bethlehem. She re-trieved the cross on which Jesus died and is known as the Discoverer of the True Cross.

There are things we do in our lives and at the time of doing them we do not understand why. I remember when Mt. St. Helens erupted in 1980; I contacted the U.S. Geological Survey people and obtained pho-tographs of the eruption. The photographs held me spellbound; in many of the photographs you can see spirit faces.

When the angels called me to experience Mt. St. Helens with them, I was emotionally moved by the energy of the mountain and the great-ness of God. It was a humbling experience. Let us never forget who really has the power. God is in control.

While at Mt. St. Helens I was guided to spend time in meditation weaving together with the energy of prayers, Bible verses, songs, and harp blessings the light of Archangel Michael; the light of God's fire that burns within each of us—a sacred/cosmic fire; the light of St. Helen; the light of the "Fire Sisters" and volcanoes on earth; the light of God's Will, God's Power, and God's Protection; the light of Divine Order. Additionally each grid point was connected with an ethereal body chakra. Mt. St. Helens was the foundation chakra. It contains the energy of building one's life upon faith in God. In traditional chakra teachings, the base or foundation chakra contains energies that support us in having our needs for food, shelter, and clothing met. The grid weaving included the message of John 6:48: "I am the bread of life." Each of the grid points established the energy of our relationship with God. God is the food that sustains us. Feed your faith in God and all your needs will be met. God will not fail you.

At Mt. St. Helens, the angels reminded me of how inspired I was by the book *Angels of Pompeii*, photographs by Stephen Brigidi and poetry by Robert Bly. When I first learned of this project in the works, I called Stephen Brigidi and gave him a blessing from the angels. He expressed that the project was behind schedule and he seemed a little frustrated. I told him not to give up on this project; it was very important. As a sign from the angels of the importance of this work of art, I was to purchase the first issue of his Special Edition. I have in my home Special Edition No. 1 of 200 of this incredible book.

On the front leaf of this book are the words, "When photographer and teacher Stephen Brigidi traveled to Pompeii for the first time, he was captivated by the luminous frescoes of angels on the decayed walls of the ancient city. Here, long after the destruction by Vesuvius in 79 A.D., the angels remain, timeless and transcendent."

Vesuvius is a volcanic mountain in Naples, Italy. No matter what is erupting in our lives, God sends the angels to remain around us—"timeless and transcendent."

The "Fire Sisters" that were part of the weaving energy are Mt. Shasta, Mt. St. Helens, Mt. Hood, Mt. Adams, Mt. Rainier, and Mt. Baker. The voice of God spoke to me through the volcanoes. The voice assured me that even when our whole world is erupting and our old ways are being destroyed; know that at the same time space is being made for new things. New life is to take shape. New experiences. New creations. A whole new world is being birthed from the ash.

Following the sacred weaving ceremony, I was inspired to purchase books, videos, and posters of Mt. St. Helens. One of the films showed the eruption of Mt. St. Helens and the fires that followed and gave a biblical quote that spoke to my soul:

---

*"And behold, the Lord passed by and a great and strong wind tore into the mountains and broke the rock in pieces . . . and after the wind an earthquake . . . and after the earthquake a fire . . . and after the fire a still small voice." 1 Kings 19:11-12.*

---

I felt God touch my soul with His words. In my own life I have experienced winds of change that tore my life apart; my life being broken into pieces; the ground beneath me quaking and shaking; emotional fires burning with me. After all of this, I found myself at a place where I heard the still small voice of God whispering to me, "It's a whole new world being created inside of you." Have you experienced this in your life?

In Exodus 13:21–22 the appearance of Yahweh was recorded as "A pillar of cloud by day, and a pillar of fire by night." This pretty well describes the volcanic spirit energy.

To help align yourself with the spirit of God during the winds, earthquakes, and fires of your life, I suggest that you align yourself through sound with the sound of YAHWEH. You can do this by chanting praise to God through the "ah" vibration such as *al*-leluia. The vowel sound of "ah" opens the heart to love. You can also chant *aum* emphasizing the *ah* such as *ahhmmmmmmm*.

The message of the first grid point was that true power belongs to God, and that we are to express our faith by expressing our trust that our lives are in divine order even in the midst of upheaval. You can utilize the affirmation, "My life is in divine order," to support your standing steadfast with your faith when the ground beneath you is quaking and shaking. Even if it appears your life is on shaky ground, affirm with conviction that your life is in divine order.

The experience at Mt. St. Helens mirrored to me that there are times in our lives when we are each a phoenix resurrected from the ashes. We arise as newborns from the ashes of our own personal eruptions. When I returned home from Oregon, I found my furnace had been stopped up by a chimney sweep's cleaning service and as a result ashes were strewn throughout my home. I knew that I was witnessing a physical manifestation of what was happening spiritually inside of me.

In February 1996 I was called to rendezvous with the angels in Ft. Lauderdale, Florida. A friend who knew that a special assignment with the angels was bringing me to Florida, arranged for me to stay at the private home of someone she knew. So I was to stay at the home of a friend of a friend. What occurred is one of the most bizarre incidents in my travels. The first evening of my stay the angels told me not to un-pack anything because I wasn't staying beyond this first night. They indicated I needed to unpack the angel art that I travel with and place one painting facing out to the west, one to the east, one to the north, and one to the south. I was setting up a protective wall of energy. I had no idea what I was being protected from. The next day I left my hostess's home and drove to Butterfly World in Coconut Creek, Florida. This would be the site of the weaving energy. While in the sacred energy of the conservatory, I asked for divine inspiration about what to do re-garding my living arrangements. I was inspired to go back to the home and wait for the hostess and tell her I needed to leave. I definitely did not handle this situation properly. I was certain that something was not correct in the neighborhood or the angels wouldn't be moving me out so fast. I didn't want to alarm the hostess, but at the same time I was concerned for her safety and my own as well. When the sun began to set, I wanted to "get out of Dodge," and so I decided to leave her a note. I made that choice on my own. It was not divinely inspired. And it is a decision that I look back on with disappointment in myself. I called her later that evening and with good reason she was very angry with me. I tried to express to her that I had been inspired to move on, and I at-tempted to smooth things over. I explained that it could be an under-ground energy source that was not abundant for my own energy. In the conversation she blurted out that she had already decided to put the house on the market because of drug transactions taking place next door. When she said that, I felt myself rejoice inside for her decision and for the protection of the angels around my service.

Whenever you are called to serve God's Light, there is always an energy that wants to see you fail and wants to stop you. I experienced this energy in some form throughout the entire grid-weaving project.

Once I had left this home, I quickly realized I had no place to stay. I could not reach the person who had made arrangements for me to stay at the home I had just left. Quite frankly, I knew that this individual wasn't going to be too happy with me either. The angels came to my rescue by whispering Rachel Salley's name into my ear. Rachel Salley is a British medium, who now lives in Florida. I called Rachel in Port St. Lucie. When she heard my voice she said, "Jayne, I knew something was going on with you. I have been thinking about you all day long. How can I help you?" I asked if she knew anyone living near Ft. Lauderdale who would allow me to stay in his or her home. Rachel had very good friends—John and Sandy Martinez—in a community near Ft. Lauderdale. Rachel gave me their address and told me to go to their home and ask for their help.

Through the grace of God I easily found their home and parked on the street. Sandy and John came home from work and found this strange lady sitting in a car by their home. I approached Sandy, told her that I, too, was a friend of Rachel Salley's, and explained my problem of having no place to stay. Sandy replied, "Sure you can stay with us. Come on in." As I unloaded my belongings, I heard her husband asking Sandy as he followed her into the house, "Who is that woman?" "An Angel Lady? What's an Angel Lady? Well, then, she's staying with us!"

I give thanks for Rachel Salley's help and for Sandy and John Martinez's kindness to me. Their home became my home base for the weaving of the energy in Florida. As I shared, Butterfly World was selected as the site for the sacred weaving. When Butterfly World opened for business in the spring of 1988, it became the first and largest butterfly house in the United States. It is truly a paradise to behold. At Butterfly World you will find gardens, waterfalls, tropical plants, flowers, and butterflies. Butterfly World promotes itself as the largest single butterfly habitat in the world with over 5,000 butterflies enjoying a natural rain forest environment.

A few years prior to my grid–weaving experience, I had been gifted an angel painting that I treasure. It depicts an angel seated by a stream. There's a small waterfall across from the angel. A tree is nearby with a white dove perched in the tree. The angel stretches her arm out and a butterfly touches her fingertip.

During one of my visits to Butterfly World, I was seated inside the conservatory. There was a small stream in front of me with a waterfall. A tree was near me and I looked up to see a single white dove in the tree, cooing to its heart's content. Just then I heard the angels whisper, "Art imitates life." A beautiful butterfly fluttered by. I stretched out my arm and it gave me a flutter–bye blessing as it touched my fingertips.

The second point of the Creator's Star was woven with the light of Archangel Jophiel; the light of the element of air; the light of St. Benedict; the light of butterflies; and God's light of illumination, wisdom, and understanding. The second grid point contains the energy of the second chakra, the chakra of identity, as well as the verse from John 8:12—I am the light of the world. The essence of this grid conveys to us our identity with the Christ Consciousness and relationship with the light Christ brought to the world.

The message of the second point on the grid is God's teaching that comes through butterflies. Butterflies are symbols of freedom and light. In many countries people consider butterflies as messengers from loved ones in heaven. There's a legend that butterflies developed from the tears of the Virgin Mary. In China butterflies symbolize the soul, trans–formation, and rebirth. Butterflies inspire us to remember we are evolv–ing from our life as caterpillars, and in the process there is a time in which we are in transition. We each are no longer the caterpillars and we're not quite at the point of becoming butterflies. This time period requires trust and faith in the process of pushing through old barriers into becoming our true butterfly–self, complete with glorious wings.

Additionally, the blessing of understanding was taught to me. In a dream, God appeared to King Solomon and asked him, "What shall I give you?" Solomon could have asked for anything. His response is found in 1 King 3:9: " . . . give to your servant an understanding heart to judge your people, that I may discern between good and evil . . . "

This answer was very pleasing to God in Solomon's time and is very pleasing to God today when we choose to ask for an understanding heart for our own lives. In our prayers we can ask for the ability to understand with God's illumination, that which is good and evil for us. When you find yourself confused by events going on in your life, still yourself and ask for God's understanding. "God, what would you have my heart understand about this problem?"

St. Benedict's blessing was woven into the star grid because of his life serving as an example of a messenger of God's wisdom, discretion, and loving kindness. St. Benedict built twelve monasteries. His monasteries were sanctuaries of light and learning. Without the monasteries, which kept focused on transcribing manuscripts of the Bible and on preserving the teachings of God's wisdom and illumination, the Dark Ages would have been even darker.

When St. Benedict was dying, he asked his fellow monks to assist him in standing in the chapel of one of his monasteries. He raised his hands in praise to God as he died. I was inspired when I read this, because he was creating a "Y" with his body, arms raised to heaven to honor the glory of Yahweh. Benedict established an order or rule for monastic life which many orders still function under to this day. Interestingly enough, the second chakra energizes our duality energies. All of us have masculine and feminine energies within us. St. Benedict was a twin. His sister Scholastica founded the Benedictine order of nuns.

The element of air, woven into the second grid point, is representative of our mental faculties, our using the gift of our minds to become great thinkers. Identify yourself as someone whom God has blessed with the gift of free will. With that freedom of choice, choose to think of yourself as a God-thought. Exercise your mind muscles daily.

In the spring of 1996, I was next called to Whitney, Texas, to the Chapel of Light to weave the energy of the third point of the star grid. The energy was woven together with the light of Archangel Chamuel; the light of the heart of God; the light of the divine heartbeat; the light of St. Anthony; the light of the joy of puppies; the light of the love of God and adoration to God.

The third grid point's weaving contained the energy of the third chakra—the solar plexus. This is the power point of the body. In ancient times it was believed by some that our mind was actually in our solar plexus—the area beneath our ribs—because we would get "gut" feelings there. The message of John 10:7—I am the door of the sheep—is expressed in this grid point. A gentleman who was involved in the early years of Alcoholics Anonymous established the Chapel of Light. He was a leading speaker for AA conferences. The Chapel has twelve steps that lead up the church. Once inside there are twelve stained glass windows—each in a different color. The grid point blessed the healing that AA has given to thousands of people on the planet. The message from John conveyed that AA is a "God-door" that is opened to people who need to be gathered together through their AA meetings and through the strength of God, the strength of the group, and the God strength inside of each of them, they are able to turn their lives around and look to God's light.

I remember as I was leaving the Chapel after having completed the grid weaving, and walking down the twelve front steps of the Chapel, the angels saying to me that an additional blessing about AA is that people go to AA first seeking help for themselves; i.e., they walk the AA "steps" to help heal their addiction to alcohol. However, at some point the energy shifts and they become one with the "steps" and become support to others who follow in their footsteps to join AA for help. And this is true; each new AA member has a sponsor who is someone who has themselves walked the steps of AA.

I cannot write or talk about St. Anthony without feeling my heart expand with love. I treasure St. Anthony's support and friendship in my life. He is known as St. Anthony of Padua. Many people know Anthony as the Patron Saint of Lost Property. If ever you misplace something, call upon Anthony for help. I always say, "St. Anthony, St. Anthony, please come round. Something is lost and needs to be found."

Anthony was both teacher and preacher. He was very charismatic and because of his popularity he usually spoke outdoors rather than inside of churches because of the large numbers of people who came to hear him speak. St. Francis chose Anthony to teach the friars at Padua and Bologna. He was so loved that he was recognized as a saint one year after his death in 1232.

When I was in Portland, Oregon, relics of St. Anthony were touring the United States. As I was beginning the first leg of quite a lengthy odyssey with the angels, I was comforted when I learned Anthony was in town.

Anthony is a blessed soul who from heaven continues to work wonders and miracles for the glory of God. He truly is a messenger of the light of the heart of God and just thinking about him lightens my heart.

The blessings of "puppies" was also woven into the grid energy at Whitney, Texas. Some years back I attended a Sacred Art class and one of our assignments was to draw a picture of a childhood memory that conveyed the message of happiness to us. I didn't hesitate in knowing what I would draw. My parents have a photograph of this precious childhood moment. I have my favorite red wagon and I am taking six puppies for a ride. I adore puppies. I honor William Wegman for his beautiful healing service provided in his book *Puppies*. I have gifted family members and friends this book because it's page after page of pure joy, happiness, and goodness.

While in Whitney, Texas, I participated in an angel conference. Under the front steps of the church where I was speaking a mommy dog had given birth to puppies about a week or two earlier. The mommy dog had kept the puppies underneath the steps, and no one in the church community had yet seen the puppies. I was obsessed with the hope, wish, and desire that the puppies would come out to play. I gave my angel lecture and before the next speaker took the podium, we had a short break. I went outside to the steps, still carrying the hope in my heart that the puppies would appear. At that very moment chubby, furry little balls of love came bouncing out into the light. Puppies smell like goodness. All of the children came running to see the precious puppies. The mommy dog watched us; however, I got the feeling she was happy to have human babysitters take over to give her a break. She could tell that we loved them abundantly.

The conference organizer came up to me and said, "Jayne, no one is going to come inside until you do." I knew I had to go inside however much "little Jayne" wanted to be outside with the children and the puppies. I handed the puppies over to the children and went inside.

The next speaker came to the podium. Directly behind her was a large glass window that was the entire width of the front of the church. This window revealed the front of the church where the puppies had

just appeared. While the speaker began sharing her words of inspiration, the children came to the window with the puppies in their arms
showing them to all of us inside. The conference leader leaned over to
me and said, "You're responsible for this." God wants our lives to be
filled with goodness. Puppies are proof positive.

Following the completion of the grid work in Texas I waited for the
call to anchor the fourth point of the Creator's Star. Prior to being given
my travel plans, I was told by the angels in meditation, "The Hand of
God raised in blessing/benediction will be appearing. When you know
of it, you are to go stand witness to it." I was expecting a large hand to
appear in a dream and point to a location on a map and that would be
my marching orders. However, that wasn't God's plan at all.

In May 1996 an article appeared in the *Baltimore Sun* on the front page
of the feature section. The article was copy only, no picture. The headline read: Raphael Drawing Unveiled. The copy went something like
this: A hand raised in a blessing or benediction, drawn by fifteenth
century artist Raphael has been discovered in the archives of the Art
Institute of Chicago.

I was drawn to the article initially when I saw the name "Raphael" in
the headline. As I've shared, my assignment was being fulfilled in conjunction with Archangel Raphael and the Blessed Mother.

I called the Chicago Art Institute and spoke to the head of the department that was involved with the uncovering of the Raphael etching
in the archives. I asked when the public would be allowed to see the
drawing. I was told spring, 1997. I explained my assignment with the
angels and asked if I could come visit them now and be allowed to see
the image. I was granted permission.

I did not know the date the angels wanted me to go on this assignment. It had always been clear in the past that I was to leave immediately upon hearing of my mission. However, I felt that this wasn't what
God wanted in this instance. As I've shared before, when something is
right and something is true, your whole body chimes in the key of you.
I stood in the center of my living room with numbers of calendar dates
that started with today and went forward through the month of May.
When I stood on May 30 my whole body vibrated in oneness with
God's Will. I was a human bell. I asked the angels, am I correct—it's May

30? I heard them respond, "If it is confirmation you want, go to your saint calendar." I rushed to my office and flipped excitedly through the calendar to May 30. There before me was a drawing of St. Joan of Arc (1412–1431) on the date of Thursday, May 30, 1996, with Joan's own words: "I was born to do this." On May 30 I flew to Chicago to visit the Chicago Institute of Art because I was born to do this.

Raphael the artist was born on Good Friday and died on Good Friday. Even though he only was on the earth for thirty–seven years, he painted over 700 works of art. The Chicago Institute had wanted to purchase a Raphael for their collection and they were blessed to discover a Raphael had been gifted to them. It was waiting for them to discover it in their archives. So often we go seeking for treasures in our life and they are in our own backyard waiting for our discovery.

The drawing by Raphael was in preparation for a painting of St. Peter that is in the Vatican in Rome. The importance of the drawing is that it is an image of God blessing our lives with wisdom that was imparted to us by Jesus when he spoke to St. Peter.

In Matthew 16, Jesus asked His disciples who everyone in the community was saying Jesus was? The disciples told Jesus there was talk that he was John the Baptist, Elijah, even one of the prophets.

He then asked them who they said that he was.

Peter responded from the truth of his heart. He said to Jesus, "You are the Christ, the Son of the living God." Because of Peter's response, Jesus blessed Peter and said to him that upon Peter he would build His church. He goes on to give Peter the keys of heaven.

The teaching from the Raphael drawing is that people around you will project upon you their feeling of who you are. However, when you look yourself in the mirror in the morning and see the man or woman looking back, imagine the Christ asking you: "But who do you say that I am?" And respond with an answer that resonates with the truth of your heart. For myself, I respond to Christ's question by saying, "I am an earthangel4peace. I have answered your call on the Mount to be a peacemaker and walk in your footsteps peacefully." When we respond with that which is revealed to us by our Father in heaven as the truth of our hearts, Christ answers back that He will build His service upon our lives.

In the spring of 1997 I was traveling through Chicago and stopped again at the Chicago Institute of Art. I smiled when I saw that the Raphael drawing had been placed in a prominent position so that it literally blessed everyone who walked into the museum.

The actual weaving took place in the center of the museum where a glorious set of six glass panels entitled "America's Windows," created by Marc Chagall, is on display. "America's Windows" was designed in 1977 in commemoration of the American Bicentennial. The weaving brought together the energies of the light of Archangel Uriel, the light of the Holy Breath of Holy Spirit, the light of St. Joan of Arc, the light of doves as messengers of peace, the light of the grace of God, and ministration to others through selfless service.

The grid wove together energies of the fourth chakra—the heart chakra—and the words from John 10:7, "I am the good shepherd."

The message of the grid point is for each of us to be a good shepherd, guardian to our hearts and the love that God has placed within each of our hearts. A shepherd is one who takes good care of that which he is watching over, i.e., a flock. Do we sometimes put our heart energy in harm's way? As a good shepherd we need to love ourselves and to take actions to prevent possible harm. In respect of the love God has given us, housed in our hearts, it is important that when someone is being unkind and abusive to us that we express to them that we prefer that they not speak to us in that tone or display a certain behavior while in our company. Boundaries that we put in place when someone is acting out are to be compared to the fencing that the good shepherd surrounds his flock with to keep the wolves out. Are you keeping the wolves away from your heart?

Additionally, the energies woven in Chicago connected the energies of the grid with the star grid energy that is already in place beneath the city of Jerusalem. Chagall's "Windows" can be found in Jerusalem. In the Synagogue of the Hadassah–Hebrew University Medical Center, as part of the hospital's golden anniversary celebration in February 1962, the Chagall "Windows" were unveiled. The "Windows" represent the Twelve Tribes of Israel. Marc Chagall commented that as he worked on the "Windows," "I felt my father and my mother were looking over my shoulder and behind them were Jews, millions of other vanished Jews of yesterday and a thousand years ago."

In some way I felt that through the light weaving and the creation of the energy Creator's Star, the "America's Windows" and the "Windows" in Jerusalem were coming together to glorify God. The legacy of the faithful people of God was woven into this grid point. I recently heard a song sung as part of the Sight and Sound Production of Abraham and Sarah in Lancaster, Pennsylvania. The words ask the question: Will those who come behind you find that you had been faithful?

The inspiration of the doves and their role as symbols of peace is shared in more detail in the chapter "Earthangel4peace."

In September 1996 I was called to New England. At America's Stonehenge in Salem, New Hampshire, the fifth grid energy was woven together. America's Stonehenge may be one of North America's oldest megalithic sites. The stone walls and large standing stones cover well over thirty acres. It's been compared to England's Stonehenge because ancient people who had knowledge of astronomy and building with stone configurations were responsible for the creation of both sites. America's Stonehenge can be used to determine both significant solar and lunar events of the year. It is one of the most important archeological sites in the western hemisphere. In this beautiful wooded setting the light of Archangel Gabriel, the light of the element of earth, the light of St. Theresa, the light of trees, and the light of God's goodness and purity were woven together.

It was a blessing of the fifth chakra—the throat chakra—and the message of John 10:11, "I am the resurrection and the life." The throat chakra is known as the will center of the chakra system. So often we "will" or allow and tolerate things in our lives by what we do or do not communicate. The throat center is a communication chakra. In Eastern traditions, the base of the neck is recognized as a spiritual doorway, and meditation directs concentration and focus of energies upon this power point. By energizing this chakra point, a spiritual doorway is opened and the individual is in the flow with divine communication. God speaks to us through this grid point with clarity of communication, Christ's words: I am the resurrection and the life.

The nature kingdom's message of this grid point came from the Mother Earth and trees. The trees are the ancient ones on our planet.

Trees inspire us to be connected to both heaven and earth. Trees are vital to the earth's life support systems.

Dorothy Maclean communicated with the tree devas when living in Findhorn, Scotland. Here's one of their messages spoken to her; yet the words are for all of us to hear:

---
❧
---

*"We are guardians of the Earth in many ways, and humans should be a part of what we guard. We are not active young things; we are, in many ways, like a school of benevolent philosophers with nonhuman purity and a great wish to serve humanity. Trees are vital to man and to life on this planet, and we are eager to experience this contact with some of you humans before the others of your kind destroy all that trees have built up."*

---

On December 10, 1997, a twenty-five-year-old woman named Julia "Butterfly" Hill climbed up into an eighteen-story high perch in an ancient redwood in California in protest of the destruction of a 600-year-old redwood, scheduled to be chopped down by a lumber company. It was only after two years of living in her treehouse that the lumber company negotiated an agreement that would spare the redwood and a 200-foot zone from logging. Hill is a woman who walked her talk. During those two years, Hill slept under a tarp on an eight-by-eight-foot plywood platform, bathed in a bucket, and hauled up food and supplies by rope. She weathered winds and rains and chilly winters. Hill remarked, "There is no way to be in the presence of these ancient beings and not be affected."

The essence of the fifth grid point contained God's purity and goodness. If there ever was a saint on the planet who conveyed that message, then it was St. Theresa. She is known as the Little Flower.

St. Theresa entered a Carmelite monastery at the age of fifteen. She literally went to Pope Leo XIII and begged him to grant her permission to enter the convent as such a young age. She lived the life of a cloistered nun until her death at twenty-four years of age from tuberculosis.

She wrote her autobiography, *The Story of a Soul*, only after she was ordered to do so by her prioress. In this book St. Theresa wrote that after she died she would "let fall a shower of roses"—miracles and favors—upon those who called upon her for help. This sweet young woman made a pledge to those who read her book that she would be there to help them when they needed her, even after death. So many miracles were attributed to this precious soul following her death that she was canonized just twenty–eight years after her death.

Prior to my leaving for New Hampshire, I received a phone call from Michele Livingston. Michele is someone who truly embodies the same goodness found in St. Theresa. Michele herself had answered a personal call from the Blessed Mother to serve by painting twelve images of Mary and writing the book *Visions from Mary*. This book is filled with words of encouragement and guidance for those who wish to forge a deeper covenant with God.

Prior to the public release of the book, the Blessed Mother asked Michele to invite twelve women—selected by Mary—to come to Michele's art studio and receive a blessing from Mother Mary. Each of the women chosen embodied a message that was conveyed in one of the twelve paintings. Not only did Michele ask me to come to the unveiling of the art, but she also asked if I could come a half hour sooner than the others as the Blessed Mother had sent Michele shopping. Michele indicated to me that she had a gift the Holy Mother wanted me to have. Now I know what I am going to share next is going to sound crazy. However, I am a big fan of Michael Bolton's. The same evening as the unveiling, I had already obtained a ticket for his concert in York, Pennsylvania. As a member of his fan club, I am able to buy a ticket within the first two rows of his concerts. I, of course, wanted to receive all the blessings of Mary; and at the same time, my inner child wanted to go to the concert, too. During the grid project, I rarely went to concerts or movies. There just wasn't time. At the beginning of 1996 the angels asked me what I wanted for myself in the year ahead. I remarked that I wanted to see Michael Bolton in concert. I was so excited when I saw in the newspaper that he would be appearing in concert one evening in September 1996 at York Fairgrounds in York, Pennsylvania. It is less than an hour from my home. I quickly bought a ticket for the show and looked forward with anticipation to the concert until Mother Mary made me this offer I couldn't refuse.

I explained my dilemma to Michele, and she saw the answer. She indicated that the event would be held early enough so I could do both.

I drove to Michele's studio in Camp Hill, Pennsylvania, on September 8, 1996. This is the date recognized as Mary's birthday. The gift I was given was a music box with a painting of Our Lady of Mt. Carmel—the image of Mary holding Christ as a baby—on the lid of the music box. Michele explained to me that Mary was blessing my service with children. Michele's words were, "I don't know what you are doing in service that is blessing the children; however, Mother Mary does and this is her way of saying thank you for answering the call."

Shortly after this private meeting with Michele, the eleven other ladies arrived. Each of us was given a personal blessing from the Holy Mother upon our lives. I was seated in the first position of the twelve paintings. My service was mirrored to me through the painting entitled, "The Annunciation" and Mary blessed me with the word: Obedience. Obedience or obey originates from the Latin *obedire*, which means to listen to. It combines the prefix *ob*, which means "to" and *audire*, which means, "hear." When we are obedient or obey God, we hear God's will for us.

Annunciation means to announce and my life has been dedicated to announcing to those who are willing to hear, that God loves us abundantly and gives us so many gifts as blessings, one of which is the angelic kingdom.

The beautiful ceremony unveiling the twelve paintings that reveal Mother Mary's divine, healing essence, rather than Her actual physical appearance, concluded at 7:30 p.m. and I was able to easily make the 8 p.m. Michael Bolton concert. God is good!

Prior to the final grid anchoring in California, I was guided to the Serpent Mounds in Peebles, Ohio, where God asked that I be joined by three of my girlfriends, Judy Stipanovich, Sandy Milczarek, and Susan Roos, for the creation of a sacred celebration. Each of my three friends contacted me separately and shared that they had received a divine inspiration that there was a project I was fulfilling with the angels and they were being encouraged to offer their help. In short, God had told them, "Call Jayne, something's in the works and you're part of it."

At the same time they were receiving messages, I was being told that a ceremony involving four people was to be created to honor the four religions and faiths inside the gates of Jerusalem. God wanted us to host a celebration of His light united on the planet, not divided.

We created a holy ritual with sacred readings, prayers, song, and messages honoring the community of Jerusalem in all of us.

In the chapter "Angels with Fur," I share the symbolism of bluebirds who are God's messengers of happiness. When the four of us gathered for prayer and ritual dedicated to visualizing a community of peace within the walls of Jerusalem, we were the only humans, other than the park ranger; however, we were joined by hundreds of bluebirds in the trees. I truly believe these winged messengers of happiness were holding the energy of God's desire for people of all nations to live happily and in peace on the planet together.

Once this holy service energizing the oneness of God within Jerusalem was celebrated, I was asked to be the chauffeur/driver of the energy across the United States via Route 66. I was driving the Divine Mother across the "Mother Road." I had enjoyed the movie *Driving Miss Daisy*. In this case I was "Driving Miss Mary."

The Creator's Star configuration being woven by light energy was a blessing of the New Jerusalem, which is in each and every one of us. As the Bible reflects, the New Jerusalem is a presence of God that is so brilliant and shining that no sun or moon is needed for light. I felt that the angelic assignment was a form of God's blessing upon all those who sincerely wanted to be closer and more connected to God. Its purpose was to enhance people's consciousness of God's Presence.

One day during this incredible odyssey experience when I was feeling "the spirit is willing but the flesh is weak," I asked for divine insight on what was being created by this energetic star configuration. I was inspired by the angels to turn on the radio and heard the playing of the Walt Disney classic tune, "When you wish upon a star, makes no difference who you are . . . When you wish upon a star, your dreams come true." I knew God was expressing His support of our dreams and this energy star would be a blessing to all the dreamers who were dreaming of a better world for the children.

William Wordsworth has written in his "Intimations of Immortality":

---

*"Our birth is but a sleep and a forgetting:*
*The Soul that rises with us, our life's Star,*
*Hath had elsewhere its setting,*
*And cometh from afar:*
*Not in entire forgetfulness,*
*And not in utter nakedness,*
*But trailing clouds of glory do we come*
*From God, who is our home."*

---

The Creator's Star was being put in place by God's order. Nature, saints, angels and archangels, the power of the words of the Bible, and the peace of the harp's vibration were fulfilling the order given.

So I drove to Illinois and connected with Route 66—the Mother Road. I drove Route 66 through Missouri, Oklahoma, Texas, New Mexico, Arizona, and California.

Many interesting occurrences took place on the journey. One of the most precious occurred in Oklahoma. Twenty years ago, while vacationing in New Orleans, Louisiana, I had shopped at a Women's Exchange where I bought an antique quilt. The quilt was a signature quilt; that is, the women who had stitched the quilt had embroidered their names on the quilt. The quilt was made in the 1930s in Sayre, Oklahoma, and had been a project of a group of women who belonged to the Methodist Church. I had totally forgotten about the quilt. In fact, it was packed away in a linen closet in my home. I stopped for lunch in Sayre, Oklahoma. As I ate my lunch I kept searching in my memory as to why Sayre, Oklahoma, had a feeling of familiarity. Then it hit me! The signature quilt stitched by the women of Sayre.

After lunch, I drove through town and looked for the Methodist Church. I found the First United Methodist Church. The church and its office were both open, which in this day and age is a miracle in itself. I chatted with the staff about the quilt. They indicated they would love to

see photographs of the quilt. They commented that the ladies had created the quilt as part of a fundraising effort to support the new church
that was being built in the 1930s. I knew that I had merely been the
guardian of the quilt and that the quilt was going to be heading back to
Sayre, Oklahoma, when I got home to Maryland.

Route 66 is a 2400-mile highway that runs from Illinois to California.
Unfortunately, a good part of this incredible route is disappearing. So at
times it was no easy task finding where the road went. Route 66 literally
brings you to the Pacific Ocean at Santa Monica. I remember having
parked my car at the end of the route in California and hearing the
angels say to me, "There's one more road you need to drive." Considering the Pacific Ocean was right in front of me, I thought I was going to
receive a crash course from the angels on how to walk on water. Instead, the road they were referencing was Route 101—the Mission Road
of California. The angels asked that I drive to as many missions as possible and do a light-weaving blessing in the chapels of the missions. I
visited nineteen of the twenty-one missions of California. I found, waiting for me to discover, sacred sanctuaries and gardens and a treasury of
religious art that gave me an experience of inner peace and serenity.
The final mission experience was at the San Rafael Mission in San Rafael,
California, and my visit to that mission occurred after the completion of
the anchoring of the grid light for the sixth point of the Creator's Star.

The final point of the grid was woven at Questhaven Retreat in
Escondido, California. Questhaven is a Christian retreat situated in
northern San Diego County. Founded in 1940 by the Reverends Flower
and Lawrence Newhouse, it encompasses 640 acres of pristine wilder-
ness preserve consecrated to the Lord Christ.

The angels chose Questhaven because of Flower Newhouse's earthly
service in cooperation with the angels. After my first encounter with
my guardian angel at eleven years old, I began seeking information for
myself about the angels. As I delved into researching the angels and
validating my own personal experiences, Flower Newhouse's books
were divine blessings in my life. Though I never met her personally, I
was touched by her Christward Ministry and service with the angels.
For me, Flower Newhouse was the pioneer spirit in awakening America's
consciousness to angels.

Several weeks prior to my arrival at Questhaven, the land surrounding the property experienced horrific destruction due to raging forest
fires. Over 8,000 acres of land were reduced to ash because of the fires.

I remember arriving at Questhaven and seeing how close the fire
had come to the church on the property. On the front porch of the
church was a plastic flowerpot that had melted because of the intensity
of the heat. The church was spared. I looked across the fields and saw so
much of the land black with ash. My eyes were drawn to a hillside that
was totally black from the fire's charring effects, except for one object. A
single white cross stood untouched at the top of the hill. It mirrored to
me the energies Flower had put into place at Questhaven. Her devotion
to Jesus was so powerful that it withstood threatening fires. Both church
and cross did not burn.

As I walked the property of Questhaven and saw the impact of the
fire on the environment, I was reminded of the devastation that was left
in the wake of Mt. St. Helen's eruption in 1980 in Oregon. I knew that
from the ashes of this fire new life would come forth. I was walking up
a hillside when the light of the sun reflected on an object in the ash. I
reached down and there was a rune. The word "rune" means "secret."
Runes are sacred symbols that originated among the Germanic tribes
and were used as divination oracles. There are twenty-four rune symbols and one blank rune in a runic set.

The rune that I picked up from within the ash is Perth. It is the rune
of initiation, new pathways, quantum leaps in consciousness, and evolutionary change.

On the hillside of Questhaven the grid energy was that the Creator's
Star was completed. The light was woven with the light of Archangel
Raphael and the Blessed Mother Mary; the light of the element of water;
the light of St. Francis of Assisi; the light of dolphins and whales—the
angels of the ocean; and God's light of healing, consecration, and inner
vision.

St. Francis is a man whom people of all religions know as a saint. He
walked away from his family's fortune to serve God by serving the
poor. He was the founder of the Franciscans. His order has spread
throughout the world. He saw God in everything. He considered the
sun, moon, stars, and animals all family members and would refer to

each as brother or sister. He was a messenger of the importance of loving all the creatures God made.

He believed that in serving the poor, he was serving Jesus. In his Canticle of the Sun, written just prior to his death, he gave thanks for all of God's gifts. He even recognizes death as a gift. In the *Canticle to the Sun* he is a messenger to all of us, telling us not to fear death. For when we close our eyes to earth we will be opening them to God, Christ, the angels, saints, and our loved ones.

Canticle of Brother Sun and Sister Moon of St. Francis of Assisi:

---

*Most High, all-powerful, all-good Lord,*
*All praise is Yours, all glory, all honour and all blessings.*
*To you alone, Most High, do they belong,*
*    and no mortal lips are worthy to pronounce Your Name.*
*Praised be You my Lord with all Your creatures,*
*    especially Sir Brother Sun,*
*Who is the day through whom You give us light.*
*And he is beautiful and radiant with great splendour,*
*Of You Most High, he bears the likeness.*
*Praised be You, my Lord, through Sister Moon and the stars,*
*In the heavens you have made them bright, precious and fair.*
*Praised be You, my Lord, through Brothers Wind and Air,*
*And fair and stormy, all weather's moods,*
*    by which You cherish all that You have made.*
*Praised be You my Lord through Sister Water,*
*So useful, humble, precious and pure.*
*Praised be You my Lord through Brother Fire,*
*    through whom You light the night*
*    and he is beautiful and playful and robust and strong.*
*Praised be You my Lord through our Sister, Mother Earth*
*    who sustains and governs us,*
*    producing varied fruits with coloured flowers and herbs.*
*Praise be You my Lord through those who grant pardon*
*    for love of You and bear sickness and trial.*
*Blessed are those who endure in peace,*

*By You Most High, they will be crowned.*
*Praised be You, my Lord through Sister Death,*
   *from whom no one living can escape.*
*Woe to those who die in mortal sin!*
*Blessed are they She finds doing Your Will.*
*No second death can do them harm.*
*Praise and bless my Lord and give Him thanks,*
*And serve Him with great humility.*

---

The energy of the sixth chakra—the intuitive center—was woven into the grid along with the message of John 14:6—I am the way, the truth, and the life. For me the sixth chakra represents God's revelations in our life, revelations through intuitive flashes and inspirations. As I wove the energies with the team God had brought together, I knew the Creator's Star was being put in place to reveal a pathway to the Lord, the truth of the Lord, and eternal life with the Lord. The sixth chakra blessing reveals that in all death experiences, God creates sacred space for the birthing of something new. God doesn't close a door without opening a new one. Doors closing; doors opening. Death, birth.

I have learned in my life the importance of completions. When a door closes, I respect the closure and look for the new door opening. If you do not close doors behind you and leave them closed, you will experience a draft in your new endeavors.

Additionally, I recommend that in all your activities you make certain that there is the element of completeness. For example, you are leading a business meeting during your workday. Before leaving the meeting, ask if everyone is complete on what was discussed and what their assignments are. If you get into the ritual of asking yourself if your activities are complete for the moment, you will find you are not leaving bits and pieces of yourself scattered about from the day's activities. Have you ever had a conversation or meeting that you reflect upon later in the day and wonder who is supposed to do what? Completeness is not the same as finishing. Completeness is the action of having some sort of closure to whatever activity is taking place. One of the reasons I believe people experience the energy of fatigue syndrome is because of the lack of completeness. When we build upon the feeling that things are left without appropriate closure, we convey to ourselves in an unconscious language that we are not achieving anything. And as a result of this confused message, we start feeling frustrated and tired. When you end a meeting, ask, "Are we all complete here?" Everyone walks away feeling they accomplished something from a meeting that had a beginning and an end. Life becomes a blur when you lack completeness in your life. You cannot tell where you stop or start. Experiment with taking charge of your life and asking for completeness in your conversations and meetings.

An even more important message of the final grid blessing was for us to fully immerse ourselves in God's love. Jump in with both feet into God's love. Be fully alive. Flow with your passion. As the ancient Sanskrit blessing I mentioned earlier tells us: Sat Chit Ananda—Be the fullness of your joy or bliss. In living and loving in your life with passion, joy, and bliss, you are glorifying God. God's love gave you your life. The greatest thanks you can give back to God is to love the gift of your life.

Even though Questhaven is not next to the ocean, the water connection is very profound. Questhaven was created with an energy of a divine "wellspring" and the essence energies of the grids beneath the earth of Questhaven are very supportive of and are supported by the dolphins and whales in the nearby Pacific Ocean. While walking the property of Questhaven, there were many times I would have an experience of "bleed through" energy where I thought I was on an island in the Pacific. I strongly believe that Questhaven's energy is in some way connected with Lemuria.

Ted Andrews has created a tarot deck called the Animal-Wise Tarot. In his accompanying book he shares that whales bring the message of greater depths of creativity to support making our life more wondrous. He writes that three of the most ancient and powerful creative forces have always been water, sound, and breath. Dolphins come as messengers that these three powers are coming together in our lives. I knew that God had chosen these totems for the final anchoring in the grid light weaving assignment as a blessing of encouragement. God is encouraging us to make creative choices to make life more wondrous.

Once I completed the grid light weaving of the Creator's Star at Questhaven, I drove to San Rafael Mission via Route 101. The route took me right through San Francisco and to my amazement across the Golden Gate Bridge. I remember coming upon the bridge and being so awe–struck that I actually drove across the bridge in a state of numb–ness. I wasn't able to absorb the incredible scenery. I was in a state of shock at actually driving on the Golden Gate Bridge. I looked forward with excitement to the return drive home, which would allow me to cross the bridge again in a more conscious state, I hoped. That was not to be God's plan for me.

After completing my light blessing at San Rafael Mission, I once again got in my car and headed toward the Golden Gate Bridge. I remember coming up over the hill of Sausalito and fully expecting to see the bridge, but instead it was the tollbooth. I thought to myself, "Oh, it must be after the toll booth that I get on the bridge." However, once I paid the toll I was back in downtown San Francisco. The bridge wasn't part of my route home. I couldn't figure out where the bridge went.

When I got back to the home of my hostess and was having dinner with her and her husband, I questioned the husband about how it was possible for me to cross the bridge one way but not cross the bridge going the same route home. This man is an engineer, and from the way he looked at me I could tell he definitely thought I didn't have both oars in the water. He simply remarked, "It's not possible. You have to go over the bridge to get back home." I could sense that my adventure was making him a little nervous about who was sleeping under his roof, and to be quite frank, the episode made me a little nervous as I didn't know what had happened.

That evening the angels would awaken me and explain what had transpired. In the middle of the night, when the angels awoke me, they had me look at my toll ticket. The time I crossed through the tollbooth was 13:13. I thought to myself that this was an incredible numerical message as the Creator's Star grid project had begun with a vision of the Blessed Mother in the Great Pyramid in Egypt on 12:12—December 12, 1994. Now in November 1996—almost two years later, the project was complete. The angels were now showing me the message of 13:13.

Was this in some way conveying the next step now that the 12:12 project was complete?

The angels encouraged me to do one of my favorite tasks—research the number 13. In a symbology book I carried cross country with me, I found the description for what is called the "Thirteenth Aeon." This is a sort of dimensional doorway. It occurs when a student of enlightenment is ready to cross the "Golden Gate" into Shamballa or God consciousness. I read and reread the words "Golden Gate." I realized I had been gifted the experience of teleportation into God consciousness. Why? Because my life is dedicated to delivering God's messages. God wanted to give me an experience because quite frankly, I would pass it on to you. The message of this experience is that we oftentimes worry about how things are going to happen. Through God we can literally be picked up and put down where God wants us to be without ever really knowing how it happened. It's God being God. By immersing ourselves in God, things happen that just plain go beyond any rational explanation.

In my lectures I often come across people who are concerned about the catastrophes that earth changes may cause. I know from the Golden Gate Bridge experience, that you can focus all your energies on the fear of what might happen and then in a divine blink the earth change experience happens. You'll find yourself in another reality where God has placed you and you missed the whole "catastrophe" part. Won't you feel really foolish? I was given the ride of my life and I wasn't even conscious of the scenery. Where was I when the ride was going on? I cannot answer that. I know I was here in one moment and there in the next. What came in the middle I missed by blinking. This life is really just a blink in the divine reality. As I drove my car up over the hill to where the Golden Gate Bridge was in the third dimension, God teleported my car with me in it—thinking I was doing the driving—to the opposite side of the bridge in a divine blink of the eye. God was giving me a glimpse of the reality that exists beyond my earthly sight. I was so focused on seeing the Golden Gate Bridge that I totally missed the holy instant I was "out of here."

One of my favorite poems is entitled "Earth Blindness," and it conveys the message that we get so used to seeing everything through earth eyes that we are blinded to what is beyond our earthly sight.

---

*Last night an angel met me at the door;*
*He said, "Time is no more!*
*I have been sent from Heaven to say,*
*Tomorrow dawns for thee a New Day.*
*Time will become Eternity for thee;*
*Sleep thou tonight; tomorrow come with me."*
*And then I wept, my face unto the wall;*
*I heard a thousand earthly voices call,*
*Unfinished tasks, loved faces, children dear,*
*And in my soul I cried: "Oh leave me here!*
*Come not tomorrow, angel, to my gate;*
*I crave more time; I pray thee, wait!"*
*Then turned the angel with so sad a smile,*
*"Thou foolish one, to pray to wait the while.*
*Open thine eyes! If thou couldst only see.*
*The visions just beyond awaiting thee!*
*Wouldst those abide where days dissolve in night?*
*How blind thou art to things beyond thy sight!"*

---

How truly blind I was on that sunny afternoon on the Golden Gate Bridge to things that were beyond my human sight.

I do know that on the Golden Gate Bridge I was traveling at "Godspeed." I believe there is no coincidence that John Glenn was selected to go into outer space a second time. On his first voyage in 1962 he was wished a safe journey by Scott Carpenter's words: "Godspeed, John Glenn." Scott Carpenter, the Mercury astronaut who was Mr. Glenn's backup in 1962, came up with the inspiration just seconds before the final countdown. The words were re-echoed to us when John Glenn returned to space on October 29, 1998. Following the launch, NASA played a tape for the crew onboard of a greeting from Carpenter, "Good luck, have a safe flight, and once again, Godspeed, John Glenn."

Imagine your body is a spaceship. It's the vehicle in which you travel through life. As you raise your vibration, your spaceship oscillates faster than before. Oscillation is the speed of vibration. The speed of the vibrational level of your spaceship is determined by your physical condition, your moods, your energy, your environment, and so on.

Your life unfolds according to the energy frequency you choose to operate your spaceship in. Positive inspirational experience will be of a higher frequency and vibrational speed than negative, limiting ones. Once you begin loving yourself and respecting God's gift of your life and your spaceship, your energy moves fast and faster, and the faster frequency creates a dimension of greater positive energy in your life.

The fast frequency leads you away from negative events or lesser frequency situations. Energy seeks its own level. You cannot have two discordant energies sharing the same space. An energy of 25,000 cycles operating next to an energy of 250,000 cycles will attempt to keep the speed for a short time and then eventually will fall away.

When your energy is high enough, you experience "disappearance" or becoming invisible. As you move your life into operating at a higher frequency through experiences that are uplifting, you move toward a oneness with God's speed or infinite light speed. Your life becomes infinitely large and expansive. In such a space, Mother Teresa was able to serve in a ghetto environment and see Christ in the face of everyone she served. In her service everything disappeared around her except the face of the divine and the call of the divine to serve. Like the Beach Boys' song, it's about "picking up good vibrations."

On November 1996, I drove home to Angel Heights. It would be nine months before the Blessed Mother and Archangel Raphael would call upon me again to drive Miss Mary.

# CHAPTER 7

# *Protect My Children*

*I*n September 1997, I was called upon by Archangel Raphael and the Blessed Mother to perform a spiritual service. I was told it was time to activate the heart energy of the Creator's Star grid that had been created at six points of light in the United States.

I was asked to drive to Kansas City, Missouri, where I would be guided to a forest with heart. I don't know why I doubt the messages that I am given, because there hasn't been one instance in which God hasn't guided my path. Yet, when I first heard the words "forest with heart," I thought of the acres of forest that must exist in Kansas City. And I wasn't initially taken with the idea of walking in the woods looking for a heart.

Prior to my leaving home, the angels gave me one more clue. They shared that while in Kansas City I would have an experience similar to that of *Brigadoon*. *Brigadoon* was the title of a Broadway show created by Lerner and Loewe. It's the story of two American tourists who stumble into a Scottish town that only reawakens for one day every hundred years. Like this community in the mist, there was a group of people in another dimension waiting for my arrival. When I got to Kansas City their presence would be made known to me. This message didn't enhance my comfort zone. Not only was I looking for a heart in a forest, but also now there were people who were going to appear from somewhere else walking out of the mist into my life. However, I am obedient, and so I headed for the highway that leads to Kansas City. Rather than proclaiming, "Let the games begin!"—my decree has always been, "Let the angelic adventure begin!"

On my way to Kansas City I spoke at a Unity Church in Columbia, Missouri. While giving my sermon I shared my reason for being in Missouri. After the church service, a woman came up to me and said point blank, "You are looking for the Heart Forest." I replied, "Yes!" And I asked her its location. She remarked, "I don't know where it is, but you'll find it when you get to Kansas City."

I had several other speaking engagements en route to Kansas City, and at the end of each lecture someone would come up and share that it was, in fact, the Heart Forest I was looking for. No, they didn't know where it was exactly, but I would find it in Kansas City. I have to admit I felt a peace knowing that people had heard of a forest with a heart.

I arrived in Kansas City at the home of Anna Franke. Upon my arrival I asked her if she knew of a Heart Forest. To my amazement she stated that not only did she know of it, but also she knew the man who had been instrumental in the project. She went into her kitchen to look up his phone number and get him on the phone for me. While she was in the other room calling the Heart Forest contact, the angels were aflutter in her living room.

The angels told me that I was to go downtown to the main library of Kansas City. I was to go to the microfiche and find the names of all the people who were killed in the Hyatt Hotel accident some years ago in Kansas City. The angels indicated that these people were in fact the ones about whom they had inspired me earlier, and they were waiting to come forth from spirit into service. These individuals would be participating in the activation of the heart of the Creator's Star grid in the Heart Forest.

When Anna returned to the room, she shared that she couldn't believe her good fortune because the gentleman she was contacting on my behalf travels the world extensively; Bob is an architect by trade. She indicated that he was willing to lead me himself to the Heart Forest and that arrangements had been made for that to occur the very next day—a Sunday afternoon.

I expressed my gratitude to Anna for her service on my behalf and said that I needed to get to the public library before it closed. I explained that I had to obtain a list of the names of all those who died in the Hyatt tragedy. Anna's face turned white; she told me that her own sister-in-law was one of those who died in the accident at the Hyatt Hotel.

Anna and I drove to the library and I obtained copies of the newspaper articles on the accident. The news reports listed 114 people who died. With the information in hand, I went back to Anna's home and, using her computer, typed out the names of those who had died.

On Friday afternoon, July 17, 1981, a tea dance in the hotel lobby of the Hyatt Hotel was attended by 1500 people. As the people listened to the Steve Miller Orchestra play Duke Ellington's "Satin Doll," a walkway that spanned the lobby collapsed into another walkway. Both walkways then crashed onto the lobby floor. There were 114 people killed and nearly 200 injured. It was one of American history's worst hotel catastrophes. Thousands of lives were adversely affected by this accident. I knew of the tragedy and loss of this incident, but I also knew that those who had died were sending a message of hope as part of the heart activation for the Creator's Star grid. What were they telling us from heaven's side?

As I read the articles on the accident, I was touched by the comments that family members made about the loved ones' deaths and the tea dances at the Hyatt. Family members explained how much their family members loved dancing and that it comforted them to know they were doing what they loved when they died. I paused from my typing and thought to myself: These people danced into the light. They danced into heaven. At that moment the angels revealed, "Yes, they are God's light dancers. They will be with you Sunday in spirit. They will bless the Creator's Star grid with the message that life is a dance—remember to dance!" I was then inspired to find a copy of Garth Brook's powerful song, "The Dance." It was no surprise to me that Anna just happened to have a copy in her tape collection.

The following day I was joined by a caravan of cars of people who I had met in Kansas City who wanted to be a part of the Heart Forest blessing. Bob led all of us to the Heart Forest.

I offer you a brief history of the Heart Forest as given at the Web site www.creativeprocess.net/heartforest:

"The first planting day for the Heart Forest took place on April 28, 1990, to coincide with the twentieth anniversary celebration of Earth Day, but the idea of a heart forest first took root with a suggestion made by Dr. Robert Muller at 'The Future is Now', Second Annual December 31 Peace Celebration in 1987.

"Dr. Muller, who had recently retired as Undersecretary of the United Nations and taken on the post of Chancellor for the University for Peace in Costa Rica, had returned as the keynote speaker for the second event. The day before the celebration a breakfast was held with civic leaders where two other visitors to Kansas City were in attendance, Iroquois Chief Leon Shenandoah and Mohawk Chief Jake Swamp.

"After Dr. Muller had given his remarks at the breakfast both Chief Shenandoah and Chief Swamp shared their feelings about Kansas City and the heart of the country.

"The next morning at the early morning celebration, Dr. Muller proposed a heart shaped avenue of trees be planted around the city, large enough to be seen from space, as a way for Kansas City to proclaim itself as loving the world with a global heart."

From the efforts of many visionaries the Heart Forest became a reality. On twenty-two acres of land near the Kansas City Airport a grove of 550 red cedars surrounded by concentric heart-shaped bands of flowering pine and shade trees paints a picture of love for the entire world to see. In Margaret Mead's words: "Never doubt that a small group of thoughtful citizens can change the world. Indeed it is the only thing that ever has." And a small group of citizens of Kansas City gave to the world a forest with a heart.

And so through the honoring of those who danced into light by reading their names aloud, and supporting with prayers, songs, and uplifted hearts the blessing of their message to always remember to dance, the heart of the Creator's Star grid was officially opened. There were tears and hugs and an overall feeling of a greater peace embracing all of us who participated in the service.

I turned my car homeward with a sense of this angelic assignment coming to completion. The evening prior to my leaving Kansas City, Anna included me in her prayers asking God to watch over me on my trip home. During her sleep she had a dream that something was wrong with my car and she was being shown a snake under the hood. The next morning Anna couldn't wait for me to get my car into the local auto repair shop. Sure enough, my serpentine belt was on the verge of breaking. The snake under the hood was God's way of conveying that the "serpent" belt needed to be replaced. The repairman indicated that I was one lucky lady in having this fixed without having it break out on the road. I knew luck had nothing to do with it; I am blessed with friends who care about me.

On my drive home, the Blessed Mother appeared to me. She held a dove of peace in her hands. She inspired me with the message that with the opening of the heart of the Creator's Star grid within the Heart Forest, her blessings for all people to have peace in their heart were pouring forth on the planet. She said to me, "Know yourself as my child of peace." That was one of the first times I would feel my service with the angels being directed to spreading the importance of peace in our hearts and in our lives and identifying myself as earthangel4peace.

The words that followed caused me to shudder: "Protect my children. Protect the innocent ones. Protect them from harm and sexual exploitation."

When I got home to Angel Heights, the angels revealed Mary's plan of service. I was asked to gather together a group of my friends who were willing to dedicate twenty-one days to the project. Each person was directed to the Web site www.childsearch.org. This organization posts pictures of children missing and lists them state-by-state. They have a motto: Missing but not forsaken. I was asked by the Blessed Mother to have every child listed in every state assigned to one of my group's members. We were then asked to print out the pictures of the children. Every morning and every evening as part of our prayers we were asked to focus on each child. We were told to look them in the eyes and send God's love to them. We were told to say to them, "You are not missing in the eyes of God. God sees you. God who is all knowing knows where you are. We reclaim you in service to God." We then envisioned a double circle of light—a double halo—protecting the child. It is called the ring-pass-not. It is created by visualizing the power of God flowing in the shape of a circle of light around the child in a clockwise direction. The second circle is the love of God flowing as light to protect the child in a counterclockwise direction. The two circles together form a protection energy known as the ring-pass-not.

No matter where the child may be, the God energies will reach them. If someone is harming the child or doing harm to the child, the ring will create a "spotlight" effect and in some way God's light will eventually cause the captor to slip up and attention will be drawn to this individual. You may have heard the saying, "turning up the heat." The Blessed Mother asked us to turn up the lights. I have been asked to continue the service of printing out the pictures of missing children and praying for them and reclaiming them with the light of God.

I know in order to assist the families in finding their children, the children have to be posted as missing; however, the Blessed Mother is saying that with God *nothing* is ever lost.

Did you know that every day in America three children die from abuse and neglect; six children and youths commit suicide; thirteen children and youths are murdered; sixteen children and youths are killed by firearms; 100,000 children are homeless; 14.7 million live in poverty in this land of abundance? Mother Mary is calling us to take a stand and to answer her call to protect the children from hunger, pain, and harm.

I was asked by the Blessed Mother to visit Bosnia. In Bosnia I learned of the service of International God-Parenthood for the Herceg-Bosnian Child. On the island of Jakljan, this organization makes it possible for hundreds of widows and children to come for spiritual renewal and retreats. These are woman and children who have lost husbands and fathers in wars. One of the little children shared, "It was the hardest for me on August 19, 1992, when I lost my dad. I was very close to him. I just couldn't believe that I didn't have him any more and even today, I can't believe that four years have gone by already and that my love for him has grown stronger. Two months after Dad's death we had to leave our city, our home, everything that belonged to us. But this wasn't half as hard as losing my dad."

Children come to the island with heartache and loss. They find a place of comfort where they can share their loss and pain and receive healing. One child expressed the most beautiful moment on the island was when she became convinced that she was not alone. She came to realize that there were those who were concerned for her and prayed for her. Mother Mary asks all of us to pray for the children of the world.

In the inspirations given to me by the angels and the Blessed Mother, I have been told to pray with my heart. I know that the Blessed Mother's guiding me to the Heart Forest was to convey to me the message of the importance of praying with a big open heart; praying with the energy of a twenty-two-acre heart.

As I prepared for my trip to Bosnia, the angels told me to pack one suitcase with what I would need for myself personally on the trip; a second suitcase was to be kept empty and in readiness for the children in Bosnia. As my departure date drew nearer, I asked the angels if I needed to go shopping to purchase what the children needed. I was told simply to keep the suitcase empty and in readiness.

The day before my departure, I spoke in Montoursville, Pennsylvania. During my lecture I shared that I was going to Bosnia on an angelic assignment. At the end of the lecture, Becky Huff asked if she could speak to me. I knew Becky as the creator of a line of dolls called Angel Babies. Her adorable baby dolls are dressed in actual human baby clothes. The Angel Babies have been used in seminars to support people's healing efforts to nurture their own inner child and many incredible healings have resulted from the experiences.

Becky shared that she had taught a class of elementary school children to make Angel Babies. The children wanted the babies to go to children in need and were waiting for a sign as to who was to receive the baby dolls. Becky knew the Angel Babies were meant for the children of Bosnia who had been orphaned by the war. When I arrived in Bosnia, the angels arranged for me to meet a director of the orphanage where the Angel Babies were to be "delivered." I feel so blessed to have been the "stork" in delivering these precious gifts from the little children of Montoursville, Pennsylvania, to the sweet children of Bosnia.

On behalf of the children, open your heart in prayer to God and ask to be shown how you can be a blessing to a child. I would like to share some ways that you can be of service. Take a child to a concert or to a museum. Spend time with the children in your neighborhood and your church. Hire a youth in your community. Offer your services as a chaperone for a school field trip. Give games to local rec centers. Praise a child. Say hello to children. Be nice to children. Become a big brother/ big sister. Make a donation to Toys for Tots. Ask your elected officials what they are doing for children. Plant a tree where children play. Pay your child support. Know where your child is and who your child's friends are. Clean up the neighborhood. Volunteer to help out in the nursery of your local hospital. Read to a child.

One Sunday I was invited by a Baltimore church to do the children's program for the service. I learned a valuable lesson that Sunday morning. I had chosen a book that was too long to read to the children in the time allotted. I thought to myself, no problem, I'll just read a few pages, and then summarize the point I want to make. That might work for adults, but not for children. When the Children's Sermon Time arrived, I sat in the front of the church with the little children of the congregation gathered round me. I started to read the first few pages, and then I started to turn the pages quickly as I gave the children of a synopsis of the message of the story. The children would have nothing to do with being shortchanged out of being read to by me. One little girl flipped the book back to where I had stopped reading, and said, "No skipping pages. You're supposed to read the whole book to us."

I supported her right not to be shortchanged; however, I pretty much pleaded with the little people to have mercy on me in this situation. I explained that in order to share time with the pastor and choir and everyone else who had a part to play in the program, we had to cut short the reading. I asked all the children if it was OK with them if I cut the reading part short this morning. They knew they had me squirming, and so they agreed. The audience was in stitches over the whole incident. The children had made their point. In fact, their point is the Blessed Mother's point, too. Don't shortchange the children. God wants us to always be looking for ways to make a child's life better. What better service is there than to make the world a better place for the children and to make a child's life better now?

# CHAPTER 8

# Happy Girl ISO Happy Guy

*U*pon our *entering the earth* experience, God gives us humans a
coat of skin that allows us, as new arrivals to the planet, to
feel our own separateness, i.e., our own individual identity. As
the human experiences "self" and the needs of "self" fulfilled, a dimin-
ished focus on being one with the creator, or one with the place from
whence "self" came, oftentimes occurs. The sacred walk of being human
offers many opportunities to regain that sense of union with the divine.
Because angels, radiant ministering spirits that serve the creator, know
no separation from the divine, my service has been to encourage people
to open their awareness to the angels. Opening to the angels affords
one's consciousness the experience of embracing this state of original
wholeness through communion with God's messengers, who are pure
radiating energies of God. We do not worship the angels. I see them as
God's spiritual training wheels. They are always close to our human
identity, helping us aspire to a consciousness where we do not need the
training wheels but rather can operate our human vehicle in direct
oneness with God.

Another communion experience is the merging with another human being in the sacrament of marriage.

I was married for eighteen years and, after a challenging divorce experience, decided I never wanted to go through that again. I was sure that the safest way to avoid the heartache was to avoid marriage entirely. In my next relationship following my divorce, I drew to myself an incredibly wonderful man who shared an equal disdain for the thought of marrying someone. In fact, Walt Blatt's first words to me were, "I don't want to get married but I would love to date you." My response was, "Would you put that in writing for me?" We were a healing to each other as we grew closer and closer and broke down the walls we had each built around ourselves because of painful divorce experiences.

This relationship taught me that commitment transcends a piece of paper. We dedicated our hearts to each other. I was there for Walt as he was there for me. I feel so blessed to have been by his side during the final five years of his life and to have been a part of his sacred dying experience. Through it all Walt and I continued to equally embrace a dislike for the "M" word—marriage in the traditional sense.

One Christmas Walt gifted me a gorgeous diamond ring and as he handed the box to me he stated, "Now this is not an engagement ring." Walt's past love relationships following his divorce had been conditional, with each partner making, ultimately, the demand of marriage. As a result of those experiences he wanted to make certain there was no mistake as to what this ring represented. I joyfully reflected total respect for his wishes, as they were my wishes, too. I proudly proclaimed to Walt, "You bet it isn't. There are no strings attached to this ring." We both laughed and realized that we were truly kindred spirits. Both of us were so afraid to go back into the waters of traditional marriage. In our minds marriage was a shark and the wedding march could have easily been the soundtrack from *Jaws*. We both feared that at the end of the walk down the aisle we would be eaten alive.

The more I denied myself the opportunity to explore the pain I felt around the experience of traditional marriage, the more the Universe called upon me to step up to the plate and face the ball that was coming at me in so many different pitches. As an interfaith minister I was asked to perform the ceremony for marriage after marriage of beautiful souls who were dedicating themselves to becoming closer and closer together in honoring God, serving God, and loving God through joining their separate lives together. God kept reflecting to me that what I perceived as a bitter experience was in fact quite sweet, as I officiated at these blessed events. The bliss and faith of these precious earth angels who stood before me exchanging vows written from their hearts began to rub off on me. I could hear the angels whispering, "Lighten up." I felt I was being called to shine light upon my fear of marrying again.

The angel d.j.'s would see to it that whenever I was driving to a speaking engagement they would bring across the air waves Faith Hill singing the words, "Hey, Baby, let's go to Vegas, bet on love and let it ride!" Faith's tune talks of two people jumping into a pickup truck and driving to Vegas to be married in one of the many wedding chapels. I heard this song so often that I finally responded to the angels, "All right. I get the message. 'Bet on love and let it ride!'"

In the Book of John in the Bible the story is told of how Christ performs a healing by asking a simple question, "Wilt thou be made whole?" The man Christ questioned had been afflicted for thirty-eight years and replies, "Yes." Christ empowers him by telling him to rise up and walk. I knew in my heart that God was telling me that if a healing was to occur within me regarding marriage, I had to allow it.

In my service as a pastoral counselor, as well as one who introduces people to the angelic kingdom, I find that many people want to marry simply because it is just too scary to face life alone. Sometimes it appears that people are saying, "It is better to have someone there, no matter how wrong they are for my life, than to be alone without anyone." I can talk until I am blue in the face of my reality with the angelic realm and that we are truly never alone even when we are totally by ourselves. This is something, however, you have to believe for yourself. That's the way it should be. The greatest gift given to us is the gift of free will. Oftentimes rather than choosing to look within our own souls to experience a divine union with the creator, we look outside of ourselves and stuff our lives full of relationships that are distracting and negate our true identity.

I work with people in helping them attract to their lives the relationship they desire. One of the first things I do is inquire about the person's schedule, asking what they do each day and night of the week. Usually the person's life is overflowing with activities and there is no free time or free space. I ask the person, "Just where in your life do you plan to put this relationship?" I encourage you, if you want to have a relationship in your life, to look at your weekly date book and take one evening and "x" it out as Sacred Space for Divine Love. You do not fill this evening. When the evening arrives, you allow spirit to give you an inspiration as to how to fill your evening. This exercise is your way of communicating to God that you are ready, willing, and able to make room in your busy life for love.

Another way of conveying your ability to make sacred space in your life for love is to go to your closet and make room in your closet for someone else's clothes to be placed there. It doesn't mean that the next person you meet will move in with you. It is a symbolic gesture to God that you are willing to share your space, your time, your energy, your love, and life with someone. I have heard a story about a woman who took this exercise so seriously that she dedicated closet space and drawer space to her future husband, and even went out and bought a man's bathrobe and hung it in her bathroom. She did magnetize to herself an abundant relationship.

In exploring my own perception of marriage I realized that I had gone to an extreme. Rather than believing the extreme of "someone in my life is better than no one," I had run to the other direction, making no room whatsoever in my life for the possibility of marriage. I had chosen to remain a spectator, as it is a lot safer than being a participant. As a result I held rigidly to the perception that "nothing" or "no marriage" is better than being courageous and exploring the possibility of someone wonderful waiting in the wings for me. I had allowed my fears to limit my life experience. I was living my life through fear rather than love.

I found it was time to examine closely those fears. I have witnessed rigor mortis in marriages and one of my fears was the dismal life expectancy of marriage. I had bought the Cinderella fairy tale that as a couple you are to live happily ever after. My first marriage didn't turn out that way. How does one keep marriage alive, and vital for life?

Romantic songs speak of how lovers become one, but in marriage

you become much more. You come together. You are together at breakfast, dinner, in bed, in the car—together in the best of times and the
worst of times. Before one plans on getting together with someone else,
shouldn't the first question be, "Am I myself together?" or "Do I have my
own life together?"

How can you sustain a partnership of equality when you bring yourself into the union feeling less than whole and complete? If you enter
the union feeling "Have I found the part of me that was missing?" you
enter this union as less than complete and rather than this new person
filling the void, the void will be enhanced or accentuated by the marriage union. Relationships enhance or mirror how we feel about ourselves. When people reflect to me on their "needs," I encourage them to
transmute the word "need" to "desire" because need is a word that expresses the thought, "If I do not get this, I will not be complete." I believe
that God made us whole and complete. We just have a brain problem in
accepting that as truth. We have to perceive the wholeness. Once again
it is our free will's choice to decide how we will perceive ourselves. Are
we whole and complete or needy? By expressing desires for your life
you are asking God for what you believe will enhance and enrich your
life.

If you believe that by getting married your internal unhappiness will
go away, you are going to be disappointed because the only way to be
happy is to be happy yourself. If you are saying, "I want to be happy," I
ask you: What is stopping you from being happy? Explore the choices
you are making about being happy with yourself and your life. From
the musical *Annie Get Your Gun* come the words, "I've got the sun in the
morning and the moon in the evening and I'm all right."

If you had a difficult childhood, or something else significant ails
you, marriage is not intended to be its cure. Joseph Campbell referred
to marriage as an "ordeal" or a test of endurance. People oftentimes
enter the marriage commitment feeling the union has the power to last
forever. This will occur only if each of you in the relationship has the
power and commitment within yourself to energize the relationship so
that it happens.

The angels are nonjudgmental beings. They never reflect to us, "That
was a stupid mistake." When we stumble on our path, they merely in-

spire us with the thought, "Choose again." Life is an opportunity to make choices. We make lots and lots of choices every day. Marriage is a choice. We choose whether or not to desire marriage for ourselves. We choose whom to marry by either being the person who asks or the person who answers. We choose how we are going to maintain the commitment to marriage once we are in the commitment.

Through our life experiences we learn how to choose what is best for our lives. When you marry, your choice is important. Is the person someone who loves you? Do you love them? Does this love shared by the two of you encompass the energies of your physical, emotional, mental, and spiritual bodies? Some people have made marriage selections based on a mental thought that this is a good move socially. Do you care about each other and support each other's individual goals and goals held jointly? Do you give each other space to dream, grow, and expand? And here goes the biggie—are you willing to accept the changes that will occur in each of you and in your marriage?

You can choose marriage to be a joyous or a miserable experience. A marriage can turn a home into a love nest or a battleground. As changes occur, and they will occur daily, you can choose to become closer together in your relationship or grow farther apart. What happens to you is not the reason you grow farther apart. It is how you choose to respond to either the change or event and to each other in the midst of that change. My parents have been married for seventy years. At their fiftieth wedding anniversary party my mother was asked, "Did you ever contemplate divorce?" She replied, "Divorce, never! Murder, often." My parents' sense of humor has been their choice of response throughout their many years of marriage. It has kept them young and their marriage young.

I remember hearing Barbara Marx Hubbard speak and she stated that it is a lot easier to be spiritual when you are not in a relationship. I have observed relationships in which people show up for the wedding ceremony and then are absent for the marriage experience.

I also believe that marriage is a three–party contract between you, your spouse, and God. If two people are not harmonious in their attitude toward God, then it will be very difficult for the marriage to be harmonious. I recommend that there be a place of worship inside the home where the couple can give thanks to God for all their many blessings, especially the blessing of marriage to each other.

There is an expression of God in each of us. When we marry we are vowing to be responsible for keeping the God light shining both within ourselves and helping our spouse to keep it shining inside. Marriage is an opportunity to treat each other with the same respect, reverence, and love which you give to God. In loving each other, you love God, and in loving God, you love one another.

If you choose to see the marriage as a physical union only, then your marriage will be limited to your becoming one in flesh only. If you choose to see marriage as being wed to God as well as each other, you will become one in spirit. The only true soul mate experience is with the divine and the mystical union that exists between God and us. God is the ultimate beloved.

In *Commune with the Angels* one of the meditations I was inspired to share is called "Dedication to the Light." We should always be rededicating our lives and light to the fulfillment of God's plan for us. If we choose to marry, we should consider dedicating and rededicating our marriage to God's plans for that marriage, such as bringing the expression of heavenly inspired marriages into reality on earth. The angels can fulfill their role as ministering spirits by working through those who are expressions of love for each other, expressions of love for God, and expressions of love for a higher purpose.

The angels have always inspired me that experiences in life can either be viewed as blessings or lessons. I came to realize that after my divorce I looked at marriage as a harsh lesson. In my response to Christ's question, "Wilt thou be made whole?" I chose to look at marriage from the view of seeing it as a blessing. Because of this choice I was able to rise up and walk away from the pain. I realized the divorce was a blessing that allowed sacred space to be created for Walt to step into my life. I would later come to realize that Walt had made his transition at the divinely appointed time for his life and that sacred space was being made for his life to continue in heaven and for Charles Feldman to come into my life on earth.

I share with you an angelic marriage blessing:

---

Be *happy with yourself. It's the greatest dowry you can bring to marriage and to your life's experience.*

Laugh *a lot. Make time for fun and play together.*

Embrace *each other with loving words, loving touches, loving gestures. Remember "Show and Tell" in elementary school? The angels inspire us to show and tell our spouses we love them every day of our marriage.*

Set *up a family altar. Observe rituals together whenever possible. Make God the center of your lives and marriage. Say grace at mealtimes. Give thanks to God repeatedly throughout the day. Live your life in an attitude of gratitude.*

Safely *support each other's growth, expansion, and evolution by allowing each other to take risks, knowing that the marriage is a safety net on the high wire of life.*

Inspire *each other. Encourage each other. Believe in each other.*

Nurture *each other and empathize with each other's feelings and thoughts.*

Glorify *God by your union. Dedicate your marriage to God's glory. Treat each other with the same love, respect, and reverence as you give to your relationship with God.*

---

I joyously admit that a healing occurred in my life with regard to the "M" word. If anyone questioned me as to whether or not I believe earth changes were occurring, I would respond to them that I had experienced a complete pole shift around marriage.

I began contemplating and desiring a relationship with the special person that God wanted for me as a helpmate. I embraced marriage as a healthy choice. It is a union of two precious God creations. In my healing and seeking the angels have gifted me with the term "star mate." I was encouraged to seek my star mate in life. Each of us has our own God-given light. You are your own individual bright star energy. When you seek your star mate you are seeking someone who has their own bright light and which, when merged with yours, will create a "conjunction" of light that shines even brighter than the two of you could have shone individually. The two lovers, when joined as one, fortify and intensify the light of each other, and each experience their own individual brilliance simultaneously with the brilliance of the light of the "silent partner" in the marriage. The silent partner always present is God. It's quite a light show.

There is a belief that the Star of Bethlehem was in fact two stars shining together in the same sacred space of the night sky. The brilliance of the combination of their two lights together guided the Magi to Christ. Marriage can be the merging of two stars—you and your spouse. From the mergence an even brighter light emerges that impacts not only your existence as a couple, but can be a guiding light to the hearts of others around you.

In March 1999, Mary Dansicker participated in the Whole Life Expo in Baltimore by renting a booth for Joshua's Lighthouse Angels. She invited Celeste McDonald and myself to come "play" at her booth for the weekend. We both leaped at the opportunity as the weekend's programs offered so many wonderful speakers.

Upon our arrival Friday evening as I scanned booth participants I discovered that my ex-husband had rented a booth also. I had not spoken to him or seen him for eight years. I decided that I would avoid him wherever he went in the expo center. I rerouted myself Friday evening and all day Saturday. Then on Sunday morning the angels had had enough of this nonsense. "Don't you know? If you avoid facing your past, you are avoiding the stepping stone to future love." I knew I had to march myself over to his booth and simply wish him well. That's exactly what I did. I want to share that I am certain my ex-husband didn't recognize what an important step for me individually this action was. It really didn't involve him, except he was the "cast member" whom I had given my power to when he left in 1989. He didn't ask for my power. I gave it to him on his way out the door. It was time to reclaim it. In all truthfulness, the encounter was uneventful in its exchange of words. All words were kind and polite. However, as I turned and walked away from him I was literally walking on air. I had never felt lighter in my life. Needless to say, Celeste and Mary were awestruck by the choice I had made.

Within a half hour after going up to chat with my ex-husband, I met Marta Robinson. Marta and I have been long-distance angel friends. We hadn't seen each other for some time and so laughed and shared stories from our lives. Marta asked me if I was open to a relationship in my life and I said absolutely. She shared that she had discovered Americansingles.com—an Internet matchmaking service. She had found that the men she had met on the Internet through this Web site had been delightful dating experiences. She encouraged me to post an ad. I remember feeling uncomfortable initially with her suggestion. When we finished chatting and I turned to walk back to Mary's booth, I heard Marta's parting words. As I heard these words I knew Spirit was talking to me through Marta because the vibration of her words rang through my whole being. It was as if God was saying, *"Now hear this, Jayne!"* The words were: Post that ad, Jayne.

I went home and struggled with the thought of posting a "love wanted" ad on the Internet. The angels weren't giving up on me. The movie *You've Got Mail*, starring Tom Hanks and Meg Ryan, was showing at the movies. I didn't know what the movie was about. I just chose to go to the movies for purely recreational purposes. As I sat in the movie theater I kept hearing the angels chime in, "Post that ad, Jayne." After leaving the movie theater, I drove home and was listening to a talk radio program. The guest was a woman who had written a book about the success of meeting someone via the Internet. The Trinity Blessing had struck again in Jayne's life. I went home and posted an ad on www.americansingles.com.

I decided I wanted the ad simple and so I wrote "Happy Girl ISO Happy Guy." I consider myself a very happy person and I wanted a happy man in my life.

On April 2, 1999, I received a reply to my ad. His name was Charles Feldman. He was a widower who wanted to date and find love in his life again. He indicated he was sixty-five years old. His two children were raised and had families of their own. He was an engineer. He stated that he lived in Gaithersburg, Maryland, and commented that since we lived so close together, he would love for us to meet at a place I considered safe and have dinner together. Gaithersburg is an hour and a half away from Upperco. I decided that was just too far away for a relationship. I e-mailed him back that we did not in fact live close enough to date.

I would like to take this opportunity to thank God and Charles for not giving up on me. The angels were aflutter with what I had done. They flew into the consciousness of my friend, Mary Blackert. I had performed the marriage ceremony for Mary and her husband. The angels told Mary, "Jayne is making a *big* mistake. Call her immediately." Mary called me and asked if I could meet her for dinner. She shared she had something important to discuss with me. Mary and I got together that same week and over dinner Mary asked me what was new in my life. I told her I had posted an ad and one sweet man had responded; however, he lived in Gaithersburg, which was too far for him to travel, to reach Upperco.

Mary looked me straight on and said, "Jayne, you have answered God's call and have traveled to such remote places as Bosnia in fulfillment of your service. You have been willing to go to wherever on the planet your service was required by God. Let this man come to you. Let him come to Upperco and take you out to dinner." I knew God had just chewed me out, and I was humbled.

I went home that evening and turned on my computer and Chuck had e-mailed me again. He indicated that he sensed I had a problem with the distance and he wanted to emphasize that he didn't mind at all driving closer to my home to a place where I felt safe and comfortable in meeting him. I e-mailed him back that I agreed on one condition. I asked that we go double-Dutch. Chuck quickly responded, saying that was out of the question. Chuck shared that God had blessed him financially and he felt it was his responsibility as a gentlemen to treat me with respect and to offer me this respect through paying for a lovely dinner. When I read his beautiful e-mail, my heart was warmed by this man's graciousness.

We met for dinner at the North Star Restaurant in Reisterstown, Maryland. It is about ten minutes from my house. We met for an early dinner. When I arrived the parking lot was almost totally empty. I was a nervous wreck. Instead of just pulling into a parking space, I chose to back my car in so I could pull out quickly if things didn't work out. I was planning an easy getaway. I backed the car in, and pulled out. I backed the car in and pulled out. This went on for about five minutes. Finally I left the car in the space, turned off the ignition, and got out. To my embarrassment, Chuck had been watching me parking the car for five minutes. He smiled and questioned me, "Jayne?" I sheepishly admitted I was one and the same.

We went inside and shared the stories of our lives with each other. I was so enchanted with everything about Chuck and I am happy to say he felt the same way. We literally closed the restaurant. He walked me to my car. We held each other's hand. I had never given a whole lot of credence to the character in the movie *Sleepless in Seattle*, who shared that he would know the special someone for him when he held her hand. When Chuck took my hand in his, it felt so very "right." I knew that we were reunited. I don't know if it was from past lives or other dimensions; however, Chuck and I had been together before and we both were so very happy that we were back together in each other's life.

Interesting enough, Mary Blackert sent me a card the week of my first date with Chuck. On the front of the card are the words: "We're all invited to the dance—the dance of Joy, the dance of Being, the dance of Life!" Inside the card reads: "Let your dreams run wild and free and always, always follow where they lead." Mary added in her own handwriting, "Dear Jayne. Saw this! Thought of you! I'll be dancing at your wedding. It's sooner than you think. Love, Mary."

Chuck and I found that separating from each other was very painful every date we had. We both wanted to be together permanently and as soon as possible. On August 6, 1999, beneath the two-hundred-year-old tulip poplar tree on Angel Heights' property, Rev. Michelle Livingston, a dear friend and author of *Visions of Mary*, married us. We chose to walk down the aisle together and we selected the music from Disney's Cinderella, "A Dream Is a Wish Your Heart Makes." The words were so true. No matter how much you may be grieving from losses in your life, never stop believing in love.

Because I am someone who observes the symbology in happenings in my environment, I want to share all the things that went on at Angel Heights on our wedding day. Chuck and I were walking out the front door together and the whole door came right off its hinges. The purchase of a new front door was necessary and how appropriately, as a new door was opening in both of our lives. Even though we had contacted the septic waste removal company weeks prior, the company chose to arrive that morning to clean out the septic system. I think you can figure out the appropriateness of that message. There were a number of things that occurred in which a "second time" was involved. We went to pick up chairs. We had to go back a second time. Because this is the second marriage for both Chuck and me the importance of being willing to do something a second time is a clear message and blessing in our lives. We went to pick up flowers. We later discovered something missing from the order and had to return a second time.

As Chuck is of the Jewish faith and I am Christian, we had two ceremonies. Rev. Livingston performed the first ceremony on August 6. This date was chosen because it is the Feast Day of the Transfiguration. This is an event that occurred in Christ's life when he was transfigured before the disciples. Christ's "face did shine as the sun, and his garments became white as light. And behold there appeared unto them Moses and Elijah talking with him." (Matthew 17:2-3) We were divinely inspired to select this date for it is a celebration date for a biblical teaching that included Jesus and Moses. We celebrate this date as our anniversary. The second ceremony was performed by Rabbi Joseph Gelberman, the founder of the New Seminary in New York, on September 29, 1999—Michaelmas Day—in Bricktown, New Jersey, at Chuck's mother's home, with his brothers and their wives present. Both ceremonies were divinely blessed.

For those of you who desire a relationship in your life, I would like to offer these suggestions in support of your quest:

*Ask God's blessing. Daily ask God to send the star mate/ helpmate that God knows is best for you and for the other person. Let God be involved in your life, especially your love life. Believe me, He already is.*

*Create an altar in your home that honors the forthcoming relationship. You may want to have a candle that represents your light; a candle that represents the partner's light; and a larger candle that represents God's great light.*

*Make room in your schedule, in your home, in your closet, in your life for new love.*

*Because your bedroom is the most intimate room in your home, energize the feng shui sector that deals with relationships. As you stand in the doorway of the room, facing into the room, look to the far right-hand corner of the room. This is the relationship section of the room. You can stand in the front doorway of your home and face into your house. The farthest right-hand corner of your home is the relationship corner. You can do this room by room as well. For the relationship section have a picture or object that mirrors the energy of two people in love. Someone once asked me if they could have two angels in that space. I don't recommend it unless you want a non-human experience. It's amazing how many people tell me, after I have shared this exercise with them, that they have in that corner a picture of a lone individual. Juice the space with images that carry a loving couple vibration.*

*Write a love letter to God outlining all the God-ideals that you desire this person to have. First, read this letter with the intent of asking that the individual have these divine attributes. Keep them all in positive expression, i.e., "he is free of substance addictions," rather than saying "he does not smoke." The angels have inspired me to align myself closer to the divine mind consciousness by making use of positive affirmations and statements wherever possible. Rather than expressing a life choice with a "not" or a "no," I select wording that focuses on positive choices.*

*Then, second, read the letter dedicating yourself to being all the things you ask of this individual. You must be willing to give what it is you want to receive.*

*The characteristics that you should be asking for in your partner are those essential for a successful relationship. Loyalty, generosity, honesty, compassion, kindness (and that includes being kind to everyone), reliability, and humility. All of these are divine attributes.*

*You may want to include other secondary human attribute requests, such as being nice looking or being someone who shares an interest that is important to you. However, sometimes we sell ourselves short when we meet someone with human attributes that fill our wish list. Then we are amazed when the "perfect" relationship turns out not to be so perfect after all. Perhaps the person was lacking honesty. The truth is that you were blindsided by the human attributes and never explored the question of whether or not the person came with the divine attributes that are important to a long-lasting relationship. You were not honest with yourself about what you truly wanted in a relationship.*

*Following your prayer request to God, I encourage you to then make a call to your beloved. I discovered this exercise from a fairy tale of old where the heroine called upon the hero to come stand by her side. You are sending out messages to God, Christ, the angels, the heavenly host, and the star mate/partner that you are ready to love and be loved by.*

*Finally, don't give up on love. Love never gives up on you. Hang on to the hope of love finding you and your finding love.*

---

Chuck Feldman is an incredible individual. Our life together as husband and wife is an opportunity to serve God by being messengers to others to not give up on love. He's kind, reliable, and honest and is so very funny. He is as devoted to God as I am. I remember when I wrote my prayer list to God, asking for specific qualities in a partner, my number one request was that this man love God with his whole being. Chuck does. Chuck immediately loved my Jack Russell terrier, Benny, and it was love at first sight for Benny, as well. I remember during my prior dating experiences, I met a gentleman who shared with me that he was allergic to dogs. I politely shared with him my blessing that he find the love he sought and explained that it was not to be me. It was the shortest date in history. Another record-breaking short date was a gentleman who asked me, after seeing my angel pocketbook, "Are you religious or something? Because I don't want anyone who is hung up on religion." I knew I was most definitely "something" this man wasn't quite prepared for in life. I again blessed his quest for life and we parted ways quickly.

My married life with Chuck is filled with happiness beyond my wildest dreams. We have since gotten a second Jack Russell terrier, a five-year-old female named Riot. Life is a riot with Riot. If someone would ask me what has been the toughest adjustment for me in my marriage, I would say learning to let someone help me. Chuck has to be one of the most giving people on the planet. He always wants to help me. In talking to others who have dedicated their lives to being caregivers and servers, I find that I am not alone in having to learn that it is blessed to not only give but to receive.

The happiest time of day for me is the evening. At this time, Chuck and I have completed a day's worth of service. The sun has set. We are moving toward a night of rest. Chuck and I are in bed together reflecting on the day's adventures. Our two Jack Russells are being their usual adorable selves. I just pause and say a prayer of thanks to God for the gift of Chuck's love in my life. And I thank Mary Blackert for being a messenger to me from the angels to let love come to me. I pass this sweet blessing on to all who desire love in their lives: Let love come to you.

In May 2001, I led a group of eighteen ladies and my husband on an Angel Tour of Ireland. Even though I had the itinerary mapped out in advance, while reading my guidebook on the flight over to Dublin I discovered that in Dublin there was a church called Whitefriar Carmelite Church that many of the locals attended. In the church were shrines to a number of saints and an altar dedicated to Our Lady of Dublin. After arriving in Ireland and completing a full day of touring, my group members were exhausted and wanted to catch some winks. My husband wanted that, as well. I am known as being the "Energizer Bunny" and so I took off on my own to explore Whitefriar Carmelite Church. I believe the saints—like the angels—are part of our holy family and they are brothers and sisters that watch over us and root for us just as the angels do. They offer us fellowship, friendship, and inspiration through their faithfulness. I believe the saints' service is to all of us, not just members of one faith or religion.

The next morning at breakfast I shared with the ladies that in the church are the bones of St. Valentine and that there is an altar where the locals believe that if you say a prayer to St. Valentine he will help you find true love. A number of the single women on my tour asked if it would be at all possible for them to go to the church prior to our starting the day's scheduled events. I am a believer that all things are possible, and so we squeezed a side trip to the church into our itinerary.

One of the ladies who made that side trip was Mary Margaret Hetrick. I don't believe that Mary went on the Angel Tour expecting to find love, but I do believe that by her going to the church she was saying to God that she was ready and willing to let love come to her. And it did come to her—rapidly! Our bus driver and guide for the tour of Ireland was Maurice Joseph O'Brien, one of the dearest, sweetest men on earth (second only to my husband, Chuck). He and Mary fell in love with each other. On April 20, 2002, they were married and are living together in Ireland. Fairy tales still do come true.

# CHAPTER 9

# *What on Earth Is Going On?*

*s an individual who first* experienced angels at the age of eleven and who has consciously been serving with them for thirty-plus years, I am very much aware that there are more angels on the earth than ever before. These beings of light are here as ministering spirits. The angels minister to our needs during these changing times. They come bearing gifts from God—gifts that include divine inspiration, divine support, divine healing, divine guidance, divine peace, and divine love. They deliver a wide variety of gifts because each of our needs is different, for the changes we are experiencing individually are different. What is commonly shared by all of us is that we find ourselves gathered together in the midst of an awakening like none before and in the midst of a dramatic acceleration of energy. What on earth is going on?

About five years ago the Los Alamos National Laboratory reported that electron showers bombarding the earth had been detected by satellites above the earth. The satellites reported that showers were dumping a billion watts of energy a second into the atmosphere and creating the appearance of a new energy field that is being stepped down into our physical plane. In short, we are getting pelted with light.

It is my belief that this new energy is only one form of "bombardment" we are experiencing. Ask yourself; don't you feel bombarded by life at times? We are being bombarded with information. We are receiving more written and verbal information than ever before. At least 1,000 different books are printed every day. It seems as if new talk shows air on television weekly. New game shows are on television where questions are asked and answers are given—all resulting in more information being shared. We are receiving and processing more information than we can cope with. Are you becoming weighed down with information? I know at times I feel overwhelmed just going to the post office and getting my mail. My thoughts are: Do I have time to read it? Do I file it? Do I trash it?

And if my post office mail wasn't enough to deal with, there is now e-mail and the Internet making information accessible—information on everything imaginable. When I do research on the Internet, I lose track of time, as there is so much information available.

The energy and information bombarding our lives are creating mental and emotional chaos as never before. What's a person to do? I suggest that we embrace the bombardment as a gift—not a curse—from the Creator. The gift is the reflection that we can no longer slide through our lives with no responsibility for ourselves. We are being forced to be responsible for choosing what we do and do not want in our lives and in our "space." We are being forced to love ourselves enough that we make conscious choices every second of our daily lives.

The angels are assisting us by lifting veils, which made it possible for us in the past to believe in a separation from God. Now more light is being beamed upon us to inspire us to "lighten up." It is as if the light is being beamed onto a part of us that maybe we weren't fully aware of or maybe didn't even know existed. We are truly "seeing the light." The "light show" is showing us a divine essence of ourselves that can talk to angels; a divine part of ourselves that is given visits in our dreams with our loved ones in heaven. Christ taught us in His words, "All this and more you shall do." We are discovering the "more."

Each of us agreed to come here and to be part of the planetary family at this time of momentous change. We agreed to be fully human. Some of us have forgotten that part of ourselves—the part that is here to experience love and to be loved as the precious human you are. Yes! We are here to have a love life! We are here to experience the love in our own life and to share that love with others. Oftentimes when the love part of us calls to us, we make certain we muffle its call to us by cramming our lives full of activities. These activities fill our lives with distractions that attempt to muffle the call from within. We pretend we don't hear the call.

Not only are the angels supporting us by responding to the call for *help* from the divine love essence inside of us, but the planets that God created are supporting us, too. Uranus, the expression of God that reflects rapid change and awakening energies moved into the divine wardrobe department and chose the clothing or outfit called Aquarius. Uranus started wearing this outfit in 1995 and will continue to do so through 2003. Uranus feels comfy in Aquarius garb. Aquarius is Uranus' favorite lounging outfit. The last time Uranus came home to Aquarius energy was ninety years ago when there was a time of revolt on earth: including World War I, the Russian Revolution, and the Industrial Revolution.

Where is the revolution now? It is a personal revolution that each of us is experiencing inside of ourselves. We are revolting against limitations and restrictions we have placed upon ourselves. We are revolting against fears, suffering, separation, death, and destruction. We are revolting against other people's perceptions of what we are to be and choosing to move toward the original vision the creator held for us at the time we were created from the full power of divine love. In Einstein's words: "I want to know God's thoughts. Everything else is detail."

It is truly a time of a new heaven and a new earth and the working model for this new existence is being created inside of each of us. Years ago John White's book, *Pole Shift*, prepared readers for a shift of the earth's poles. I believe the shift has occurred inside each of us and the shift is causing personal revolution. How many of you have experienced your world being turned upside down by unexpected changes? That's a personal pole shift.

The revolution is inspiring us to make changes that will allow us to evolve into the realization that we are universal beings. We are making quantum leaps in the perception of who we are and all of the potentials and possibilities that are within us. Many of us are awakening to the realization that things we thought would be "everlasting," i.e., job security, relationships, are not so eternal after all. These changes in our lives are causing us to seek a personal answer to the question: What is really eternal?

As these major changes occur in our lives, we experience new doors opening to us—doors inside ourselves that we have not dared look behind. One of those doors is the Heart Center—the doorway to the love of God that exists in each of us. One of my favorite songs is by the recording group ABBA. It is entitled "I Had a Dream," and one of the verses says: "I believe in angels. I see good in everything I see." Be a love finder. Look for love inside of yourself. See the good inside of you! And so if there is still evolution taking place on earth, and revolution taking place inside of each us, how can the heavenly host help us cope? Years ago in meditation the angels gave me a very simple message that sums up what the angels are all about. It is a message I shared in *Commune with the Angels*. If you take the word ANGEL and apply these words to each letter—Accept Now God's Eternal Love—you have the message they bring to each of us. Open your heart and accept God's eternal love. You can count on it. You can depend on it. You can build your life on it.

There are two things that are constant in life—*change* and *love*. We don't always know the changes that are coming our way, but we are one with the love that will help us get through these changes.

How can you attune yourself to being open to love and experiencing more love in your life during a time that feels like your whole world is being turned upside down? The angels have inspired me with three words of guidance: Simplify—Exemplify—Glorify.

Keep your life simple. Take stock of what is no longer useful and purposeful in your life and lovingly release it. Clean out the closets of your house and your mind. Make room for more light and more love. The angels encourage us to look to the stars—our kindred spirits in the night sky. Even though there are truly billions of stars, notice the space they give themselves to shine.

Give yourself space. Make time and space to meditate, to pray, to breathe, to dance, to play, to laugh, to love—to experience the all of God inside of you—and the all of God around you.

Not only can we learn from the stars the importance of giving ourselves space to shine, we can also simplify our outlook on life through stargazing. James Mullaney is an astronomy writer, lecturer, consultant, former director of both the Buhl Planetarium and the DuPont Planetarium and a past editor of *Sky and Telescope* magazine. Years ago Jim and I were co-presenters at an A.R.E. Conference in Virginia Beach, Virginia, and from that weekend a precious friendship grew between Jim and his lovely wife, Sharon, and myself; a friendship I treasure. They are truly cosmic sweethearts.

I found out personally that weekend why Jim's passion for stargazing has earned him the title of "celestial evangelist." I guarantee that if you attend one of Jim's lecture, at the end of the evening you will be thinking about buying a telescope or at the least subscribing to an astronomy magazine. His enthusiasm for stargazing is contagious.

Jim shares with his audiences that whenever you're feeling stressed about the state of the world, simply step outdoors at night. In Jim's words: "When you go out at night and look up at those distant serene stars, you are looking at what God used to make you—a part of them is inside of you. Realize that you came from them. We are made of the same substances as stars. We are destined to someday return to the Creator and claim our heritage as a child of the living God who created the universe in all its radiant splendor." No wonder Jim's license plate reads STARMAN. Jim has a wonderful video entitled, "The Heavens Declare!" One of the declarations made by the stars is that quite simply we are made of stardust, so we truly are a star race.

Exemplify the goodness of God in your life. Be the best you can be. If there are habits that are not supporting that program, take steps to change them. They don't have to be gigantic steps. Start with baby steps. Remember that light gives the appearance of being a continuous stream but it really is made up of little steps—one following right after the other. Love yourself and be kind to yourself for you are deserving of behaving toward yourself and others in a way that reflects your recognition of the preciousness of life—including your life!

Glorify God in all that you do. Open your heart to the love of God inside of you. Let every sense experience it and let it overflow from you in the expression of your service. We can be of help to each other in this time of tremendous influx of energies just like the angels. Be on the lookout for ways that you can serve as an earthly angel to someone today.

The angels inspired me with the following information to assist us in this time of rapid acceleration of energy. These suggestions may help you cope with the new energy dynamics your body is experiencing. You can remember the helpful hints with the word ANGELS:

**A**cknowledge *that you are in the midst of change. Don't be an ostrich. Remember what part of the ostrich is exposed when it sticks its head in the sand. Don't deny that things are not what they used to be—and neither are you! It is time to be conscious and responsible for your life. Being responsible means taking good care of yourself.*

**N**urture *yourself with naps. All the acceleration is tiring out our precious physical bodies. Give yourself permission to rest. Nurture yourself with natural supplements. Mother Nature knows how to deal with change. Nurture yourself with adequate sleep, nutrition, and movement.*

**G**o *to God. Make time for talking to God in your life. Make time for prayer. Have a refuge room in your house. Have an altar in your home. Spend quiet time with God. Commune with nature. Take walks. Mother Nature is a wonderful teacher as to how to grow through change gracefully.*

**E**liminate *stress. You've heard it before and the angels are saying it to you again. Let peace on earth begin inside of you. Embrace peace by releasing that which is stressful. Fill your life with calming experiences, i.e., movies and music that soothe your soul. To help eliminate stress and toxins in your body, drink water—lots of water. Acquaint yourself with Edgar Cayce's readings. The readings are filled with information on healthy living Cayce received while in a sleeping trance. Check out the Association for Research and Enlightenment in Virginia Beach, Virginia, where* *you will find out about Edgar Cayce.*

Love *yourself and live in this moment. Do not keep your cir-cuitry plugged into the past. It only juices the past and doesn't help you one iota in this eternal moment. Stay focused on the now for that is where you are. Take your eyes off the dramas of the past and turn your attention to the glorious present. Live in the now.*

Seek *help and support. When you feel overwhelmed mentally, seek the professional help of a counselor; when you feel over-whelmed and your energy is bouncing all over the place, get a massage or go to a Reiki healer; when you feel overwhelmed physi-cally, talk to a doctor and ask about exploring natural supple-ments such as herbal remedies. The energy overload is requiring different diets. Talk to your doctor about vitamin supplements.*

Our dear precious bodies are trying their best to adjust to all the changes taking place. Listen to your body. The angels aren't the only ones trying to inspire you. It is time to go within and listen to the voice of God right inside of you. This voice is the Master Physician placed there by God. Begin by trusting yourself. Listen to your inner voice to know what to avoid and what to embrace. Your inner voice will guide you as to what is unworthy of your time and what is supportive of your spiritual growth. When you learn to trust yourself you will always know what you need to know at any given time in your life.

In the spring of 2000 I had an incident that occurred during a visit to the dentist. Though the dentist didn't mean to do it, during a root canal a piece of filling went up into my sinuses. I had to go immediately to an oral surgeon who rectified the problem. Even though I went back to the surgeon and was told everything was healing fine, there was an infec-tion taking up residence in my sinuses. During the next several months I found myself having a running nose and feeling draggy, but I brushed it off as the sinuses being opened from the surgery.

One morning I awoke from sleep hearing a voice loud and clear telling me: Eye, ear, nose, throat doctor—*now!* I knew it was the Master

Physician. It was Dr. God speaking directly to me. I made an appointment and the end result was I had to have emergency surgery. I trusted that voice with my life and it saved my life!

You are responsible for the evolution of *you*! You are not here merely to survive. You are here to evolve into the incredible being that God perceived you and conceived you to be! See yourself through God's eyes! See yourself with "Light Sight."

As I shared in the last chapter, I have an agreement to do art shopping for God. One of those shopping expeditions occurred while I was in Egypt in 1994.

Following the completion of the "12:12" prayers to God ceremony in the Great Pyramid, my angel team told me my service for that day was not complete. I was inspired to take a taxicab to Old Cairo. Prior to going to Egypt I had given a lecture in Virginia. During the lecture a man stood up in the middle of the audience and proclaimed, "I love the angels! I love you!" I graciously thanked him and proceeded with my lecture. This gentleman later called and left this message on my answering machine, "My name is Jorge. I am here to tell you St. George will protect you in Egypt." I remembered thinking, "How wonderful! I'll take all the protection I can get."

When the angels told me to hail a cab in Egypt and head for Old Cairo, that's what this earth angel did. Our prayer ceremony had been an all-night vigil and it concluded at sunrise the morning of December 12. I arrived in Old Cairo just as the stores were opening for the day. The angels guided me to a Coptic museum. While inside the museum, I was thrilled by the displays of ancient images of the angels. I just wanted to be alone to meditate and pray with the art. That was not going to happen. Being a single American female tourist I was hassled beyond belief by the people that proclaimed they were tour guides for the museum. It's quite different from going to the Walters Art Gallery in Baltimore. I remember saying to an American in Egypt that I wasn't coping very well with the aggressive sales approach of the Egyptians. The person said, "Jayne, be kind on yourself. They've been doing this for 2,000 years and this is your first experience." This person was correct. By the time I left Egypt I had become known as "Hard-Bargain Woman," and people on the tour would solicit me to get the lowest prices for them.

There was an additional factor that also played into my emotional fragility on this trip. I knew that I was on an angelic assignment; however, in December 1994, Walt's health was worsening. In fact, the day I arrived in Egypt, Walt went into the hospital. I felt torn by the service in Egypt and the service to Walt at home. I came to recognize that it was in divine order that Walt went into the hospital the entire time I was in Egypt. It was God's message to me that Walt was in good hands and that I should remain focused on my assignment at hand in Egypt.

And so there I was in the Coptic museum. My physical body was tired from the all-night vigil. My emotional body was stressed from concern over Walt's condition. I just wanted to rest in silence with the art and attempt to rebalance myself. However, the tour guides weren't going to let that happen. I left the museum in tears. As I walked down the cobblestone streets of Old Cairo I saw a church and felt a peaceful presence come over me as I read its name: St. George Coptic Church. The blessing that Jorge had left for me on my voicemail came into my thoughts: "St. George will protect you in Egypt." I went inside the church and my heart was lifted heavenwards by the mosaic art of Christ. Holy images surrounded me in all directions. I felt myself drawn to a mosaic of Archangel Michael. I knelt before Michael as if I were sliding into a church pew next to my brother to join him in worshiping God. I said to Michael. "Michael, my spirit is willing; however, my flesh is weak. I am so tired of being hassled. My heart is so heavy over concern about Walt. If it be God's will, may I be given a sign of your presence, sent by God, to protect me and help me rebuild my strength on this trip, so I may do what God wants me to do." I rose up from my prayer feeling hopeful.

I walked outside of St. George Church and immediately saw a store across the street where the shopkeeper was sweeping the front entrance. I walked up to the gentlemen and when I opened my mouth, the Holy Spirit took over. Before I knew it, I had asked him, "Do you have any icons?" I was amazed as to where the words came from and equally amazed by his response: "Come inside. I am the only store in Egypt that sells icons." I have no way of knowing if that is the truth or not; however, I followed him inside the store passing all the statues of Egyptian gods and goddesses to a room filled to the rafters with icons. There were beautiful icons of Mary and Jesus, and the Holy family. I looked and looked and yet didn't find what I was looking for. The storekeeper said to me, "What is wrong? Aren't my icons beautiful?" I agreed that they were exquisite in beauty; however, I was looking for an icon of Michael. The warmest smile came over the storekeeper as he asked me, "Do you like Michael?" I nodded and said, "I love Michael." He left me for a few moments and came back with a contemporary painting of Archangel Michael. He said a local artist had painted it. He went on to say that it was painted in the hope that a church would buy it; however, that had not yet happened and thus it was for sale. The painting was magnificent. It depicted Michael with one hand raised in a gesture of blessing and one hand stretched out extending an image of sacred geometry. I knew immediately that it was conveying the blessing of God that the angels bestow upon our lives. The sacred geometry is the energy of creation and what God gives to us as the incredible gift of acting as our own creators of goodness in our lives by our thoughts, words, and deeds. I inquired about the price, and it was quite a bit to my single woman's budget. I asked the man if he had a smaller one. I no sooner had that question out of my mouth than the heavenly host broke into a roar of laughter. Yes, angels do love to laugh. I heard my angel team tease me as they commented that God had guided me out of the cornfields of Upperco, across the ocean to Egypt. God had guided me to the narrow streets of Old Cairo to this particular shop where this painting was waiting for me to buy and share with the world. And here I was asking if there was another smaller version of this painting. I know the heavenly host finds me an absolute hoot at times, and I have to agree with them. I got the message loud and clear, and so my second question was: "Do you accept credit cards?"

The painting of Michael—Messenger of God's Sacred Geometry—has traveled with me throughout America as part of my ministry. Whenever I share the painting with my audiences, I always observe that people come up to the painting after my lecture and a personal interaction occurs between them and Michael. As I mentioned earlier, I am just the one who gets to buy the art.

Archangel Michael, himself, is an incredible artisan. He has used the sky as a canvas. When I led a group of eighteen ladies on an Angel Tour of France in 1999, we visited Mont St. Michael. I will never forget seeing the Mont rise up out of the ocean as our tour bus approached it. As we arrived at the Mont, the angels said to me, "Have your camera ready. Michael has a gift for you." For the balance of the day I was looking around me and above me for a Kodak moment being provided by Archangel Michael. Later that day, just before the sunset, our touring of Mont St. Michael was over and our bus had taken us to a hotel that was very near to the Mont. I was seated on a bench outside of the hotel with my precious angel friend, Celeste McDonald. We were reflecting on the joyous day we had spent at Mont St. Michael. We looked up above us and were speechless from the sight that seemed to have appeared out of nowhere. The sky was a heavenly blue background for the single white immense angelic image that Michael had shape shifted from clouds. The divine artistry was breathtaking. We captured that image on film. Celeste and I would later share the picture with members of the HA HA Group. Deb Curry took one look at the picture and said, "Jayne, that's an exact replica of the angel image on the front cover of *Commune with the Angels.*" Celeste and I were amazed and in total agreement with her discovery. Archangel Michael had mirrored to us the image that talented Chris Arbo had created for the cover of *Commune with the Angels.* I can't help but think that this was Michael's way of sharing a God message with all of us. In all the ways we serve, being a nurse, author, teacher, programmer, and so on, we may not realize what purpose our service fulfills. God's "sky art" message is a reminder to us that there is a bigger picture always being painted that we may never witness. It's our mission to keep serving.

# CHAPTER 10

# A Sound Choice

$S$amuel Taylor Coleridge who owned an Aeolian harp was inspired to write these words:

"And what if all of animated nature be but organic harps diversely framed, that trembled into thought as o'er them sweeps plastic and vast, one intellectual breeze, at one of the soul of each and God of all."

When I first came upon Coleridge's quote, I felt a union of our hearts. I, too, am a promoter of the "one divine soul" experience that the harp offers.

One of the most healing instruments on earth is the harp. It has been written that in 500 B.C. Pythagoras played a three-sided lyre and through his playing transformed negative energies into peaceful ones. Pythagoras has been quoted as saying, "Music heals."

Your body is nurtured through sound. The sound of the harp is masterful in its nurturance and comforting faculties.

In the Mesopotamian Royal Tombs of Ur harps were found buried with the deceased. The harps were held by the deceased ruler's personal attendants when they were entombed in the inner chamber. The harps and harpists were recognized as valuable in assuring the deceased ruler a safe transition into the next world. The body truly listens when music begins. To hear harp music is to give your body the gift of listening to angelic tones—listening to the music of the spheres.

Laurie Riley, one of the foremost contemporary players of the double-strung harp, was asked in an interview published in *The Harp Therapy Journal 1998-99*, "What is unique about the harp as a therapeutic instrument?"

"The wide pitch range and range of overtones are significant. Cymatics has shown that our bodies are like an orchestra. Literally each part has a frequency or group of frequencies produced by its function (although the ears don't pay attention to those sounds). When our internal 'orchestra' becomes disharmonious, we become out of tune, out of balance. The harp, with its many strings, consistently generates a profound response in the listener . . . there are many effective healing instruments, but the harp seems to be the epitome of a healing instrument." There is a new movement taking place in which the vibrations from harp music are used to promote wellness, relaxation, and reduce stress. People are researching the harp's therapeutic possibilities and Harp Therapy training programs have been created.

I am filled with delight every time I hear of someone serving with the harp or read an article about the healing role the harp is playing.

Earthly harpists are also bringing peace to the dying. Chalice of Repose is one of the groups providing that service. The founder, Therese Schroeder-Sheker, had an encounter with a man she calls an angel and from that experience was inspired to provide for the dying a "blessed death" with the support of harpists who play songs to ease pain and soothe the soul. For more information visit their Web site at www.saintpatrick.org. I've listed their contact information in this book's list of resources. Music Thanatology helps meet the needs of the dying through individually prescribed musical selections played on the harp. St. Joseph Hospital in Towson, Maryland, offers "Harp Prayer: A Musical Passage Through Sacred Song."

Having grown up with the angels, I learned at an early age the harmony that emanates from the harp. I think I came out of my mother's womb, loving the sound of the harp. In 1995 I was speaking at a conference in Texas where Barbie Edwards, aka The Harp Lady, was present. During a conference break I was at Barbie's booth and had the opportunity for the first time in my life to pick up and hold a zither harp. It is a harp that originates from a harpsichord. I remember that moment as if it were yesterday. I have never been blessed with children, but in that moment I was holding my child. I remember feeling a oneness with the harp. Then the reality of the cost of the harp and my limited budget came into my consciousness. I handed the harp back to Barbie and said, "Someday I will own a harp like this." Barbie handed the harp back to me and said, "The angels have told me that you are to take this harp today and it will become part of your service. If you can only pay me $1 a month, that will be OK with me because the angels want you to have this harp now." I stood there in disbelief at what I was hearing but at the same time feeling the grace of God once again manifesting in my life. I explained to Barbie, "You don't understand, it may only be $1 a month." She laughed and said again, "Do *you* understand. I would rather receive a dollar a month from you than to have you leave without this harp after the angels have clearly told me it is to be yours." And so I left Texas with harp in hand, and it did become part of my service. I bless Barbie Edwards for being the open channel to God that she is. And I need to share with you, that after that weekend God brought people forward who blessed me financially so that I was able to send Barbie the money faster than $1 a month.

When I was back home at Angel Heights with my harp in hand, I recalled Walt's words to me just before his death, "Don't forget to use music in your work. The music is important."

I had the harp in my possession for a few months, not quite knowing what I was to do with it, how to include it in my service. However, when God has plans they will be revealed in God's time. I was in Florida lecturing at a United Metaphysical Church where a medium was giving messages from spirit to the people in attendance. Everyone was receiving blessings of love from relatives in heaven. The medium came right up into my face and said to me, "The angels want to know, why aren't you singing and playing your harp?" The medium didn't know I had recently obtained the harp. God did.

So I began closing my consultations with a "harp blessing." I would sing a blessing or prayer. I have to admit I was a little sheepish about "singing in public." Additionally, my "playing of the harp" consists of allowing Spirit to come through me and do the strumming. Even though people would tell me that my voice and playing were angelic, there was a part of me that just was not willing to accept it. God just wasn't going to accept my not accepting my service. One summer I was at Guilford College in Greensboro, North Carolina, attending the joyous Southeastern Conference held there annually. I was in a private room offering a consultation, during which time I concluded with my singing and playing of the harp. In the room next door was Alan Seale. Alan is an ordained Interfaith Minister of Spiritual Counseling himself, Peace Elder, and a spiritual/clairvoyant counselor, as well as a professional singer and voice teacher, in New York City. Alan has appeared as a soloist with the New York Philharmonic, the New York City Opera National Company, the Spoleto Festival (Italy and USA), the Baltimore Chamber Orchestra, and in solo recital throughout the United States and Europe. He has a CD recording and is the author of *On Becoming a Twenty-first Century Mystic: Pathways to Intuitive Living* (Skytop Publishing, 1997) and *Intuitive Living: A Sacred Path* (Skytop Publishing, 2001).

Needless to say, Alan's an exceptional singer and judge of singing voices. After my session was over, Alan and I crossed paths on campus. Alan approached me and asked if I would be open to exchanging sessions as he truly wanted to experience my singing and playing of the harp. I have to tell you that there was a part of me that wanted to reject the offer because of total fright at performing for a master voice instructor. However, I could feel the angels nudging me and reminding me of Anthony Robbins' inspirational message: "What you can't do, you *must* do!" And so I gave Alan a harp blessing, and I can say without any ego, because I truly understand now that it is God's grace that flows through me, Alan was moved to tears.

At that same conference I was asked by a professional harpist to give her a harp blessing. She, too, was touched by the angels through my singing and playing the harp. She was so inspired by the experience that later her husband would build her a small harp similar to mine. I am certain you can identify with those times in your life when God is whispering, "Beep. Beep. Please get out of your own way. Service is coming through."

I have performed harp blessings at Joshua's Lighthouse Angels. I place my small harp directly upon the chest of the person I am blessing. The individual holds the harp as if it were a small child in the lap. I then strum the harp and sing the individual's name, as well as prayers and blessings that I receive through inspiration. The majority of my blessings are for those who have experienced the loss of a loved one, and many have lost children. As the Bible states, "Blessed are those that mourn, for they shall be comforted." My service is as one who comforts through sound. I am just one of many who have answered the call to go forth and bless and soothe troubled souls with the gift that was written about in the first book of the Bible—Genesis 4:21: "His brother's name was Jubal [Enoch's great—times seven—grandson]. He was the father of all those who play the harp and flute"—as well as in the last book of the Bible, Revelation 14:2: "And I heard the sound of harpists playing their harps."

In my travels I have had the blessing of meeting other earth angels who serve with the harp. One of these precious healing harpists is Carol Cox of Pottstown, Pennsylvania. Carol provides her clients with a truly beautiful and soothing experience. Carol's harp is attuned to angelic notes that balance the seven energy centers of the body, as well as surrounding the individual with the enveloping presence of God's peace. Carol's sessions provide heavenly upliftment for body, mind, and soul. I remember the first time I met Carol, I felt her expanded light energy even before she came into the room. I knew immediately we were angelic sisters of the heart and harp.

Another angelic harpist disguised in human form is Fay Byrd. Fay is a classically trained soprano who channels healing energy with her voice and angel harp for groups and for clients in private sessions. I had the joy of serving with Fay in an angelic workshop we have offered together for a group called Baltimore Angels. When the sweet harp sounds blend with the healing vibrations of Fay's truly angelic voice, this powerful combination is a divine experience. Fay's angel harp is a restructured, retuned autoharp, the divinely inspired creation of Carolyn Weislogel of Hudson, Ohio. Each harp created by Carolyn is accompanied by an angel; the angel Ariannah sings through Fay's harp. Together, Fay and Ariannah have just completed an incredible CD entitled, *We Are One.*

I have found that angel harp music is a wonderful way to connect with the angels. I truly believe we are here on earth to sing our own unique melody. Angelic harpists such as Fay Byrd are accompanied by the sound of angels that join with them in glorifying God, and together the sweetest music is produced through perfect harmony. I know there have been times that I have been doing harp blessings and I have felt a second pair of hands close to mine when I am strumming the harp. Together with the angels we serve God.

There are activities that you can do to bless your life and your body with nurturing "sound choices":

*Purchase harp music tapes—and play them in your car, and in your home—tapes by Erik Berglund and Laurie Riley—fill your life with the healing harp vibration. I recently discovered a wonderful DVD called* Fairy Faith *by John Walker. One of England's leading harpists, Elizabeth Jane Baldry, is featured on this DVD and she has produced a lovely CD of Victorian fairy harp music.*

*Take a walk in nature and commune with the peace and quietness.*

*Become aware of your sound environment and your body's reaction to sound and music.*

*Purchase a small harp for yourself.*

*Subscribe to* The Harp Therapy Journal, *9 East 3rd Street, Bethlehem, PA 18015.*

*Read* The Mythic Harp, *by Sarajane Williams, published by Silva Vocat Music.*

*Experience your life as a living prayer. Experience oneness with St. Francis' words: "Lord, make me an instrument of Thy Peace." Bring harp awareness into your life. Let yourself experience the vibrations of the healing harp. The harp is an instrument of peace that can transform you into "an instrument of Thy Peace."*

In the 1920s, prominent astrologer Marc Edmund Jones with the as–

sistance of Elsie Wheeler brought the Sabian Symbols into modern–day consciousness. These inspirational symbols have been called the American I Ching. There is one symbol for each of the 360 degrees of the zodiac. As an introduction to Sabian Symbols and a tie–in to my message of *healing harps*, I would like to share with you one of the 360 messages; in fact, it is the only Sabian Symbol that mentions the harp: For *Capricorn 9* the Sabian Symbol is *an angel carrying a harp*. The keyword is *attunement*.

I share this Sabian Symbol as a blessing and healing to all who are reading my book. Throughout history angels have been depicted carrying harps. The harp is an archetypal symbol of a sound that links heaven and earth together. The Vikings referred to the harp as *Joywood*. In Greek legend, following Orpheus' death the Muses placed Orpheus' lyre in the heavens and it is known today as the star Vega. Vega became known as the Harp Star. It shines boldly with a light that is fifty times brighter than the sun. Because of its prominence in the night sky as the fourth brightest visible star, many of the sacred temples of the past were built on a divine or cosmic ley line with Vega. When I uncovered this fact, I felt God inspiring me with the message to "hitch" my energy to the star quality of the harp. It truly is a healing instrument.

In the Bible, David plays the harp to comfort Saul and the harp's sound harmonizes the discord within Saul. Perhaps there is discord in your own life. Just like Saul you find yourself tossing and turning in your sleep; worries and anxieties keeping you awake at night. Your yearning for peace and restful sleep in your life has brought you to my words. The sound of peace—the music of the spheres—the angels with their healing harps are inspiring you to take steps to create heavenly harmony in your life on earth.

Through harp music they offer the vibration of love to soothe you and bless you. I encourage you to consider having a CD player by your bed at night. Before you go to sleep, turn on the sound of harp music and push the continuous play button. While you are alseep, let the music play throughout the night at a low enough level so that you can barely hear the music. The sound of the harp will energize your sleep environment with healing vibrations.

Let yourself embrace the reality that there is no separation between you and the Divine. There is no separation between you and your destiny. You are in oneness with the Divine and the Divine's goodness for your life. Let yourself feel the peace of the Divine enveloping you like Angels' wings. Let the comforting vibration of the harp envelop you with peace profound. You are loved, protected, and blessed.

Open yourself to the vibration of serenity, tranquility, and peaceful-ness radiated by the sound of the harp. Let yourself feel the strumming of the harp strumming the string of your own heart. Let yourself receive an "attunement." The "attunement" energy is inspiring you to "tune-in" to your Higher Self—the God voice within—and to have a "Conversation with God." Listen to the God voice. It whispers to you: "You are loved. You are cherished." The sound of the harp is the sound of purity and of goodness. It is the sound of God's goodness in our lives.

One of my favorite psalms is Psalm 33:

> *Praise the lord with the lyre;*
> *Make melody to him with the harp of ten strings!*
> *Sing to him a new song;*
> *Play skillfully on the strings with loud shouts.*

Sing to the Divine a new song for this is a new day in your life. Sing a song of inner peace. Sing a song of belief in yourself. Sing a song of attunement with the Master Dream that is within you. Sing a song as the Beloved you are!

In concordance with attuning yourself to the healing sounds of the harp, I also encourage people to claim for themselves a "Soul Song." This inspiration came from the popular television show *Ally McBeal*. In the show Ally has a theme song for her life that she sometimes hears playing inside of her mind. The song would oftentimes be heard as a motivating energy to help her through her weekly predicaments. The "Soul Song" I've chosen for myself is "Happy Girl," sung by Martina McBride. The master dream that is within me is happiness. Whenever I need to attune myself with the vision of myself as the "Beloved," I just play "Happy Girl" and imagine that every cell in my body looks like a sunshine happy face, as I sing along with the song written by Annie Roboff and Beth Neilsen Chapman.

When I have offered blessings through harp and song, people have shared with me what they witnessed during the blessing experience. One year at Joshua's Lighthouse Angels, as part of the store's annual *Angel Search*, I gifted the winner a harp blessing. The woman who won the contest was an inspiration to us all as she was courageously battling cancer. Sherry was very weak as her time on earth would soon be ending, and so I asked her if I could offer the harp blessing right on the front porch of Mary's store with all of Sherry's friends and family members around her. She loved the idea. As I sang and played for her, my husband, Charles, was standing nearby and observed what took place. He shared that a "presence" came over me, and I glowed with light. He would later tease me that the voice that comes through during the harp blessing is entirely different from the one that is singing songs with the radio when I'm in the front seat of our Jeep. When people compliment my singing, I graciously accept the praise because it belongs to God! When it's just me singing, trust me—it's off-key; when it's God coming through—it sounds heavenly!

One year I was invited by the Life Spectrums Conference to be the leader of the Healing Program the last evening of the conference. I felt so blessed to have been chosen to fulfill this sacred assignment. The angels inspired me to bring together five musicians from the conference that would be an invocation of God's energies. There was a drummer, a flutist, and clarinet and didgeridoo players; and the fifth musical energy was provided by a young man named Richard Chad. Each participant played a song as part of the program and invocation of God's healing presence. Young Richard was learning to play the harp; he wanted to play "Ode to Joy." His harp instructor encouraged him to play something less difficult that he could perhaps play through without any hesitation. Richard was determined to be a blessing of joy with "Ode to Joy." The energies of the evening were lifted as the dynamic musical sounds filled the auditorium. And when Richard started playing there wasn't a dry eye in the place. It was a symbolic message to our souls direct from God. He mirrored to us the hope eternal that God brings to all of us through the children. God bless Richard and his "Ode to Joy." God bless the "sounds" of the children.

During my travels through Florida in 1996 with my harp accompanying me, a God assignment was given to me via a cable television program that aired at two in the morning. I was asleep in the guest room of a family that had hosted my visit. I was awakened by the angels telling me that I needed to turn on the television for there was something God wanted me to see. Fortunately there was a TV in the guest room, so I didn't disturb the rest of the household. I took the remote in hand, searching for what I was to see, and was guided to watch a program that featured the House of Harrari in Jerusalem, Israel. Micah and Shoshanna Harrari have been making biblical harps in Israel since 1984. Micah is descended from the tribe of the Levites, who were responsible for music in the Temple. The harps they make are the first and only of their kind to be made, based on the ancient origins of biblical harps, in over 2000 years. I was enchanted by the story of the truly divinely inspired service of this precious couple. I heard the angels tell me that I would at a future time be contacting the House of Harrari, asking them to build a harp for me.

In January 2000 the angels came forward with a divine message that it was time to bring forth a King David Harp as part of my service. This type of harp was played in the time of King David and in the first and second Temples of Israel.

David's Harp is a Kinnor. "And David would take the Kinnor and play with his hand. Saul would find relief and feel better and the evil spirit departed from Saul." (Samuel 16:23)

It is the type of harp that is described in the Talmud connected with the imminent arrival of the Messiah. As the Harrari House states: "The Kinnor reminds us of the potential of the unknown future scale of music that will reflect a time of joy and love."

The angels' message stated that I was to order it in the same wood used to build David's harp—cypress from Israel—and it would be a harp of healing. The angels' message went on to explain that the money to purchase the harp had to come forth from people who believed in my service; it was to be raised from private consultations and artistic commissions. The energies that conveyed belief in the importance of service were to be the energies that paid for the purchase of the harp.

I shared this message with my tape subscription members and with all audiences at lectures and seminars. Dollars built up to hundreds of dollars and hundreds of dollars became one, two, and, finally, the three thousand dollars needed to purchase David's Harp, which would be built for me in the Holy Land. Each harp created by the craftsmen of the House of Harrari is a one-of-a-kind personal devotional instrument. And the House of Harrari keeps in mind the power of the harp in religious history. It takes approximately nine months for the harp to be created—it is truly a divine birthing experience—for the House of Harrari assists God in bringing forth sacred sound upon the earth.

The day before the "topping off" money for the harp was received, my husband and I felt we wanted to take a break from working at our offices at home. We got in the car and drove to an antique mall in the nearby town of Hampstead, Maryland. We were doing our Rachel Ashwell–inspired "Shabby Chic" browsing when both of us were stopped in our tracks. There on the wall was an antique painting. It depicted King David with his Kinnor in hand. At the top of the Kinnor was an angel's head and above King David were two additional angels. The painting had this inscription: King David praises God. We delighted in our discovery, knowing the shopping angels had brought us to the antique mall. We bought the painting and left the store filled with the excitement of hanging it in our home. King David! King David's harp! Angels! Praising God! How perfect a painting for our home!

When we stepped outside of the store carrying our newly acquired art, both of us had our attention drawn to the sidewalk. Apparently many years earlier, when the sidewalk cement had been poured, someone had felt inspired to write his name in the cement. That one name was: *Joshua*. We knew Joshua Dansicker had been with us on our shopping excursion. We both looked up heavenward and said, "Thanks, Josh!"

We went home to Angel Heights and immediately hung the painting of David and his harp in the center of our home, as the harp has a special place in the center of our hearts.

The next day I went to the post office and there in the mail was a kind letter from someone who is a member of my subscription group. She explained that she wanted to be a part of bringing David's harp from Israel to the U.S.A. and wanted to make a donation to assure that it would happen. Her check was exactly the amount needed to complete the harp purchase. I truly believe that the painting was heaven's way of saying to me, "Get ready. Make sacred space. David's harp is coming."

.

# CHAPTER 11

# Angels with Fur

*T*here is a beautiful cooperation that exists between all of God's king-doms, especially between the angels and the animals. I am one who truly believes our pets are angels with fur. And I am not alone.

Alice Wilson, of Pennsylvania, shared with me that animals had al-ways been a passion of hers. She always admired angels from afar and yet never realized their interconnection with our lives and the lives of animals. Several years back she was working in an animal shelter as the veterinary technician, when a stranger brought in a stray cat with her right hind leg partially severed. It seems the cat had been in a car acci-dent. She had beautiful green eyes and a gray fur coat with a silver hue that covered her body. Alice recognized her pedigree as being that of a Russian Blue Cat. Alice observed her for some time and then decided that this "stray" cat would make a wonderful addition to her family. She approached her boss to let her know that she wanted to adopt this animal before someone put her to sleep. Since Alice worked for the shelter, the attending veterinarian performed surgery on Alice's newest family addition and took the rest of the cat's leg off. Alice's next step was to give the cat a new name. It wasn't hard to do, and so by the time she came home to Alice's house, "Bumper" had taken to her new name. While Bumper was recuperating from surgery and learning to walk again, Alice was busy doing research on Russian Blue Cats. In Russia their nickname is "archangel," and they come from the northern part of Russia, from a town called "Port of Archangel." It is believed that British sailors who were visiting the seaport of Archangel brought the first Russian Blues to Western Europe in the 1860s. Before 1900 they were often known as Archangel Blues. The most distinctive feature of the Russian Blue is its short, dense, plush coat, which is similar to that of a seal or beaver and feels silky and soft. This graceful coat is a bright, even blue, and silver–tipped hairs give the coat a silvery sheen. These cats have vivid green eyes and mauve or lavender noses. When I think of this cat, with its blue, silver–tipped hair giving it a silvery sheen, I truly can envision the blessing of Archangel Michael with his own blue essence and silvery sword radiance. No wonder someone was inspired to refer to these angels with fur as Archangel Blues. This fascinated Alice, and the more she learned about the cat the more she wanted to know about angels.

Bumper lived to be two years old; one day as she and Alice were together walking down the street, Bumper had a heart attack. Alice rushed her to the vet's office, but by then it was too late. If it hadn't been for Bumper's short life, Alice never would have been introduced to the angels and realized the joy of angelic friends. She has been involved with the angels ever since. Near Christmas time of 1994, Alice asked her guardian angel to help her find a hobby to help her relax. She was guided to learn to play a tubular harp. Prior to learning to play the harp, she had never played a musical instrument in her life. Once a month Alice hosts an angel party in her home, and at the end of the party she plays the harp with the help of her cats Orange Juice, Jingle Bells, and Peaches 'N Cream. And, of course, Bumper is accompanying everyone in spirit. Alice had been completely deaf in her left ear, but one day when playing her harp, she realized she could hear out of her left ear. Her hearing is completely normal now, and she is truly grateful to God and to God's messengers—both angels of light and angels of fur.

In *Commune with the Angels* I wrote about my dog Rebel and how, when she knew it was time for her to make her transition, she assisted me and my ex–husband with a healing that made it possible for the two of us to resolve marital property differences, complete our divorce proceeding, and get on with our lives. Before the book came out in October 1992, I was attending a party at a home in Levels, West Virginia. Attending the party was the very gifted intuitive Carl Knieberly. Carl and I were both guests at this party, but I did not know the extent of Carl's intuitive openness until I sat down beside him that evening. He introduced himself and began to ask me if I knew there was a little dog in spirit around my feet. I really didn't expect to be receiving a psychic reading at this party, and so I was rather nonchalant and said, "Oh, really?" I didn't connect with what this sweet soul was gifting me. My lack of enthusiasm did not deter him one iota, and I thank the angels that it didn't. Carl answered, "Oh, yes. But one thing I cannot figure out. Why is this dog wrapped in a confederate flag?" At that remark the tears flowed down from my eyes as I realized that this man was in fact seeing my precious Rebel by my side. I had given Rebel that name as a way to insure my former husband's acceptance of the dog when she came into our lives. My former husband was at that time fond of reading about the Civil War. So when I brought this little gray–haired "Snoodle" puppy home, I said to him, "We can name her Rebel." He loved the name and grew to love Rebel equally as much as I did.

When Carl revealed Rebel's closeness to me, I was surprised because I had felt I would have to wait until my own transition to be reunited with her again. Carl added, "She's right here and wants you to know she's right beside you always." I asked Carl to not tell me anything more as I didn't want any other thoughts to replace the pure joy that I was feeling from this incredible experience with Carl and Rebel. I would later learn that Carl is quite an amazing individual, who, in fact, is a professional intuitive who has read for many celebrities. I know that he was truly an angelic messenger for me that evening, because he brought me a gift of comfort in telling me that Rebel was back in my life—in fact, she had never left.

I truly believe that oftentimes when a stray cat or dog appears in your life, just at a time when you are at your lowest and need compan-

ionship or need to be caring for an animal to take your mind off difficulties and challenges, it is not a coincidence. There was an angel in the
bushes whispering, "That's right, kitty, kitty. That's the doorstep you are
to approach."

A few years back my own mom was making some emotional adjust-
ments in her life. All her children were out of the nest. She was getting
older—only in years, though, as my mother is eternally young at heart—
and she didn't have a clear sense of being needed. She concerned me
and my siblings because her dialogue was such that she was clearly
questioning the changes in her life. We would all repeatedly emphasize
our love for her and the importance she played in our lives. However, a
person has to feel needed. My mother had an empty place in her heart
that only service could fill, and her children were grown, independent,
and no longer in need of the service she had given before. I remember
praying to God, asking for God's wisdom and guidance, on how to help
my mother. The answer came in a small furry package.

I was driving on Route 30 in Upperco early one morning and noticed
a stray dog sitting all alone in a bank parking lot. It was as if I could
read an invisible sign around the dog's neck: I've been dumped. What I
didn't realize was that he had been dumped there by the angels. This
dog's fur was matted and dirty and to top it off he had mange. I pulled
my car up to him, and it was as if he was expecting me. I could have
sworn he looked at his invisible Goofy Dog wristwatch and said to me,
"The angels told me you would pick me up, and you are right on time."
I opened my car door and lo and behold he jumped into the back seat
waiting to be taken to his angelic assignment. I looked back and said,
"Little dog, I know who you need and who needs you." I drove directly
to my mother's home. When I walked into her home no words were
spoken but that dog conveyed to my mother, "Martha, will you look at
how they left me. I need you bad, Martha." My mother stretched out her
arms and accepted her new "baby." My mom was back doing what my
mother does best—giving love, being the incredibly caring, nurturing
person that she has always been all her life. Benji was the angel in fur
who not only was rescued but also came to the rescue. My siblings
praised me for the brilliance of my decision to find Mom a dog. I had to
confess, I was simply the taxi that made the delivery. The brilliance

belonged to God. Up until that moment I was the youngest of six children. Our family became a family of seven and "Benji" was the youngest child. Benji is short for Benjamin—in Hebrew it means "favorite son"—and without a doubt Benji became the family's favorite child.

In the fall before Walt's death, I was speaking in Minneapolis, Minnesota, and I felt Walt's energy make a shift. I knew in that moment that Walt's soul had turned heavenward and that the focus would now be on Walt's preparation for death. I needed to convey to Walt that I knew what was taking place. I went to a card shop in the airport and found a card with a photograph of two golden lab retrievers sharing one stick, dog-paddling in the water together. When you opened the card it read: "We're in this together." I wrote the following note to Walt.

---

*September 30, 1994*
*My Dear Sweet Angel Man,*

*When I saw this card in a card shop in the Minneapolis Airport, I thought of the two of us swimming together. I know at times you are frustrated in having to take pills and having to use oxygen. The cancer can be a scary thing to deal with every day and every night of your life. But one thing is for certain. I love you very much. I am right here beside you dealing with anything you have to face. You are not alone. I am here. If I could find a way to fortify you even more and give you even more of God's strength, I would. So be at peace that you are not alone. We are in this together. You have shared with me that because of the medical necessities you feel like a burden to everyone who loves you. I am here to set the record straight, Walt. You are a gift of love in all of our lives. Whatever comes our way, on our path or yours, we face as a team together. God knew what he was doing when he put us together. I thank him for His wisdom and I thank Him for you, Walt. Love, Janie*

---

As I revisit with the words I wrote to Walt in 1994, I realize that the date—September 30—is Angels Harvest Day. I wrote about this date in my first book. Angels Harvest Day is a date upon which angels of heaven and angels of earth rededicate themselves to divine service. As I wrote in *Commune with the Angels,* "On September 30, a joyous holy day is celebrated . . . the angelic host reports on the progress or 'harvest' of the efforts of the angels to being of help on earth. After the report is given, in the form of an exchange of Heavenly Consciousness, God determines what additional resources need to be made available to the angels to help facilitate their work here." I know there is no coincidence that I wrote the note on September 30. I know God heard my words to Walt and was determining what resources we would both need to help Walt make his transition from earth to heaven.

It brought me comfort to find a card with two dogs on the front, for as the gifted artist Sark so aptly put it on her poster, "Dogs Are Miracles with Paws: God made dogs and spelled his own name backwards!" Animals can teach us so much if we would only listen. Isaiah 11:6–9 speaks of a time when all creatures shall live side by side in peace.

All life has purpose. Man's relationship with the animal kingdom avails us of the opportunity to learn so much about love. Our pets give us a love that is always with us and always there for us whether we are in a good mood or bad mood. Regardless of what we look like or how smart we are, whether we are rich or poor, sick or well, our pets love us. This kind of love, which comes to us without words, is constant. For this reason I believe that our pets are truly angelic messengers, too. Animals that come into our lives often bring a tremendous healing power that we would not have found on our own. They are truly ministering spirits that chirp, purr, fetch, and "heal."

Research has discovered that pet owners live longer than non-pet owners and additionally, just holding an animal causes the blood pressure to go down. Both psychologists and psychiatrists now routinely prescribe acquiring pets for the relief of many emotional problems in children and adults. Pet visits in nursing homes and hospitals by pet therapy programs have resulted in miraculous progress by patients. There have been case studies in which individuals who are epileptic and are not consciously aware of when a seizure will be taking place have been forewarned by the pets they own. One particular case is that of Elizabeth Ruddy. Elizabeth is a vet who lives in Seattle, and she herself is epileptic. She became aware that just prior to her having a seizure her dog, Ribbon, would come to her, would sit beside her, would stare at her, would lick her hands, and would begin to cry.

Similarly, there is the documented case of a woman named Vicki. Vicki was afraid of going outside because her seizures would come unexpectedly and result in her falling down. It was only after she became aware that her dog Harley knew when she was about to have a seizure that Vicki felt safe to venture outdoors. Harley was able to warn her when a seizure was about to take place in time for her to sit down and not experience the trauma of falling. It has been speculated that animals are able to predict a seizure because they sense a bioelectrical disturbance occurring inside of their owner before the epileptic seizure.

I have been teaching for years that angels are radiating beings of a finer vibration of electromagnetic energies. The animal kingdom truly operates at the same frequency as angels.

Studies in hospitals show that patients who have received regular visits from animals recover much more rapidly than patients with similar complaints who do not receive visits. Animals bring to us a soothing sense of well-being. The action of stroking our pets, holding them, talking to them, feeling them snuggle close to us in bed is all therapeutic. Through the presence of animals in our lives we are able to experience the purest energy of unconditional love. When people tell me they have difficulty slowing down from their busy, demanding lives to practice meditation, I encourage them to sit in a chair with their cat or dog and stroke their pet. You will find that the stroking is a "hand-to-heart" meditation experience. It will relax both you and your pet.

And healing is radiated to us by creatures below the waters of the earth, too. There have been numerous books published about the connection between dolphins and the angelic kingdom. Dolphins have been described as having great sensitivity. In the book *Dolphins and Their Power to Heal*, by Amanda Cochrane and Karena Callen, dozens of case histories are given of dolphin therapy and dolphin healing. People with incurable illnesses have found that their health has been greatly improved by swimming with dolphins. Dr. Horace Dobbs is the founder of a pioneer project to establish a nationwide network of dolphin therapies in

England. He has experienced considerable success helping people who are combating depression by allowing these individuals to have dolphin encounters. Patients suffering from depression who immerse themselves in the waters where they are able to listen to the comforting sounds of the dolphins have experienced many healing benefits.

Even though the next story I'm going to share with you is not so much about how an animal was an angel with fur, I laugh every time I think of it because the angels helped me with a very furry animal.

In the summer of 1993, I was in Angel Fire, New Mexico, to participate as a speaker at Power Places Tours First Annual Angelic Conference. Because it was the same week that ended with the First Annual Be an Angel Day Celebration, I could not stay at the conference for its entirety. I had to leave midweek. I left early on a Wednesday morning in order to take a flight back home. I was going home to then depart for Buffalo, New York, where I would lead an angel workshop at the Lily Dale Assembly.

On Tuesday evening after the conference concluded there were a number of people who expressed their desire to have a private reading with me while I was at Angel Fire. Because I was leaving early the next morning the amount of time that was available was quite limited. Several people asked if I would be willing to do late readings Tuesday night. I agreed and concluded with the readings around midnight. Before retiring I packed my bags and put everything in my room in order because I knew I would be departing bright and early Wednesday morning. I wasn't finished packing until sometime between 1:00 and 1:30 a.m. I was ready to retire when I heard my guardian angels impress upon me that it would be a good idea to wheel my luggage down to the elevator and load it up in my car now. My car was parked out front in a parking space right next to the lobby doors. I remembered debating with my guardian angels that I could easily do that in the morning when I got up around 5:30, and I preferred to go to bed. But again, they impressed the importance that it be done now. In fact, I was given the inspiration that on the way back from having loaded my luggage I could take care of checking out, and all the matters of business I had with the hotel front desk would be finished. I could depart Wednesday morning without any obligations to perform. Since I sensed my guardian angels knew something I didn't, I wheeled my luggage out to the car. I followed their suggestion and checked out with the front desk night clerk and then went to my room and retired.

Since I did have to leave bright and early, I had the front desk give me a wake up call that allowed me just enough time to get up, shower, dress, get into my car, and head to the airport. Everything the next morning went according to schedule. As I walked off the elevator into the lobby and headed toward my car, one of the people who'd attended the conference approached me and said, "Did you hear about the commotion that just occurred here within the last half hour?" I replied, "No. What happened?" She went on to tell me that there was a bear in the front lobby. In this area, bears often come out of the woods. This particular bear ventured up to the hotel and when he stood at the front doors of the lobby (next to my car) the automatic doors opened and he invited himself into the hotel. He checked things out and saw there wasn't anything of real interest and so went right up the stairway to the outside of the hotel, taking the steps that lead to the ski lift and freedom in a wooded area. I realized as I listened to the story that, had I been operating under my originally planned schedule, I would have been going out of the lobby doors when the bear was coming in the lobby doors. I'm sure that my guardian angels were well aware of this potential crossing of paths and prevented me from having a close encounter with a furry angel of the *big* kind. I give thanks for the many times in my life the angels have prevented me from running head first into trouble that is the size of a large grizzly bear.

God's voice speaks to us in so many ways. Spirit speaks through animals. I have found that members of the animal kingdom often bring me messages as I observe them. I remembered shortly after Walt's death I was driving home on a country road one evening. On the road in front of me I observed a fox that had been hit and killed by an automobile. A companion fox appeared to be uncertain as to whether to stay with its dead companion or go on. Then suddenly the fox took off into the woods. I remembered my heart almost breaking from the loss mirrored to me by the foxes. And I knew that I was being told by God, the angels, and even Walt, that I, too, had to go on with my life.

I recommend that everyone's home library have a copy of Ted

Andrews' *Animal-Speak*, published by Llewellyn Publications. I am to-tally convinced Ted is a leprechaun disguised in a man's body. I have had the good fortune of hearing him lecture on numerous occasions and have been enchanted by the depth of his wisdom on the sacred symbols mirrored to us through animals. The book is filled with insight on animals as messengers through myths, legends, and animals' natural behavioral patterns.

Several years ago I was having groundhog encounters. I would look out the window and there would be a groundhog sauntering through the yard. I would be driving and would catch the sight of a groundhog popping its head out of a hole. It got to be comical. I didn't "get" that the groundhogs were messengers to me until one day I got a glimpse of a groundhog with its little hands in the air and I am totally convinced it was saying in groundhog language, "Yoo-hoo! Jayne!" I went home and read *Animal-Speak* and learned from Ted's wonderful book, "It is not unusual to have a groundhog appear at a time when a new area of study is about to open up. Since a groundhog does not fully mature for about two years, its appearance as a totem can reflect an endeavor that may take two years to come to full fruition. This may reflect two years of intensive study, digging and building." That groundhog most defi-nitely was a messenger from God because I was starting to research the Sabian Symbols, which, after two years' research, I would be sharing in my spiritual astrology classes.

In 1994 during the weekend of Be an Angel Day, an angel with fur named "Miracle" was born in Janesville, Wisconsin. On Dave Heider's forty-six-acre buffalo farm, on August 20, 1994, a rare white buffalo was born. My attention was immediately drawn to the news. I loved her name and the fact that she was gifted to us by God the weekend of Be an Angel Day. I could easily remember her birthplace: "Janes-ville." I bought the issue of *People Magazine* that featured Miracle's first baby picture and talked about the Heider Family and Miracle at all of my seminars. At 6 a.m. on August 20, 1994, Dave Heider went out to check a buffalo cow ready to give birth. He fully expected to see a reddish-brown calf. What he found was that a miracle had been born. Accord-ing to the National Buffalo Association, the birth of a white buffalo is an extremely rare event.

The story hit the news wires a few days later, and the first Native Americans arrived at the farm the next day. Miracle was viewed as a sacred sign from God by the buffalo–hunting Plains Indians. According to Indian legend, the birth of a white buffalo was a sign from God. She was a message of the need for people of all colors—black, red, yellow, and white—to come together in peace. Though there are many versions of the White Buffalo legend, they each center around a story of three hunters encountering a white buffalo calf. The white buffalo calf transformed herself into a beautiful woman who instructed the hunters to go to their village and prepare for her visit. Four days later, the white buffalo woman arrives at the village and gives the tribe the sacred peace pipe. With the gift of the pipe, she brought laws to the tribe that brought about healing changes. Though the tales may vary, the tribes are in agreement that a white buffalo is a sign of abundance and a message that humanity is on the cusp of an awakening. "Miracles" are being shown to us.

Months following Miracle's birth, pilgrimages continued to Heider's farm. Arvol Looking Horse, Nineteenth Keeper of the Sacred Calf Pipe, said that Miracle was a messenger that "a healing would begin and dreams and visions would return . . . it's an omen that's bringing a change and a new world. The twenty–first century that is coming is going to unify all of us." By the end of 1994, thousands had visited Miracle.

Dave Heider turned down many offers to purchase Miracle. She is not for sale. The Heider family believes Miracle was given as a gift to the hearts of all people.

In all of my lectures following Miracle's birth I would share my picture of the white buffalo calf. I would first ask everyone, "Do you want to see a Miracle?"

In the summer of 1995 I was invited by a Wisconsin A.R.E. chapter to speak at a weekend conference. When I arrived in Madison, I asked my host, "Have you seen Miracle?" He remarked, "She's brown now." He then added he had not gone to see her.

During the first evening's dinner I inquired of everyone seated near to me if they had seen Miracle. Everyone remarked, "She's brown now." And once again, no one had seen her.

At the first evening's lecture I didn't bring out my Miracle picture. I was intimidated by the thought of the whole audience saying together, "She's brown now!"

Back in my dormitory room I ended my day with prayer and meditation. During my meditation I was inspired with a message to share at the morning lecture.

When I began the morning session, I had Miracle's picture in hand. I told the audience of the messages I had repeatedly been given about Miracle, "She's brown now." I shared the inspiration given to me by the angels. A miracle is still a miracle even if it changes colors. Oftentimes when God gives us a miracle in our life, we are initially excited about it, i.e., seeing a rare white buffalo. However, when it becomes familiar to us, such as being the color of a basic brown buffalo, we cease believing in the "miracle." We are not to give up on miracles simply because they change in some way.

During the lunch break an A.R.E. member asked if I would like to spend lunchtime driving to Dave Heider's farm. I was thrilled with the invitation. When we drove up on South River Road, we found a field that is designated for parking. As we walked down a gravel road, we met a Native American. We shared we were there to see Miracle, the white buffalo. It was obvious from his words that he had been dealing with people who had expressed disappointment that Miracle was no longer white. He simply said, "She's brown now." I smiled and remarked, "That isn't a problem. I'm here to give thanks to God for gifting us miracles."

As we walked back toward the field where Miracle was, I passed a man who was kneeling down stirring paint in a paint can. Just as I got near to him, he turned and looked at me and said, "If you ever have a white buffalo born on your farm, don't tell anyone." I knew from the *People Magazine* article this was Miracle's guardian, Dave Heider. I replied, "Oh, Mr. Heider, God knew exactly what He was doing when he had Miracle born on your farm. You're the perfect guardian." I think I took Mr. Heider by surprise in recognizing him. My hostess chimed in, "Oh, yes, she's been telling everyone at our conference about you." I believe the angels sent me to the farm that day not only to see Miracle, but to reassure Dave that he is an incredible man and that is the reason why Miracle was birthed on his farm. My own dad is a farmer, and so I could appreciate the many sacrifices Dave Heider had made in adjusting his farm life to coping with thousands of visitors. He should be canonized.

Next to the gate of Miracle's pasture were hundreds of gifts left by the many tribes who have come to visit Miracle. The gifts included prayer bags, prayer ties, prayer flags. The Dalai Lama had left a traditional white silk scarf.

When we returned to campus, I started off my afternoon session talking about my visit to Dave Heider's farm and gave the conferees exact directions for how to find their way to a real miracle.

In June 2000, I was invited by the Angels of the World to be the guest speaker at the conference in LaCrosse, Wisconsin. My husband and I made a vacation out of the trip. We stopped and visited Joan Berg's Angel Museum in Beloit, Wisconsin, and we stopped and visited with Miracle both going out to the angel conference and on our return trip home. It was so wonderful to be able to share Miracle with my husband.

There were no other visitors on the farm on both trips. On each of our two visits, Dave's father was so gracious to us. He took us on a golf cart and drove us to Miracle's pasture. She's a large buffalo now and is a mother of two. Miracle's first calf, Millennium was born in 1998, and Miracle may be a grandmother soon. Miracle's second calf, Lady Miracle, was born August 18, 2000.

Sometimes the messengers are birds. Many people have shared with me their own personal stories of having witnessed a dove, cardinal, or bluebird flying close to their window or even close to their car following the death of a loved one. Bluebirds, symbols of happiness, have flown into my life on numerous occasions as a spirit messenger foretelling that things are going to get better and to not give up. One of the earliest bird voices heard in spring in the northern hemisphere is the bluebird. The bluebird is a messenger that winter is over and spring has finally arrived. In an earlier chapter, "Driving Miss Mary," I shared that God had guided me to create a sacred ritual at the Serpent Mound in Peebles, Ohio. I was joined by three girlfriends in fulfilling God's request to create a ritual that honored all the religions within the gates of

Jerusalem. On the morning that we staged the ritual of honoring, there was no one at the park besides the three of us and hundreds of blue-birds in the trees serving as our observers. We couldn't stop comment-ing on the sight before us of branch after branch filled with an abundance of bluebirds. We were surrounded by messengers of happi-ness. Perhaps we were being inspired with the message that if we make sacred space here on earth and choose to be tolerant of the many dif-ferent ways God is glorified by people of many different faiths and religions, then the vision will be one of happiness on earth—one of peace on earth.

Additionally, in Chinese astrology each new year is celebrated as be-ing a year of a particular Chinese totem. In my service with the angels, I have found many precious people who are serving God in their lives. I truly believe that though they may have been born in a year that was one particular totem in the Chinese calendar, they serve God with a lifetime totem—Lifetime of the Dove.

I'm always delighted to discover the ways that God reveals His affirmations of truth to us. As I was writing the above paragraph about "Lifetime of the Dove," I was inspired to go to my e-mail and check for messages. I received the following from my dear friend Sharon Shreve:

"You will love this. Yesterday a.m. I opened our front door and found a baby bird on the front step. It didn't move, so I thought it was injured. I began to stroke it lovingly, asking what I could do for it. This went on for quite a while, then finally the little bird flew up to the top of the door and hung on to the bricks. I was so relieved that it could fly. I wasn't sure what kind of bird it was, and I wanted to look it up in Ted Andrews' *Animal-Speak*. So I just asked aloud, "What kind of bird are you?" Well, it turned around and spread its tail to show me. It was a baby dove!!! No need for a response—just wanted to share my joy."

In my lectures, I encourage my audiences to pay attention to sym-bology in their lives. The word symbol is derived from the Greek word "symballein." "Sym" means together and "ballein" means to throw. A symbol is an object that conveys the message of an idea, quality, or essence. For example, through a dove, a message of an inspirational "God-thought" is conveyed to the person who sees the dove.

Ted Andrews shares that the dove has a keynote message of "feminine energies of peace." Ted explains further that the dove's song is heard more often in the "twixt times" of the day, i.e., between dawn and dusk. These times of day are when the veils between the physical and spiritual worlds are the thinnest. Numerous cultures believed that at death, our souls turned into doves. Doves share with angels the visual connection of being "winged messengers."

In Christian art the presence of a dove depicts the presence of the Holy Spirit—the third member of the divine Trinity. This interpretation comes from the baptism of Christ by John the Baptist when a dove was sent by God from heaven. The seven gifts of the Holy Spirit are sometimes represented as seven doves that surround a circle with the letters SS—Sanctus Spiritus, Latin for Holy Spirit. The seven gifts of the Holy Spirit are: Power, Riches, Wisdom, Strength, Honor, Glory, and Blessing, as taken from Revelation 5:12.

Often in chapels dedicated to the Holy Spirit, doves are depicted in the art. The dove is often shown descending to earth, which mirrors the Holy Spirit descending into our consciousness and lives.

In reading the Web site of St. Michael's World Apostolate found at www.smwa.org, I learned of their experience in 2001 with the Miracle of the Doves. "Droves of miraculous white doves inundated the sky above the Vatican Pavilion site during their February 2, 2001 vigil. The unprecedented phenomenon lasted for twenty minutes. Over 1000 doves were viewed by the awe–inspired crowd." Like the angels, doves are God's messengers of love from above.

The symbolism of the appearance of doves contains so many blessings. Seeing a dove in the sky inspires us to look up and look higher. There is a universal acceptance of doves as messengers of peace, i.e., the customary portrayal of a dove with olive branch shown in art. There are many challenges to achieving and maintaining peace on our planet. The doves are sent from God to remind us to look up for inspiration to our problems. The dove is God's messenger of hope. It's God's way of saying: "Do not give up. Do not lose hope for peace on earth." Just as for Noah, who sent out a dove after the flood to see if the promise of land had been fulfilled, and it returned with an olive branch in its beak, for us the dove is a messenger of hope. Do not lose your patience. Keep holding on to the belief in peace on earth.

So don't be surprised if you are driving one day and a dove flies by in front of your car, making its presence known to you. It's God's way of reminding us that we are here to be peacemakers and to continue believing in God's peace on earth!

# CHAPTER 12

# *Afternoon Tea with the Angels*

*I share with people that if* the concept of our all having had past lives is, in fact, true, I had to have had a life in an Amish community because of my dislike for having my picture taken. In addition, I had to have had a life in Britain, for one of my life's simple joys is having afternoon tea.

As I have traveled around the globe as a messenger for God's messengers—the angels—I have included in my lecture schedule time for afternoon tea in the cities I have visited.

I didn't always have this passion for afternoon tea. In fact, it was heaven-inspired. I was attending a conference in which I got to sit in on the lectures of other speakers. I had such a demanding schedule filled to overflowing with traveling as a speaker/lecturer and private consultations, there wasn't much breathing room and much less time allocated for fun.

While I was seated in the audience, the speaker shared the message of encouraging all of us to "get a life." I was intrigued by that remark. I was giving myself in service to others to the point that I no longer had a life of my own. One person I greatly admired was Edgar Cayce and his work as the "sleeping prophet." Mr. Cayce gave so unselfishly of himself that it resulted in his physical exhaustion and death. He just couldn't say no to anyone who needed his services. I realized that by not having boundaries and saying yes to everyone, I was saying "no" to having a life for myself.

The dilemma was brought home again when someone innocently asked me what my hobbies were. I couldn't say the angels were my hobby because service in cooperation with the angels was my entire existence. I read books as part of my research endeavors. I had no hobbies.

I prayed to God and asked for divine inspiration for a hobby that would be a blessing and healing for my life. The answer came to me in an issue of Victoria magazine. I was leafing through the magazine and to my delight discovered a feature about a charming antique store/tearoom. The best part of all was that it was located in Baltimore, Maryland. The store was called the Old Waverly History Exchange and Tea Room. The photographs of the tearoom conveyed the message, "Afternoon tea is a gift you can give to your soul." I knew finding this tearoom was a step toward reclaiming my personal life.

When I got back to Maryland, I quickly called the tearoom and made a reservation. I met the owner, Donna Shapiro, and we became fast friends. I was enchanted by the ambiance of Donna's tearoom. Donna made all the sandwiches and pastries herself. Her menu was totally vegetarian. She is not only an excellent cook but also an artist in the kitchen.

I began to visit the tearoom whenever I felt my soul needed to be nurtured. I could even call up at the last minute, and Donna would joke that, if she didn't have space when I came, she would set up a chair in the kitchen for me. It was my home away from home.

Donna wanted to spread the message of her tearoom and approached the *Baltimore Sun* about their printing a feature on her business. They indicated that they would be willing to do that if they could send a reporter to interview someone interesting who visited the tearoom. Donna remarked, "Have I got an interesting person for you!"

Donna approached me about the interview, and I felt honored to be able to be a part of promoting such a wonderful place. As I knew I was going to be interviewed about my service with the angels, I prayed to God that the reporter would be open to the angels. There have been times that people have taken a "tongue–in–cheek" approach to the angels. I wanted the article to be a blessing upon all who read about the angels and afternoon tea. When I met the reporter at the tearoom on Saturday, June 6, 1992, he extended his hand to me and said, "Hi, I am Rafael Michael Alvarez." I beamed with delight. The following morning, on the front page of the feature section of the *Baltimore Sun* was a photograph of me smiling as I enjoyed tea with my dear friend, Ann Bell. Here's an excerpt from Rafael's article:

"The old–fashioned tearoom where Ms. Howard and herbalist Ann Bell enjoyed scones and strawberries, cheese biscuits and leek tarts, has become a favorite spot for believers to talk about the kingdom of angels.

"'It's so soothing to the soul,' said Ms. Howard, who visits the tearoom with special friends about one Saturday every month. 'There's so much stress in the world, and it's so healing to come here . . . One of the things we have lost in this age of technology is taking time to sit down and talk with one another, to appreciate each other the way people used to do, and this is a place to do that.'"

The article was a huge success in promoting the tearoom. And the tearoom was a sanctuary for my soul. I feel blessed that in June 1999, just prior to Donna's decision to close the Old Waverly History Exchange and Tea Room because of her desire to pursue other business adventures, Charles Feldman came into my life. Together, Chuck and I were able attend the last teatime at Old Waverly. Needless to say it was an emotional afternoon for me as the tearoom and Donna were such dear friends and had provided a healing for my soul.

The Old Waverly History Exchange and Tea Room had not only served as a place of refuge during the writing of *Commune with the Angels*, it had also been the place at which I chose to have friends join with me in celebrating my birthday. I called the celebration: "It's an Otterly Wonderful Birthday." In lieu of gifts I asked my friends, if they felt inspired, to make a donation to benefit the sea otters. When my friend Rosemary Ellen Guiley's book *Angels of Mercy* was released, I hosted a celebration party to honor her artistic achievement. My mother's eightieth birthday party was held at the tearoom.

Hearing all my stories about the importance that Donna and the Old Waverly had played in my reclaiming playtime and a personal life, my husband decided to surprise his new bride with a complete set of Victorian dinnerware purchased from Donna. Whenever I take a break from my angelic service and create my own teatime, I look at the teacup and remember a corner table where I spent many enjoyable hours having afternoon tea with the angels.

Just after my discovery of Donna Shapiro's tearoom, I began a subscription to a magazine called *Mary Mac's Tea Time*. The magazine promoted tearooms around the country. In one issue a woman shared an antique pamphlet she had purchased, published by Lipton Tea Company, entitled, *Your Fortune in a Teacup*. I immediately thought that perhaps the copyright had expired and I could reprint the booklet as a fun project. Since I was becoming connected with tearooms all over the country, I briefly considered the possibility of making this booklet available for sale to the tearooms. I first had to find out the copyright status.

I sent the woman author a letter; however, the address given in the magazine was simply to identify the part of the country where she lived and was insufficient in delivering my mail. When I saw the returned mail posted insufficient address, I knew I was going to have to call the woman myself. I obtained her phone number from directory assistance and dialed the number. The day I called was the Friday before Mother's Day.

When she answered, the energy that came through loud and clear on the phone made me aware that I had called at a "bad time." I could tell this dear soul was having a challenging day. I explained as fast as I could that I saw her article, and was interested in paying for having a copy of the pamphlet made. I then went on to say that I could tell this was not a good time for her to talk and that when I got to California in November I would try again to reach her. And perhaps then I could visit her and pursue the idea I had about reprinting the pamphlet.

Before I could excuse myself she asked, "Why are you coming to California in November?" I shared that I wrote *Commune with the Angels* and that I was invited by A.R.E. to speak at a conference. She then remarked, "Oh my God!" I asked what was wrong. She shared that her only son had been killed in Desert Storm. This was her first Mother's Day without him, and she had said a prayer to God to send angels to help her get through this weekend. I then remarked, "Here we are!"

I asked for her mailing address and offered her a gift copy of my book wrapped in her son Bill's love.

As a result of that phone call, she and I became pen pals. We shared a passion for afternoon tea. In the fall of that year her husband came to Washington, D.C., for business and Barbara came with him. We made a tea date to meet each other at the Willard in Washington, D.C. Prior to my joining her for tea, I stopped at a shop to buy her a small friendship gift. I was thrilled as the store had a lovely collection of ceramic angels. I chose to give her an angel that was holding a bouquet of flowers. The angel reminded me of Barbara. I heard a voice say loud and clear, "Buy her the one with the light. Give her the light. I want her to have light." I explained to the voice that Barbara ran a Victorian tearoom. She gave her guests Victorian hats to wear during their tea experience. The flowers reminded me of the Victorian clothes she loved to wear. There was no change in the emphatic voice, "Buy her the one with the light. Give her the angel with the light. I want her to have light." I bought the angel holding the light.

Barbara and I met each other for the first time in person at the Willard. It was as if we had been best friends for years. Immediately Barbara started telling the story about the last time she saw her son, Bill. He had come to her home to help out with yard work. He realized that the outdoor light over her garage had burned out. She remembered seeing him standing on the ladder replacing the light for her. He turned to her and said, "I'm replacing this light, Mom. I want you to have light." I then realized and shared with Barbara that it was her son who was shopping with me as I selected a special present for her.

I thank God for the inspiration of making time in my life to have afternoon tea. It's important that all of us remember to stop and smell the roses.

People often ask me how they can become closer to God's angels. One way to do that is to focus on the now—focus on the precious present. Sometimes we live for the future and it creates a state of impath birthday celebration. In that interview, Ms. Astor shared her belief that people rush about, "no one sits down, has a chat, or dances in the afternoon." I was enchanted by her statement and thought of the wonderful British tea dances that afforded an individual afternoon chats, tea, and dancing.

The angels encourage us to live in the moment. Take time to watch the sunrises and the sunsets. Even though you feel that by some prognosis there is an even greater uncertainty as to the continuance of your physical body, that uncertainty is a reality for all of us. The angels inspire us not to focus on a future that is uncertain. But rather on rediscovering and finding the meaning of today. Value the "todays" of your life. Focus with certainty on the opportunity given to us every minute to fill our life with joy.

Sometimes in our life, something that we thought was going to happen gets changed at the very last second. It may create within us a feeling of disappointment; however, I have found that usually the change is to allow something better to occur.

The angels gifted one memorable afternoon tea experience to my husband and me as part of our honeymoon. We took a honeymoon cruise and embarked on the Island Breeze at the docks of the Canary Islands. The cruise ship was scheduled to visit Casablanca one day and then go on to Madeira. We were scheduled to visit Madeira, Portugal, arriving in port early in the morning and departing 3 p.m. the same day. Because of rough seas, the trip to Casablanca was cancelled. The captain made the decision to arrive one day earlier in Madeira. As a result we would arrive at 2 p.m. in the afternoon and leave at 3 p.m. the next day. It seems the majority of the passengers were saddened by the Casablanca cancellation. My husband and I had in fact chosen the cruise because Casablanca was one of the ports of call. So when we heard the news we both wondered what new surprise was coming our way.

When it was announced that our destination was a Madeira arrival at 2 p.m., I heard the angels proclaim, "Reid's Palace Hotel." I was re-minded of a front cover article featured in *Victoria* magazine about this world-celebrated hotel built by Scotsman William Reid in 1891. The hotel sits on the clifftops overlooking the Bay of Funchal and the Atlan-tic Ocean and is truly a heavenly setting for afternoon tea. I remem-bered the front cover photograph showing afternoon tea with a breathtaking view. I am an avid reader of books and magazines. I love reading about people who have been inspired to create places of beauty on earth—people who have built something beautiful in the physical structure of the building, at the same time maintaining a respect for the natural setting that God has provided.

When the ship pulled dockside in Madeira, I informed my husband we were going on an angelic adventure, and so we hailed a taxicab for Reid's. Once at Reid's, we went into the hotel to the front desk where I explained that we had just arrived on the cruise ship and didn't have reservations for tea. I asked if it would be possible for us to have after-noon tea with them. Reid's is known for being a home away from home to many of the most prominent people on the planet, and I must say that they made us feel like royalty.

The exact table shown on the front cover was the table where we were seated for our afternoon tea. We spent a romantic afternoon at a table for two. Our palettes were pampered with tea and sandwiches, scones, and pastries. The view was as fulfilling as the delectable delights served.

When teatime ended, my husband and I went to the front door of Reid's and asked the doorman to call a cab for us. We also asked if we could stroll through the lush gardens behind the hotel. The doorman first commented that the gardens were restricted to guests of the hotel only. We indicated that we respected that and waited on a bench for the taxicab to arrive. The doorman came over to us again and indicated that we could walk through the gardens until the cab's arrival, which would be in about ten minutes. Once again we were beaming like a pair of kids who were just invited into the secret clubhouse. In advertising, Reid's Palace Hotel promotes itself as "a destination of its own." I would like to add the adjective "divine" destination of its own. The gardens give one the feeling of having arrived in paradise.

My love of afternoon tea experiences has introduced me to so many enchanting places around the world and I have been doubly blessed when I have shared them with my husband. We have treated ourselves to one afternoon tea experience whenever we go on vacation. We experienced the delight of sipping Empress blend tea, served in Royal Doulton china at the Empress Hotel, one of Victoria, British Columbia's most beautiful landmarks. The Empress has been called "The Jewel of the Pacific." The hotel serves afternoon tea to over 100,000 visitors annually. The Empress was designed by Francis Rattenbury and opened in 1908. It was built in the Edwardian style and was recently restored to its original grandeur with antique furniture and luxurious decor. We were so blessed when we were seated at a table that looked out over the city's inner harbor. Prior to our visit to Canada, I read that the chef of the Empress had taken the British tradition of tea time and raised it to an art form. Chuck and I both agreed that there truly was a master artisan in the kitchen as we witnessed the stunning presentation placed before us: blueberries and Chantilly cream; tea sandwiches of smoked salmon and cream cheese, carrot and ginger, egg salad and cucumber; and fresh scones and crumpets, and other scrumptious pastry delights.

It's interesting to note how many tearooms create a soothing atmosphere with harp music. I feel I would be remiss if I didn't share where afternoon tea originated. It's a perfect example of someone painting outside of the lines and becoming a trailblazer in the process. In 1840, Anna, the seventh Duchess of Bedford, found that there was too large a gap between lunchtime and dinner. Her solution was to ask for tea, breads, and butter to be brought to her room. She soon started asking friends to join her for the afternoon tea break and the new trend was off and running in England.

I encourage you to incorporate tea into your celebrations. Consider a bridal tea; have tea tasting in lieu of wine tasting; host a teddy bear tea or Alice in Wonderland/Mad Hatter tea party for children; have a tea picnic, a mystery tea—the ideas are endless. More inspiration around tea celebrations can be found in Frances Norton's *A Victorian Cup of Tea: A Guide to Victorian Entertaining*. Frances shares the inspiration that "Your tea should not turn into a drudge of perfectionism, but one of the gladdest occasions that both you and your guests partake of." Additionally, Frances encourages readers in her belief that Victorian tea brings "surprises to your life because it has a tendency to bring forth the creative *'secret self'* that lives within each of us." I was blessed to meet Frances and learned that we share a love of tea and a love of the angels. Because of the many blessings God has given to Frances, she always puts an angel somewhere on all her work and personal correspondence. For example, there's a cherub on the front cover of her book.

Just as Frances doesn't forget the angels, I encourage everyone not to forget to invite the angels to share teatime with you. Make a place setting for your guardian angel. The angels love to partake in joyous celebrations. One holiday season my travels took me to New York City. I remember having afternoon tea and feeling self-conscious because everyone was with someone, couples and groups of girlfriends surrounded me. My mini-pity party abruptly ended when the angels reminded me that I am never alone and to invite them to have tea with me. I immediately offered them the place across from me that was vacant of human company and started having a "telepathic" conversation with my friends from on high. I felt if I started talking to those who are visible to me and invisible to everyone else in the room, it would be grounds for management to call the men with the white jackets. Christmas carols were playing as background music and at that moment, the tape got stuck and one line kept playing repeatedly for several minutes. The angels were definitely getting their point across as throughout the restaurants these words were being heard over and over: "Oh hear the angels sing! Oh hear the angels sing! Oh hear the angels sing!" The angels love to sing! Love to celebrate! Love to party with you! Love to have afternoon tea with you! They are God's messengers of joy. Another author who likes the angels and spreads the message of beauty, peace, and tea celebrations is Alexandra Stoddard. Alexandra is a prolific author and my library overflows with her books, one of which is *Alexandra Stoddard's Tea Celebrations: The Way to Serenity*. Alexandra writes, "As the end of the twentieth century approaches, it is more vital than ever before that we learn to treasure ourselves and our planet . . . Tea is a perfect place to begin. Put the kettle on. Make yourself comfortable near a window. Sip, and let the world boil down to just this cup, this moment, and let the warmth slowly spread from your fingers, throughout your whole body to your soul. Reflect, analyze, dream and plan. For now, the world is right here."

The word "serendipity" means to happen upon abundance when not really looking for it—when blessings just seem to happen on their own. Horace Walpole coined the word in his book *The Three Princes of Serendip*. Serendip is located in Ceylon. Walpole's heroes experience good fortune without seeking it, and the term "serendipity" was born.

I would like to invite you to experience "sippindipity." It's the experience of abundant blessings of peace when you take time to nourish your soul with tea. Peace just happens when you pause for tea. As an earthangel4peace, I offer that you can reclaim peace in your life. Teatime is a special time to pause, reflect, and find peace. One enjoyable sip at a time.

# CHAPTER 13

# *Angelic Feng Shui*

**O**ver *3,000 years ago the* technique *feng shui* originated in China. Feng means "wind" and "shui" means water. In my studies of this technique I have come to recognize that feng shui is a way to align your home and your own personal energies so that you are supported by both heaven and earth.

I have integrated practices I have learned through reading feng shui books with angelic inspiration to create Angelic Feng Shui.

By applying Angelic Feng Shui in your life, you can support your mental faculties with a symbolic "wind" energy that blows you in the direction of your highest good. In short, it's the wind behind your back that is found in Irish blessings. Angelic Feng Shui can support your emotions with a symbolic "water" energy that has you flowing to your highest good.

Energy imbalances in your home impact you physically, mentally, emotionally, and spiritually. Not only do the angels watch over your personal body, they watch over your home as well. The angels welcome the opportunity to bless you and your home through Angelic Feng Shui.

I encourage you to embrace the angels as divine feng shui consultants who are available all hours of the day. I have often been fascinated that people are easily intrigued when someone shares that their house has a ghost. Angels abide in everyone's home. I have been contracted by hundreds of people who have invited me into their home to "feel" the energy and make suggestions in support of what they desire for themselves in their lives. The first thing I "feel" when I enter the home is the angelic welcoming committee. The angels are so joyous when I arrive; not because of my presence, but rather because of the homeowner opening to the reality of the importance of balanced energy in our lives. It is almost as if I can hear the angels saying, "One small step in bringing peace to this home and its owner; one giant leap for peace on earth." Peace on earth begins inside of each of us and we support the energy of peace within us through allowing a peaceful vibration within the walls of our home.

Invite your angels to walk around the inside of your house with you. Ask your angel team to "inspire" you by directing your vision or your thoughts to places in your home that could use an energy boost or even a healing. One of the easiest healings can be found in two simple words: *Lighten up!*

Take a walk with the angels and let your attention be drawn to places that energy has accumulated in piles or stacks. Allow yourself to be inspired to let go of anything and everything that is no longer useful and purposeful in your life. The angels are assisting you in bringing divine order into your life, so let your attention be drawn to any areas that are in disorder or are disorganized. These are energy traps.

Your home is truly a sacred space and you are now taking steps with the inspiration of the angels to reclaim the space as holy ground and to move forward supported by this positive energy. So even though you are not literally moving out of your home, let yourself imagine that you are taking the same steps as you would in preparation of a move. You are moving forward, embracing peace in your life. You are moving forward to embrace your life's sacredness and holiness. Ask yourself—room-by-room—what items do you want to take forward with you? What items do you want to release?

The objects that you retain in your sacred temple, a k a your home sweet home, convey a message to you about your life. For this reason, release to the trash man anything that is broken or cracked. If it doesn't work and it cannot be fixed, release it. I remember visiting one home where my client had an abundance of stereo speakers that were no longer functional. This collection was conveying the spiritual message that the person was filling her life with tools for communication that just didn't work. It didn't surprise me that the client was frustrated in that she wasn't being heard in her relationships.

The country music group Diamond Rio has a great recording called "Stuff." It pokes fun at how we love to fill our lives and our homes with *stuff*. Our belongings sometimes begin to take on a life of their own. I remember one of my friends sharing with me that she had stuffed so much down into her basement that she was sure whenever she opened the basement door she heard breathing—the sound of the "stuff" coming alive.

Do you realize that having too much stuff can impact your well-being? We are guardians or stewards over all of our possessions. For example, if you own property, you are the earthly guardian of that land as long as you own it. Stuff is property, too. The more stuff you are guardian over, the thinner your energy is spread out over the possessions. Are you spreading yourself too thin for things that no longer have relevance in your life?

Don't hesitate to invite an auctioneer into your life and make a clean sweep of the household items you no longer need or desire in your life. Or perhaps you can donate items to charity. A feeling of being depressed mentally or "weighed down" can be caused by the weight of possessions. *Lighten up!* Now this does not mean you are not to surround yourself with beautiful objects that inspire you. However, our own personal energy is slowed down in our homes when it cannot move about because of too much stuff.

When Chuck and I married and made the joint decision to live happily ever after at Angel Heights, we had to put his Gaithersburg, Maryland, home of thirty-eight years on the market. Over the thirty-eight years Chuck did what we all have a tendency to do, he stored stuff in his attic, thinking that one day the things would serve a purpose. Prior to putting his house on the market, there were a lot of activities involved in making the house ready for the real estate market. The one project we most avoided was the attic. I remember one morning, after Chuck had gone off to work, I was feeling really good about his home being ready for sale. I had told Chuck I was going to Angel Heights for the day, as I missed the country atmosphere. I got into my car in our driveway in Gaithersburg and heard the angels say, "You can't leave. You've got to clear the attic. Your work isn't finished here." I rested my head on the steering wheel in total disbelief. I had never gone up into the attic. Chuck had discouraged it because the accumulation of stuff would give off energy that would transform into instant depression. And now the angels were telling me it was "my problem." I made a deal with the angels. I would contact a local handyman company we had been using for house repairs. If they could send a man over to help me that morning, someone who would arrive before noon, I would take it as a sign to stay and clear out the attic. I went inside the house, dialed the handyman company, and held my breath as they looked at their schedule. As the angels already knew, they were able to have a man meet me at 11:30 that morning. Lucky me.

The helper came right on time. We got a stepladder for him to position himself up into the attic, which didn't have pull-down steps. The man lifted himself into the attic and started handing "stuff" down to me. I had laid tarps on the floor of one of the bedrooms nearby. For half an hour the stuff poured out of the attic. The man came down and begged me, "Please, you and I cannot do this alone. Please consider this offer. I will come back tonight with a crew of four people and we will form a line through your house. I will hand it down to one person and they will pass the stuff through the house to the carport. From the carport you can examine the items, and then we can take them to the local dump for you." I asked him about how long he thought it would take just the two of us, working together, as I pride myself on being a hard worker. He remarked, "Days, madam!" He then added the amount of money that he charged to take a ton of trash to the nearby landfill. I was startled. He was measuring the stuff in the attic by tonnage. I replied, "You don't think there is a ton up there, do you?" His comment floored me. "No madam. There are two tons!" *ha ha ha ha*

I called Chuck at his office and told him that I was giving him a gift.

A crew was coming after work to clear out the attic. It took the team three hours of nonstop work to remove the accumulation of thirty-eight years from Chuck's attic. It was two tons of stuff, and Chuck will tell you himself that about a bag's worth was saved. After this purging process was complete, Chuck came into the house and got on his knees in front of me. He said, "Jayne, I want to thank you and the angels for saving my life. Had I attempted to do what the crew did here tonight I would have had a heart attack. I didn't realize myself the amount of stuff that was up in the attic. Thank you."

I am not a big believer in storage lockers unless you are in a transition stage. We learned so much from the attic-clearing project. We have an attic at Angel Heights and there is nothing in it. We have made a commitment to keep only what are treasures to us personally and items that are useful and purposeful. One of the cards in my deck of seventy-eight *Spirituals* is the Angel of Release. The affirmation of that card is: I am releasing anything that is no longer useful and purposeful in my life.

Our homes are alive with energy. Just as nature is constantly changing, we can support ourselves by making healthy changes in our home environment. An easy feng shui technique is to move 27 objects in your home. By adding the 2 and 7 together you reduce 27 to the one digit number 9. Nine is known as the universal number. It is a number of a larger vision, higher learning, and enlightenment. You can take that a step further and move 27 objects for 9 days in a row. This gets the energy moving and inspires you by your seeing the objects in a new light. I have found that when I start this exercise, there is often an object that gets moved here and moved there and then moved right out the door, because I realize that I no longer have an energy connection to it. As you move objects around your home you will become aware of things that have a sadness connected to them. Let your home nurture you with sweet memories. Our belongings have dialogue with us. What are your possessions saying to you? Walk with the angels and listen to the stories that the objects of your home share with you. Only you can determine when something that once had special meaning and supported you has ceased to be a blessing.

When you walk into your home you want to feel as if you are experiencing the energy of walking into a pair of loving arms. Arms that welcome you home after experiencing a day's worth of the harshness of the "outdoor world." Your home is your sanctuary, and it should mirror your spirit to you. The objects that fill your sacred space should radiate the energy of your own spirit. For example, one of the key ideals of my spirit is peace, so when I come home to Angel Heights, I am returning to a physical place where I give myself the opportunity to reside in peace.

You are a "God-thought." The divine mind of the creator created the thought of you and wrapped around that divine thought are your physical, mental, and emotional bodies. Let the sacred space of your home mirror to you the truth of your identity—you were divinely conceived. Let the angels inspire you with ways you can mirror your true self. Let your home be a place where you are at peace with not only your human self but your higher self as well.

I would also like to suggest that you give your home a name. You don't have to have a sign outside with this name. Let the name be a message to you about your spirit's ideals. Following my divorce, I knew doors had closed and new doors would be opening. I wanted to change the name of my homestead to reflect what was important for my spirit. Obviously, the angels are, for me, of key importance, as is achieving great heights for my spirit, as well. Together my new identity was birthed: Angel Heights.

An exercise you can do in determining how to create and support sacred space in your home, is to do a "house reading" using the cards I created with the inspirations of the angels—*Spirituals*. If you are unable to obtain a set of *Spirituals* through stores in your community, you can purchase them from me through my Web site. You can, of course, use other decks of inspirational cards. Center yourself while holding the deck of cards in your hands. Ask that God inspire you through the card with insights on positive energy changes to make in your home/sacred space. Then draw a *Spirituals* card and read the message. Perhaps you are standing in your hallway, and you draw the Angel of Decision—I am making and following through on decisions. Let yourself pause and reflect about any decisions you have contemplated making with regard to the hallway and items in the hallway.

Perhaps you move into your living room and draw the Angel of

Forgiveness. I would encourage you to reflect upon what might have happened in that room where there is still a residue of energy that needs to be smudged and transmuted into light.

Additionally, let the angels inspire you in ways to bring more light into your home and into your life. As I shared earlier, one of my favorite Bible verses is Isaiah 42:16, which states: "I will make darkness into light before them." God wants to turn on the light in our lives. Fill your home with light and you will at the same time be filling yourself with light.

Brighten rooms with light colors of paint and lighten up the energy of your home. Use mirrors to reflect window light. Pay attention to when light bulbs burn out and replace them. Keep the light bright and shining in your home and in your heart. An easy way to let more light into your home is to clean the windows; in fact, cleaning your entire home is an exercise in removing negative energies.

Once again call upon your angels to assist you. In doing this, you will receive "inspirations" that will assist you in a thorough cleansing of your home environment.

Consider house cleansing a sacred ritual. Before beginning, remove all jewelry that can possibly absorb the energies you are removing. Open windows. Light candles. Additionally, playing uplifting music is a wonderful cleansing tool as the music raises the vibrations in the house and transmutes the negative energies into a higher frequency or blessed energy. Use smudge sticks to clear the atmosphere of negative energies. A dear friend of mine, Ann Bell, sells a wonderful smudging kit for use in cleansing your home. I've listed her as a resource in the back of this book. When you have completed your house cleaning, it is important to then cleanse yourself. If possible, take a bath with sea salts. Sea salts are wonderful in cleansing oneself of negative energies.

I also encourage you to consider creating space in your home as a Sanctus Sanctum, a "refuge room." *Sanctus* is Latin; it means holy. *Sanctum* means a sacred place or a private room where one is not to be disturbed. Make for yourself a Sanctus Sanctum—"Holy Sacred Place."

One of my favorites passages is Psalm 91, verse 2: "I will say of the Lord, He is my refuge and my fortress; my God; in him will I trust." In reading that verse one day I found myself focusing in on the word refuge. I started looking for other passages with the word refuge and found: Psalm 84:5, "Happy the man whose refuge is in thee"; Psalm 27:1, "The Lord is my light and my salvation; whom should I fear? The Lord is the refuge of my life; of whom then should I go in dread?"; Jeremiah 17:17, "Thou art my only refuge on the day of disaster"; Psalm 90:1, "Lord, thou has been our refuge from generation to generation"; Psalm 46:1, "God is our shelter and our refuge, a timely help in trouble"; and finally Psalm 34:8, "Taste, then, and see that the Lord is good. Happy the man who finds refuge in him!" The word refuge means safe place, shelter, or protection. Its Latin origin "refugere" combined "re" (back) and "fugere" (to flee). A place where we are able to flee back to is our place of refuge.

I was inspired by the Feng Shui Angels to create a refuge room for myself in my home. It is my Sanctus Sanctum—my holy sacred place. This is where I take refuge and feel myself close to God. I can shut the door and be entirely alone with myself and with God. When I need to flee from the demands of life, I can go into my refuge room and give myself the opportunity to be alone and take a look at the challenges in my life. There are times when my soul wants to tell the world: Do Not Disturb.

I feel everyone needs space that is totally one's own. It is a place where you can be yourself. Don't get discouraged if living arrangements prevent you from having a refuge room. It is equally abundant to find refuge in a chair or a rocker.

There may be a little nook in your home and by simply using a screen you can create a place of privacy. Let your creative self become an interior designer and discover a sacred space—no matter what size—in your home where you keep a divine appointment with yourself every day of your life. For whatever amount of time you are able to allot, make this space totally yours. We all need time to distance ourselves from the outer world in order to be closer to God and our inner world.

There are so many things in this world that demand our attention. Look here! Look at me! Look this way! It's nice to have a place where you can go and "God gaze." A place where the only thing you are looking at is God. You may go God gazing through meditating; through praying; through reading Scripture or other inspirational writings. It is where you take refuge with God.

I also encourage you to keep the space uncluttered. There are enough distractions in this world, you don't need to bring distractions into your sacred space. Let whatever you choose to have in your refuge room be of an energy, color, and vibration that is soothing to your soul. Create a space that supports the energy of having an undisturbed conversation with God. If you want to feel like you are climbing up into the arms of God, make the sacred space comforting and cozy.

You may choose to have inspirational art, but again do not overwhelm the space with objects. Create a place of peace where your soul can take refuge, not feel like it has to take inventory. This is a place to flee from phones, computers, and television sets. A place to experience stillness, a place to experience quiet, a place to experience God. You will need to tell family members that when you are in your sacred space, you ask not to be disturbed.

By keeping your divine appointment every day, you will be light weaving with the angels a celestial sanctum or refuge room that embraces you every time you return to this place of peace.

In time you will become aware that there are angels that watch over your refuge room. When you return to the room, you will feel a "presence" that welcomes you "home."

I also recommend that you have a place that you can visit in the outside world that gives you this same feeling. This place mirrors to you the same energy that you feel in the refuge room or Sanctus Sanctum in your home. This place may be public, i.e., a garden or shrine, but once you have discovered it, let it be a secret place between you and your soul. Don't tell anyone about the special meaning of this place for your "soul self." It will be a place that you can take yourself when you need to get in touch with your spirituality and need to journey or make a pilgrimage away from your home.

If you would like to fill your life with blessings, then on your altar or somewhere in your home place an Angelic Blessing Bowl. To create an Angelic Blessing Bowl, first find a bowl that is special to you. Perhaps the design on the bowl speaks to you, or perhaps someone special gave the bowl to you and the bowl reminds you of his or her love.

In many ancient traditions bowls were utilized in sacred ceremonies to represent containers that collected blessings from heaven and blessings from the Divine Mother. The bowl also was symbolic of the womb of the Divine Mother and so items placed in the bowl represented the energies the Divine Mother would birth into one's life. An Angelic Blessing Bowl is a continuation of this celebration of the birthing of blessings in our life.

Once you have selected the bowl you wish to use, then fill the bowl with whatever items mirror abundance to you. You may place holy medals and little angels to mirror blessings from your friends in high places—saints and angels who watch over you and love you. You may have pictures of your family members and friends to mirror the abundance of love and friendship in your life. You may place dollar bills and coins to mirror prosperity in your finances. Crystals are energetic and colorful and are wonderful magnetizers of abundance. They make wonderful additions to Angelic Blessing Bowls. I also place jewelry that glimmers and shines because it mirrors to me energy that sparkles with a golden vibration.

You will find that once you create your Angelic Blessing Bowl a vortex of energy will rise up from the bowl. When you walk by the bowl, you will feel the energy moving from the bowl and blessing you and your home. Make certain that you keep the crystals and items in the blessing bowl cleansed so that the prosperity vibration that flows from the bowl is kept free of dust.

You may want to keep your Angelic Blessing Bowl in the center of a coffee table in your living room. You can fill the bowl with extra blessings such a little angels or small crystals. When people visit your home, you can gift them a blessing angel or blessing crystal. You thereby create the energy that you are sharing your prosperity, sharing your wealth, sharing your blessings.

A popular feng shui remedy for stagnant energy is the use of a fountain. The placement of a fountain conveys the message that energy is flowing in the space. When you hear the sound of the fountain's water flowing in your home, let it be an inspirational reminder that you are choosing to place yourself in the flow of God's streaming consciousness of eternal love. Your life is flowing with goodness!

Additionally, in my lectures I encourage people to make certain that furniture is not placed so close to the wall that it touches the corners. The word corner is derived from the Latin "cornu" which means horn, as in cornucopia. Visualize a horn, similar in shape to a "horn of plenty" in the corner of a room in your home. It is through this heavenly horn that energies flow into your home. It is in the corners of the rooms of our houses where dimensions come together. In my first childhood experience with the angels, my guardian angel manifested its energy through the corner of the bedroom ceiling. By keeping the energy flowing freely in the corners of your rooms, you are outwardly supporting your inner communication connections with the divine.

In Jewish tradition the shofar or trumpet was oftentimes a ram's horn used as an instrument of proclamation, announcing the presence or coming of the Lord or to praise God. "With trumpets and the sound of a horn, shout joyfully before the Lord, the King." (Psalm 98:6) When I am asked into people's homes to perform a house blessing, I always anoint the corners with holy water and ask that just as the corners are structural meeting points, may the energies of the "cornu" fill the home with the awareness of heaven and earth coming together. I offer a blessing that those living in the household are always aware of the presence of God and that they joyfully praise God in all they do within their home.

Open you mind, heart, and spirit to angelic feng shui. You'll find the angels are always available to help you make your home heaven on earth.

# CHAPTER 14

MARYLAND
DUIANGEL

# *Fairy Tales*

I n my travels around the world as Earth Angel 4 Peace, I have been blessed to have contacts and conversations with fairies. Yes, you can communicate with fairies as easily as you can talk to humans. Even though for the past twenty years I have been inspired to lecture on communing with the angels, Spirit has now called upon me to speak and write about the fairies. It is with great joy that I respond to this divine request, for just as the angels are around us, so, too, do fairies abound here on earth. My message is quite simply to make time to dance with the devas and frolic with the fairies.

One of the ways that Spirit conveyed that it was time for me to share inspirations from the fairies was that in the middle of the night I would hear my husband's printer printing all by itself. Whenever I looked at the clock it would read 4:44 or 11:11. I would get out of bed and go into Chuck's office, and there in his printer bin would be a sheet of paper with an itty bitty heart in the corner of the page. I considered these wee little hearts to be valentines from the fairies. The fairies were sharing their heart energy and asking simply that we do the same.

While working on this chapter, I had taken a printout of the pages and was sitting in a chair in my office reviewing what I had written. Just as I read over the words "itty bitty heart in the corner of the page," I again heard the printer going off by itself in my husband's office. When I looked at what had been printed, I discovered the itty bitty heart in the corner of a white sheet of paper. This was the first time the valentine had been sent during the daytime hours, and again I interpreted the message to be one of love from the fairies. My husband, Chuck, is a retired IBM engineer. It was so much fun to see him peering into the printer trying to figure out a logical explanation for where the message came from.

I once heard a Catholic priest say, "If you don't believe in angels, no explanation is possible. If you do believe in angels, no explanation is necessary." For me, it was simply God being God—communicating love through the fairies with the appearance of wee little hearts. It was God being God; however, I would soon learn the incredible message the fairies were attempting to convey to us through page after page of tiny printed hearts.

Upon returning home from my Angel Tour of Scotland, Chuck went to a heart specialist at Johns Hopkins Hospital for what he had shared with me was simply a routine checkup. When the doctor asked Chuck what had brought him in for the visit, Chuck stated that he had been experiencing serious chest pains; he had kept this information to himself as he did not want to worry me. After listening to Chuck's descriptions of the pain and giving him an EKG, the doctor determined that Chuck had classic blocked artery symptoms. Chuck was scheduled for a heart catheterization procedure the very next morning.

When Johns Hopkins did the procedure, they discovered that an artery in the front of the heart was 99 percent blocked. Because of the accessibility of the artery, they were able to put a stent in during the catheterization procedure. Chuck spent one night in the hospital and went home feeling truly blessed; if the blocked artery had not been so easily accessible, he would have had to have heart bypass surgery immediately. The doctor was amazed that Chuck had been functioning so well with a 99 percent artery blockage and was thrilled with the ease and success of the surgery.

In the middle of the first night that Chuck was home from the hospital, I once again heard his printer going. When I got up the next morning, I immediately thought of the sound and went into his office fully
expecting to see an itty bitty heart in the corner of the paper. To my
amazement, the hearts had been replaced with a line of happy faces.
Tears streamed down my face as I realized that the fairies had been
sending us SOS messages about Chuck's health with the printing of the
little hearts. It truly is time for me to share the healing messages from
the fairies.

In Geoffrey Hodson's words, fairies are "on the lower rungs of the
angelic ladder of life." The fairies often reveal themselves as a flow of
energy or a flowing force of the element they are associated with and
also at times shape shift the light force into the appearance of wee
humans or "wee people."

My formal introduction to the fairies was a result of two earth angels.
The first was Flower A. Newhouse, author of *Kingdom of the Shining Ones*,
and the second was Dorothy Maclean, author of *To Hear the Angels Sing*:
*An Odyssey of Co-Creation with the Devic Kingdom*. These two precious woman
helped me understand the identity of the light energy beings I recognized inhabiting nature. As a child who grew up in the country, I experienced an awareness of little light beings in the streams, hills, and
forests. To me they were the "light flickers," as they appeared as flicker-
ing light beings.

I grew up with the "Sparkies," the fire fairies; the "Gillies," the water
fairies; and the "Bubbles," the air fairies. You may not find these names
in any books on fairies because they were given to me by the fairies
themselves.

In my service with the angels, the angelic kingdom has tutored me to
recognize areas in nature where it is easier to connect with the little
light beings. Dorothy and Flower were my teachers in learning that
there are light beings called devas and fairies that are connected with
the elements—fairies of the earth, fairies of the air, water fairies, and fire
fairies. In *Commune with the Angels* I share two personal interactions with
fairies—one with a spirit being of the water while swimming in my
parents' pond and one with a fire fairie during a firewalk experience.

Because they are connected with the elements, you can sometimes experience fairies at certain sites, such as the water fairies being near springs or where a smaller body of water expands into a larger body of water, i.e., stream to river. Fairies of the air are to be found in the fall when a "whirlwind" whips up a pile of leaves. Usually the twirling wind distracts us from realizing we are not alone and that a fairy is present. Fairies of the earth love blossoms. There have been numerous occasions when I've seen what appeared to be a blossom and then when I'm recognized, the blossom moves and a little light appears. I am so very grateful that my service has somehow been communicated to the wee people and they feel safe enough to venture out when I pass through their communities. You might catch a glimpse of a fire fairie when a beam of sunlight shines through a forest. As the light cascades to the ground, there may appear a fairie of sunlight. Whenever I am hiking and I have a sense that two trees have created a natural doorway, I know that the fairies are near. Whenever I am near to nature and I find myself having a giggle attack for no apparent reason, I know that I have ventured into a pixie playground.

If you want to make yourself known to the fairies you need to take yourself into nature and recognize the importance of your walk. We are such heavy-footed beings. Fairies are more apt to reveal themselves if you have a gentle walk—a tiptoe—a light step or prance. There's wisdom to the popular lyrics, "tiptoe through the tulips." Fairies prance! Fairies dance! Fairies whirl! Fairies twirl! They will recognize immediately that something is different about you as a human and that will pique their curiosity and out they will come peeking. They are curious when we behave differently. They know we are not abundant in the change department.

Just as there are guardian angels for all humans, there are angels who are guardians of the fairies. One of the things we share in common with the fairies is that we are watched over by God's angels.

Time expressed in the world of the fairies is quite different from time in the third dimension. In the story of Rip Van Winkle, Rip's time spent with the fairies resulted in a hundred years passing in human time. There are instances where people have walked into the fairy world and have come away not really knowing where he or she actually had been and not able to account for a short amount of human time that is missing. The person simply thinks, "Where did the time go?" The fairies roll over with glee and laughter as they remark, "Where did the time go? The real question is where did the human go?"

If you are truly someone who wants to open you heart and life to the fairies, here are some suggestions on getting in tune with their light and vibration:

---

*Celebrate the seasons* • *explore flower essences (a wonderful source is Molly Sheehan's Green Hope Farm)* • *listen to your intuitive voice when you are out in nature* • *go barefoot in nature* • *Mother Nature loves when you give her a massage by walking gently on her with your bare feet* • *walk gently, not only with your physical body but with your emotional, mental, and spiritual bodies, too* • *experience the wind blowing through your hair* • *know that the wind loves experiencing you* • *interact with nature* • *let your little child/inner child out to play* • *take time to rest upon the earth and watch the clouds float by* • *sing a song that you make up as you go walking in nature* • *look at the world through your legs* • *look for pennies* • *look for feathers* • *get in touch with the wonders of this world* • *get in touch with the wonders of you* • *give yourself a secret name* • *share that name with only the fairies* • *imagine the woods as a secret club house where you and the fairies meet* • *create magic in your life by keeping your ears open for things people say they would like or want or wish for; if you can fulfill their dream, do it; that makes you a fairy godmother* • *fairies love their relatives* • *be on fairie alert* • *look for fairies in paintings, statues* • *worry less, laugh more* • *giggle even more* • *romp* • *be whimsical* • *be sure to have a magic wand and a jar of bubbles* • *a jar of bubbles is great to have in your car during traffic jams* • *have toys in your shower* • *make life fun and fantastic* • *spread joy* • *proclaim today National Belly Button Day and honor your belly button* • *feed bread to the ducks at the local pond* • *pick up a seashell and hear who's calling you on the God line* • *put on a dance recital just for the fairies* • *when you plant a garden, communicate with the*

*devas of the land you are cultivating • see God's presence every-
where and in everything.*

And, most important, rent the movie *Fairy Tale: A True Story* and believe! Then be inspired to make a place in your home where you place
a little fairy bed. This way the fairies will know they are welcome for
sleepovers. I love Rose Fyleman's poem "Fairies and Chimneys":

*"Blind folk see the fairies, oh better far than we, who miss the
shining of their wings because our eyes are filled with things we
do not wish to see. Deaf folk hear the fairies however soft their
song; 'Tis we who lose the honey sound amid the clamor all
around that beats the whole daylong."*

We do lose the "honey sound" amid all the yamma yamma of daily
life.

Some years ago I purchased Inner Child Cards. As promoted on the
back cover of the package: "Drawing on universal children's fairy tales,
myths, and fables such as Sleeping Beauty, Alice in Wonderland and
Robin Hood, these delightful cards open our hearts and minds to new
revelations about the journey of self-discovery." The cards are the creation of Isha Lerner and Mark Lerner and are illustrated by Christopher
Guilfoil. I openly thank them for the blessing these cards have been in
my life.

I was immediately enchanted with the cards. Fairy tales I had grown
up with came to life through the images and messages of the cards.
Through continual use of the cards I found that a "living language"
came into being between the fairy tale cards and myself.

After my divorce, when I was going through a dating stage of my life,
I remember asking for divine insight on a particular relationship that
seemed destined to remain in a platonic state. I drew an Inner Child

Card. The card chosen was Hansel and Gretel. In that first draw I knew the "God-truth" was being told to me, yet I didn't want to hear it. I shuffled and drew, shuffled and drew; and time after time Hansel and Gretel would stand before me.

The "truth" would not be buried or lost in the deck. Hansel and Gretel always were smiling at me on the card I had chosen. In time, I came to accept the truth as my reality, too. We would be best friends—like brother and sister, like Hansel and Gretel—nothing more, nothing less.

When I met Walt Blatt, he had already been dealing with cancer for five years. As I have shared earlier, he and I were together five years and on March 1, 1995, he accepted the angels' invitation to come home to God. Throughout our relationship I would repeatedly draw Beauty and the Beast from the Inner Child Cards. I came to realize the symbolism of this card. The cancer could have been perceived as the role of the beast. It was a curse that shortened Walt's life. However, when we first met, Walt had been told he had a year to live. Through the beauty of love, the spell was broken, and we were given five years together. Love is a miraculous gift!

When Walt died, it was very similar to the scene in Disney's Broadway version of *Beauty and the Beast*, where the "beast" is transformed into a handsome prince. God transformed Walt's physical body into a totally healed light body. Through Walt's allowing me to be a part of his sacred dying experience, I learned to see the beauty in all of life's experiences, including death.

Sometimes it's not the card you draw but the one that is missing that holds the message.

When Charles and I married and started our life together at Angel Heights, we hired a painter to give the inside of the house a new paint job. During packing and unpacking due to the interior of the house being painted, one of the cards from the Inner Child Cards totally disappeared. I just "knew" a card was missing. I counted out the cards and sure enough the deck was one short. I went through the entire deck and discovered it was the Ace of Wands. Because of this occurrence I realized I needed to purchase a new deck. My life was overflowing with new energies and it warranted an Inner Child Card set.

Even though I had a new deck, I was curious as to where the card went and why it had "disappeared." I searched high and low but never uncovered the card. It was frustrating because one day all the cards were there, and the next day the deck was missing the Ace of Wands. I kept asking, "Where did the card go?"

One day in meditation, the fairies came to visit. During our lovely chat they said to me, "You didn't ask about the fairy tale card?" I realized who had taken it. I asked them, "Why did you take it? And why that card?"

They explained that when they celebrate a wedding or a birthday they cannot send a card, so instead they take the card they want you to have. They told me to reread the Ace of Wands and to read it as if it were a wedding congratulations card sent from them to me. Here's the wedding card we received from the fairies:

*"In this card, a magnificent soul potential in the form of a butterfly is being unveiled by two fairies . . . The butterfly is an essential emblem of love, suggesting in China, a wedding of souls. This winged gift is a reminder to you today that love, soul unity, and art are fluttering into your life. An inspired rebirth is taking place. It is time to reveal your true colors. The flight has begun."*

Needless to say the fairies had to pass me a tissue—and a wee little tissue it was. What a truly perfect wedding card. The words they chose are so true! Love, soul unity, and art have fluttered into my life with my marriage to Charles Feldman. It is a wedding of souls with the fairies' blessings!

During my Angel Tour 2000 to Turkey, I was inspired by the fairies to connect with the relief effort on behalf of those impacted by the earth-quakes of recent years. I have had many conversations with the fairies on how our help is needed by the nature kingdom and from these conversations I learned of the need of the undines—the fairies of the waters of the earth. The fairies encouraged me to share the message that we all have opportunities to bring relief in each other's lives. The word relief originates from Latin and means to rise up with light. With our lives and the choices we make, we can raise each other and the earth up with light.

In working with the angels during the Star of David grid project, I was amazed to notice as I traveled around the U.S.A., how many people are ready and willing to toss a coin into a pool of water. If you show the public a small body of water, it will become a wishing well overnight. I have also discovered that this occurs around the world.

I decided to do a little research on wishing wells and found they are connected to the fairy kingdom. The ceremony of making a wish and then making an offering into a well or body of water originated as a sacred ritual to the divine messengers found in the waters. It was believed that the messengers would deliver the wish request to the powers of manifestation, and then, one hoped, the wish would be fulfilled.

I am encouraging people to continue the tradition of making wishes and making offerings. However, I offer a little twist to the ritual: Make Use of Wishing Wells to Wish the Earth Well.

The fairies of the waters of the earth need our help. These precious God–creations need us to bring them relief. They want to support us in the fulfillment of our hopes, wishes, and desires. They ask for our help in bringing relief to the waters of the earth—the streams, the rivers, the oceans. Make your wish and then make a donation to an organization that is actively and responsibly taking steps to support, clean up, heal, and bless the holy waters of Mother Earth. Make your wish and then toss your offering in the direction of healing the waters of the earth. Rather than the coin sitting at the bottom of a pool of water (and usually the coins are not healthy for any fish that share the same space), direct your energies and your monies as a relief effort for the water babies—the water fairies—the gillies.

Think of all the waters of the earth. Think of the powerful energies of these waters. In many religious traditions, water is recognized as a powerful protection and for this reason babies are baptized with water. The Christian ceremony originated from a pagan magical rite.

The relief that you bring to the waters of the earth you bring to yourself. We humans are comprised of 90 percent water. In the Bible, John 2:6-7 refers to the "six water pots," which are six nerve centers of our bodies, and the water of life is the fluid that flows through our nervous system.

Together with the water babies/gillies/water fairies, let us focus our intent on healing the waters of life both in us and around us. I encourage you to create a wishing–and–giving ritual around the chakras or energy centers of your body. Make a wish that is connected with each chakra, for example:

---

First Chakra—*A wish for your foundation energies; perhaps a wish of abundance.*
Second Chakra—*A wish that will support your relationship with yourself and with others.*
Third Chakra—*A wish that will in some way empower you.*
Fourth Chakra—*A wish for fulfillment of your heart's desires.*
Fifth Chakra—*A wish that will support your creativity and communication of your gifts and talents.*
Sixth Chakra—*A wish that will support a vision or dream you have.*

---

Then on behalf of each one of the six chakras, make an offering that will benefit six bodies of water on the earth. Once you make known to the angels that you want to support the waters of the earth, your path will cross with organizations that are waiting for your offering. You may support an organization in your own state that is involved in cleaning six or more rivers or streams. You will learn of cleanup efforts taking place as soon as you make the decision within yourself to make an offering. Additionally, keep the water fairies in your prayers.

I share Chief Seattle's words: "This we know: the earth does not belong to man, man belongs to the earth. All things are connected like the blood, which unites us all. Man did not weave the web of life; he is merely a strand in it. Whatever he does to the web, he does to himself."

There is one additional plea I wish to make to you on behalf of the fairies. It is to support the global efforts being made to rid the planet of all landmines. We have not only trashed our beautiful homeland with garbage but have buried millions of landmines in the earth. Princess

Diana was such a blessing in raising the consciousness of humanity around the Campaign for a Landmine Free World. To learn more about the heroic efforts being made, I encourage you to contact the Vietnam Veterans of America Foundation. You'll find contact information in the back of this book. "VVAF has transformed the experience of war suffered by America's soldiers in Vietnam into a program of service to others." We have a crisis of great magnitude on the planet. There are over seventy million landmines buried within *our* earth. Even worse, it is innocent children who are more times than not the victims. Did you know that no one who is alive today will live long enough to see a world that is free of landmines? That's a statement made by the Landmine Clearance International Organization, who promote the continued commitment to finding ways to safely remove landmines from the earth.

One person that I consider a true "earth angel for peace" is Bobby Muller. Muller is a Vietnam vet. In 1981 he led the first delegation of American veterans to return to Vietnam since the war's end. As a result of that trip and future trips, Muller answered an inner calling to establish rehabilitation centers for caring for civilian amputees. He established a prosthetic clinic on the outskirts of Cambodia's capital city. Muller cofounded the International Campaign to Ban Landmines (ICBL) in 1984, an organization that won the Nobel Peace Prize in 1997. He became a messenger to the world, spreading the need to educate the public about the atrocity of landmines and the need for action.

Back in 1996 I was visiting Bermuda. A late evening wedding was being celebrated at the hotel where I was staying. Following the nuptials the wedding party set off fireworks that flew right over the roof of the hotel. The sound of the explosion made sleeping hotels guests awake in fear that the hotel was under attack. I had traveled to Bermuda with a girlfriend and we were both in restful sleep when the fireworks commenced. I jumped out of my sleep state and said, "They're bombing the earth! Don't they know what they are doing to the devas? Doesn't anyone think about the fairies!" I then fully awoke and realized that fireworks were exploding in the sky above, and the sound was not of bombs exploding into the earth. My friend remarked that my first concern in the thought process of bombs being set off around me was the welfare of the nature kingdom rather than for myself. Nuclear testing and landmine explosions are just a few of the many ways we are self-ishly contaminating the earth—our home and home to the rest of God's earthly kingdoms, too. Shame on us. However, it's not too late to roll up our sleeves and clean up our act. I am an advocate of "no excuse living" when it comes to cleaning up the planet.

I am an interfaith minister, so I do have my moments of preaching. Here's one of them. There's no excuse for littering, dumping, or trashing the earth. I have read how Bette Midler—another "earth angel" in dis-guise—got so disgusted by what she saw in her environment in New York that she knew she had to do something, including being willing to pick up trash with her own two hands. That's exactly what she does. Bette founded the New York Restoration Project (NRYP), which currently has a workforce of sixty people who clean, restore, plant playgrounds, parks, ball fields, and trails in New York, as well as offering educational programs. NYRP has acquired fifty-one community gardens and also maintains pine barrens located in Brentwood, Long Island. Bette has put her mind and muscle into cleaning up the planet. No wonder people refer to her as the "Divine Miss M." Her vision is truly a divine one.

What's your vision for the earth? For her waters, the oceans and streams; for the woods and forests; mountains and hills? Breathe life into your vision by doing something today in your home, backyard, town, city, state, nation, and world that conveys your respect for the gift of this place we call home—earth. I remember when I was growing up and my bedroom was in need of attention, my mom would simply leave a little note: "Clean your room. Love, Mother." It's time we all heard our "Mother's" message and cleaned up the open-space room six billion of us share together. "Clean your room. Love, Mother."

Sometimes, when we look at the work that is ahead of us in cleaning up the environment, we succumb to a feeling of being overwhelmed or begin thinking "it can't be done." One quality I love about children is their belief in themselves and all that they *can* do. Ask a child what career he or she wants to pursue when grown up, and the sky is the limit. Children may tell you that they want to be president of the United States or a famous actor or actress. They believe everything is a possi-bility. What a freeing outlook to have on life! Children respond to life with a positive *"Yes, I can!"*

How do adults lose belief in themselves and what they are capable of accomplishing? And how do adults learn to become naysayers to others? Too often I hear people giving almost robotic responses of "You can't do that!" when someone shares an inspirational idea.

For the next few days take notice of how large the membership is in the tribe of "Can't Be Done!" You may be in the car with them as they remark that they won't find a parking space. They are quite certain that all the parking spaces have already been filled, and it is not possible for someone to be leaving just when they need a space. They accept that when it comes their turn, life will flash a neon sign that says: "Filled to capacity. Go home." They focus on what can't happen in parking spaces, at work, shopping, at home, and in their life in general. Sometimes I hear people comment, "I never win anything," or "That's my luck, nothing good ever happens to me." Rather than exploring new possibilities and vistas for their talents and abilities, when given a new assignment or task they respond, "I can't do this!"

The tribe includes members that sit in the background and whenever you try something new they remark, "You can't do it; that won't work." They spread a subliminal message, "Give up now."

One of the Ten Commandments is "Thou shalt not kill." I believe that applies to not killing someone's dream. Dreams are so precious. Have you had an experience when you shared a dream with someone, and they immediately discouraged you or told you, "You can't do that!" I'm certain you didn't give up on your dream because of someone else's thoughtlessness; however, just for that moment, didn't it feel like someone had burst your dream bubble?

When I find myself unable to do something, I steer away from saying, "I can't do it." I prefer to phrase my response that at this particular time I choose not to do the activity. When I notice that I repeatedly avoid a particular activity and I feel beneath the surface a tinge of "I can't do this" as the reason for the avoidance, I take a hard, long look at the activity and start developing a plan for doing it.

Anthony Robbins teaches on one of his empowerment tapes: "What you say you can't do, *you must do!*" Whenever I have followed that teaching and made myself do something I initially believed I couldn't do, it resulted in my feeling invincible and truly empowered. The more we tell ourselves we cannot do something, the more we are conditioning ourselves to believe ourselves as limited.

I have also decided that I want to make certain I am not a "dream popper." When someone honors me by sharing a dream with me, I want to make certain that I listen to this person and give him or her my attention. I truly want to hear what they believe they can do rather than drowning them in projections of my fears and doubts.

I once read a saying that has been of inspiration to me throughout my life: "He didn't know that it couldn't be done, so he did it."

Open your heart and mind to the fairies and the feng shui angels. Let yourself be inspired on how you can be involved in cleaning up the environment. Let's look forward together to making choices now that will enable us to leave as an inheritance to the children of the future a planet that is equal to the beauty that God first perceived it to be. To-gether we *can* do it!

# CHAPTER 15

# *Gardening Angels*

*I feel that one of the* most important reasons for rolling up our sleeves to clean up and heal our environment is because of the healing it provides us personally. I believe deep within all of us is a yearning to somehow and in some way return to the first garden—"Paradise." There is something sacred about spending time alone with nature. In those private moments we commune with a space that is deep within each of us. Being alone with nature is a beautiful opportunity to rededicate ourselves to God, a time of surrendering ourselves to the One who created everything—the One who loves us so much that that love is expressed to us through nature, over us, beneath us and around us.

Growing a garden is a way to obtain a passport to "Paradise." Starting and growing a garden is a new adventure every spring. You don't know what to expect from one day to the next. New weeds seem to pop up overnight; perhaps new insects arrive unexpectedly. And most joyous is the discovery of a new bloom or blossom. There's always growth taking place. There's so much that we can explore together with the angels in gardening.

When we are with our flowers, herbs, and vegetables we can feel the closeness and warmth of God as we hold a fragile strawberry in our hands and are amazed at the vividness of its color. There's also a great breath of energy that touches us deeply on a soul level as we recognize that there is an invisible hand working with us as we work with nature. God has created angels to watch over all creation. There are guardian angels that watch over us, and gardening angels that watch over nature. When you spend time in your garden, you are communing with the angels of nature. God has created a specific angelic vibration that radiates and watches over every flower, vegetable, herb, and tree. God has created an angelic consciousness energy that watches over eggplants, over tomatoes, and so on. When you grow eggplants and tomatoes you are tapping into God's angelic radiating energy for that particular plant. In addition to working with the angels who are God's caretakers and stewards over the gardens of the earth, when you are on your hands and knees weeding, planting, cultivating, you are also connecting with the elementals of the earth. These wonderful beings of creation hold by their very presence pictures and visions of perfect plants and vegetables as envisioned by God. The name elemental in Hebrew means "of the mind of God." The elementals' earthly assignment is to hold God's thoughts. I love that image. As the Bible teaches us, "In the beginning was the Word." I interpret the Word to be "thought" because it is by God's thinking that life came into existence. As Einstein phrased it, "I want to know God's thoughts." The all-knowing mind of God with infinite thoughts exists behind all life. In creation God brought forth a group of beings known as the elementals to hold His thoughts—to hold a picture of a perfect blade of grass—to hold a picture of grapes on the vine. This is what the elementals do.

In Dorothy Maclean's book, *To Hear the Angels Sing*, Dorothy shares many amusing stories of her experiences in communicating, talking, chatting, and meditating with the elementals and devas at Findhorn, Scotland. Through these conversations, the Master Gardener guided Dorothy in planting a par excellence garden at Findhorn. No one knows how to grow a garden like God. Not only are you blessed when you listen to God for helpful gardening tips, but the earth is blessed as well.

Working in a garden you can allow yourself to commune with the flowers. You can commune with the vegetables. On a sunny day you can lay back on the grass and commune with the fluffy clouds as they float against the vast blue sky. You will find God has placed angelic energy in service as the many guardians of the sky and earth. Everything exists because of God.

If you are someone who has difficulty sitting in a chair and meditating, then perhaps you can experiment with meditating with nature. Place yourself in your strawberry patch. Place yourself beside a rippling brook. Take a peaceful walk through a park. Wander through the woods. Not only will you feel yourself immersed in the richness of the natural surroundings but within the consciousness of God mirrored to you through the beauty of nature. One of my favorite gospel songs is "This Is My Father's World." The words were composed by Maltbie D. Babcock and were sung to the lyrics of a traditional English melody. "This is my Father's world. And to my list'ning ears, all nature sings, and round me rings the music of the spheres. This is my Father's world, I rest me in the thought of rocks and trees, of skies and seas—His hand the wonders wrought." Yes, when I am with nature I am resting myself in God's thought of paradise.

Another reason that the angels encourage us to grow plants and flowers is because it is therapeutic. When you are in your garden, you do not have the opportunity to dwell on the past. There's so much that needs attention in the now.

In gardening, the angels will allow you the opportunity to open up to a new awareness, to new feelings. It's a wonderful experience to make time to get outside of your house and office cubicle and get away from the electronic world. True, these are wonderful blessings in this day and age. However, to get away from phones, computers, television sets, etc., is to give ourselves time to realize there's another form of communication waiting for us to discover in nature. There's no end to the learning when you open yourself up to working with the gardening angels.

I've mentioned Molly Sheehan, founder of Green Hope Farm, in an earlier chapter. As Molly describes her farm, "We are a community of Humans, Angels and Elementals working together to create gardens and Flower Essences of the highest vibration possible." She is a true messenger of the blessings, experiences, and knowledge that can be

6
↓

re__ved in working in cooperation with the gardening angels. Molly at Green Hope Farm works with the angels in creating healing flower essences. Sometimes the angels make suggestions to her that initially she doesn't understand. She shared the story that one particular year she was inspired by the angels to dismantle a beautiful railroad tie garden that she had just set up the year before. She was inspired to take down the garden and build it again in another location on her property. She found that through the move an even more abundant garden grew. The elementals and angels are not in our lives to exasperate us, rather to inspire us to experience the fullness of God—to experience the wonderful vibration of gardening at its highest potential and at the highest good for all kingdoms. You may ask, "Well, why didn't the angels tell her to plant the garden there in the first place?" I have found in my own life that I have had experiences where God has put me in a holding pattern at one place in my life, and then when it is time to land, the landing strip becomes available. When I question why I had to bother with time spent in the holding pattern, I'm reminded that there were lessons to be learned in waiting and crashes to be avoided by not landing too soon.

Through my friendship with Molly I've learned what a blessing flower essences are. They are just one more example of God's love for us. The human body is an amazing electrical system. In a perfect world our electrical system would be operating with a clear connection to God. However, our lives are often stressed out to the max. We often feel overwhelmed and our electrical system takes the brunt of the results of our stress. Rather than our electrical circuitry juicing a connectedness to God, we turn our energies instead toward survival. Flower essences each contain the high frequency vibration pattern of a particular flower. When you integrate flower essences into your life through drinking the essences in a glass of water daily or simply taking a few drops underneath your tongue, you are asking God's natural gifts to grant a healing from the flowers. The essences, once taken into your body, go to the places in your electrical system that are overtaxed. They help to bring your energies into balance with God's light energy.

One flower essence that the angels have asked me to spread the word about is the "Eyes of Mary," the French name for the flower known in

also— Lavender tea

America as the Forget Me Not. This essence helps us to bring our lives back into alignment with what I call "light sight." Having light sight enables us to see an opportunity to be light rather than to perpetuate darkness. To look through the Eyes of Mary is to look at life through loving eyes and not curse the illusion of darkness. Rather, embrace the opportunity to love and bring light into someone's life, especially our own. Abraham was asked by God to see with light sight when he asked for Isaac to be sacrificed. Mary was asked by God to see with light sight when Christ was crucified.

In *The Magical Name*, Ted Andrews describes the Forget Me Not as a flower with energies that "make it easier to tap the higher realms and can lead to connecting with universal mind."

The gardening angels inspire us with God's message that just as the plants and flowers burst forth with new life, we too are here on the earth to burst forth and grow abundantly. In our own lives there are weeds that grow up around us and can be detrimental to our growing space.

When we plant a garden, whether it is a box garden on a patio of an apartment or condo or a large garden out in the country, we give our souls the opportunity to return to recognizing our oneness with nature. God wants us to experience a patch of heaven here on earth. Every time I am in a garden I feel Christ's words, "Thy kingdom come; Thy Will be done on earth" come to life around me. God wills life, growth, beauty, and color. Gardens mirror to us a microcosmic expression of the incredible macrocosmic thoughts of God. You cannot plant a garden and not be filled with the awe and wonder of God at work.

The energy of the infinite mind of God is in every rose and every berry. As we plant seeds, nurture them, and watch them grow into glorious flowers, we are witnessing the presence of God unfolding before us.

Communing with the gardening angels gives us the opportunity to develop listening on an inner level rather than an outer level. We get away from listening for phones to ring, listening for a boss to call out to us with an assignment to be tackled, listening to the needs of our family. When we spend time in a garden, we let go of the outer hearing faculties and tune into listening in the inner realm of ourselves. We allow ourselves to be still and know God.

Nature and gardening offer us a chance to reconnect with our inner listening abilities. When we open ourselves to communication with all life, we move away from separateness into a unity with the Creator of all kingdoms.

As you open to the gardening angels, landscaping angels, elementals, devas, and fairies you will find that one message they are whispering to us continuously is that change is part of life. The angels bring the divine message to us that we should not be frightened by change. They encourage us not to hold on or cling to that season which has passed. Nature teaches us how to go with the flow; how to change and grow; how to die to the old and allow the new to be born. Ecclesiastes 3:1 teaches, "To everything there is a season . . . "

As an earthangel4peace, I invite you to plant yourself in nature. Experience the peace of mind and peace of heart that comes with placing yourself near to God when you are near to nature. I would like to offer you an experience of peace through a meditation with a gardening angel.

---

*Close your eyes and with your inner light sight, visualize that you are in the midst of a sacred garden. At the entrance of this garden a radiant angelic being stands beneath a glowing white trellis adorned with vibrant red roses. Roses are messengers of love. As you admire their beauty, let your heart receive this Valentine from nature. "You are loved." As you walk through the trellis, you smell the richness of the roses' fragrance. You feel yourself blessed by the sweet aroma.*

*The angel welcomes you, "Come in—come into God's peace and love." You hear the angel encourage you to shed your doubts and fears. Shed your stresses and anxiety. They are like weeds to the flowers of your soul. You walk forward into the garden and a lovely flower catches your eye. You bend down and touch it. As you touch the flower, you feel an energy radiating through your whole being. It is the energy of connectedness as you have just received a handshake—a greeting from the flower.*

*As you become aware that a consciousness of God exists within all flowers, the flower acknowledges the consciousness of God that exists within you. Your attention is now drawn to the garden, filled with flowers. It's filled like a loving cup to the point of overflowing. The garden overflows with beauty and the richness of life. You see a rainbow of colors as lilacs, roses, pansies, and irises surround you. All of your favorite flowers are abloom in the garden. There are herbs, too—rosemary, thyme, and lavender. There are sweet fragrances floating in the air. You feel the divine stirring within as you stand within this sacred garden. You feel fully alive in the reflection of the plants, flowers, and trees that are fully alive with God's life force. There is simplicity to the garden. The peace of God unfolds around you. You feel yourself connected on a heart level with all that is within your vision. You realize how much your soul needs this peace. The gardening angel says to you, "Breathe in all the peace that you need. God gives you peace in this moment and peace evermore." As you peacefully breathe in and out, you see a pure white dove fly over-head. The sight of this winged messenger of peace blesses your heart. The beauty of the garden lifts your soul. There is a motion that is flowing through you and you feel yourself being raised in vibration. In fact, you become aware that you are taking flight. Your feet are no longer touching the ground of the garden. You are now floating above the garden just like the peace dove you saw earlier. There is no room inside of you for energies that would weigh you down. You are the fullness of God's light sight of you. Peace has given you wings. You realize that whenever there is the illusion of anything in your life that is attempting to deprive you of peace, you can visualize this sacred garden. Whenever you need to reclaim peace in your life, you can come to God's garden of love. Connect with the beauty. Connect with the love. Connect with the peace and let your heart take flight.*

*The gardening angel is God's messenger reminding you that God gives life to all things. God gives balance to all life. God gives peace eternal. God is the God of all creation. God breathes life out into our day with the rising of the sun and breathes peace into our night with the setting of the sun. God balances day and night and, in doing so, balances our lives. Think for a moment upon what it is that you need in your life to experience balance. God already knows your needs. Embrace the energy of peace that is within you as Matthew 6:25-26 inspires us, "Therefore I say to you, do not worry about your life, what you will eat or what you will drink; nor about your body, what you will put on . . . Look at the birds of the air, for they neither sow nor reap nor gather into barns; yet your heavenly father feeds them. Are you not of more value than they?"*

*As you experience the peaceful silence of God, let your heart be filled with the contentment of knowing your needs are being provided for by God, even before you are aware of each need.*

*You feel yourself gently touching down with your feet upon the ground of the garden. Look around the garden one more time. Let one of the flowers mirror a message of God to you.*

*If you find yourself thinking, "I don't want to leave the garden. I don't want to leave this place of peace and serenity," be assured that the oneness goes with you. You may hear yourself saying, "Oh, no, it feels different here in this garden than it feels sitting at my desk with a stack of work." Know that the gardening angel gives you this experience to show you that too often in life we weigh ourselves down with problems and concerns. We forget that we can float like birds of peace. When you connect with God, you can float through anything that appears on your life path. It is often our own disbelief that keeps us grounded. When you look at life as an opportunity to bloom in a garden of love, you are embracing wholeness with all of God's kingdoms. You recognize that you are a resident of the state of God's love everlasting.*

*Come to the garden of love as often as you need to find peace. Commune with and attune yourself to the gardening angel. Whenever you feel fragmented and isolated by life, come to the garden. Place yourself closer to God.*

*Feeling the gardening angel's blessing of God's peace, you gently open your eyes and reacquaint yourself with the light of the room. Give yourself time to journal inspirations you received from the gardening angel in God's garden of love.*

Sometimes because of all the technology that fills our lives, we don't give respect to nature and our role as stewards in caring for the earth. Without nature our human kingdom would not exist. Too often we humans have been responsible for destroying nature rather than coming to its rescue. Even in the midst of our many poor choices in decision making on our environment, nature has never given up on us. Nature continues to provide us with healing answers for our lives. Discoveries are constantly being made in nature about plants that can be used for natural healing remedies. Many Western doctors are incorporating natural supplements in healing regimens for their patients, a practice that has already been embraced by Eastern medicine for many years. Healings abound and blessings are found when we open our hearts and minds to God's wisdom, waiting for us to discover it in nature and in gardening.

The last night Christ was on earth in a human body, he spent his evening in the garden of Gethsemane. It was in the garden that He stated, "Not as I will, but as You will." A garden is a place to align us with God's will for our life. Just as you bless your life and home with an altar honoring God inside your house, I encourage you to consider creating a garden—a place where you can go and find peace and the companionship of the gardening angels and experience the will of God for your life. After September 11, I found solace and healing in gardening by creating a red, white, and blue garden at Angel Heights. I found that the images shown repeatedly on television were more than I could bear to watch. I sought for a way to help heal my heart and also energize my love of America and our country's heroes. Chuck calls this our Patriot Patch. Sometimes when we hear of heightened security alerts, we go and sit together on the bench in our Patriot Patch and connect with the ultimate "homeland security"—the eternal security of God.

C. Austin Miles wrote the wonderful gospel tune "In the Garden." As I remember the sound of the words of this song filling my childhood church to the rafters, my heart is filled with the sweetness of the words. "I come to the garden alone, While the dew is still on the roses; And the voice I hear falling on my ear, The Son of God discloses. And He walks with me, and He talks with me, And He tells me I am His own; And the joy we share as we tarry there, None other has ever known." Just thinking about the image of being with Jesus in a garden, fills me with a sweet peace. He is for me the Master Gardener.

I began this chapter with the thought that deep inside of us is a longing for the first garden on earth. The garden that God created for us as our home. I have seen paintings depicting Adam and Eve being cast out of the garden and the paintings usually show the angels wielding swords and the looks on the angels' faces and their body language convey, "Get out!" Genesis tells us that God placed cherubim at the east of the garden of Eden, and "a flaming sword which turned every way."

I am a believer that the reason the angels wanted us out of the garden was because the sooner we went out into the harsh realities created by our failure to remain in oneness with God's divine consciousness, the sooner we would find our way back into that oneness. The angels are rooting for us.

By our choices we developed a consciousness separate from God. This is why God's first words to Adam after Adam and Eve ate of the tree of knowledge of good and evil were, "Where are you?" Adam and Eve had moved their consciousness away from God's and this was the beginning of separateness.

The angels knew that the first man and woman must leave the original garden and begin finding their own way back to harmony, balance, and oneness with the Creator.

I believe that when we plant a garden and dedicate it to God, we are asking for a new beginning in our life. When we get in touch with the earth, we are allowing our lives to feel the tender touch of God. As you tend to your God-garden, let the Master Gardener tend to your heart.

Frances Hodgson Burnett's *The Secret Garden* has been enjoyed by children of all ages. There's a part of us that wants to find a secret garden where we can go and communicate with nature. In the story of *The Secret Garden* a curious orphan, Mary Lennox, discovers a hidden garden. In finding the key to the garden she unlocks many family secrets. By breathing new life into the garden, Mary breathes new life into the family and into her own life. Through Mary's life-learning experiences, readers discover that in restoring a neglected garden, a healing occurs for all family members. The healing of a neglected garden extends into the healing of neglected hearts.

A precious angel friend of mine, Sean James Bradley, lives in Manchester, UK. At the age of sixteen, Sean entered a monastic community and became a qualified nursing monk. Sean gave thirty-six years of his life to nursing. He then was inspired by God to give his time and talents to creating and sustaining an Angel Sacred Peace Garden. He is someone who now helps nurse the Mother Earth. Sean's Web site is www.angelgardens4u.com. He offers do-it-yourself angel garden design kits and in England has created the Bethany Project—a sacred angel peace garden that is incredible. Sean's garden is truly a "heaven on earth" experience.

Sean has created with the angels an Angel Magic Square that you align at your garden's entrance. The square is a divine blueprint for gardeners to use to enable them to work with Archangel Metatron in blessing your garden and the earth. The blueprint divides the garden into nine sectors, and each sector is aligned to the energies and vibration of an archangel. Sean has designs for an Angel Healing Bagua and Sacred Angel Circles. Part of his earthly service is to offer his talents as an angel garden design consultant. He's a perfect example of someone who serves God together with the angels.

I have led groups of people in what the angels have called "Inner Outings" around the world. I refer to the trips as Angel Tours. As I have planned the itineraries with the angels' inspirations, I have taken tour members to some of the most beautiful gardens on earth. One of my personal favorites is Monet's Giverny in France. Even if you do not feel inspired to become a gardener yourself, make time in your life to admire the gardens of the earth. Every time I experience a garden, whether it's the one in a friend's backyard or one that is an established tourist attraction, such as Longwood Gardens, a gardening angel at the entrance always greets me. May it bring you peace to know, that as in life, you do not seed or weed alone. God has created gardening angels to watch over nature and guardian angels to watch over us.

# CHAPTER 16

# *Earthangel4peace.com*

*T*here's a truly inspirational photograph by John Paul Caponigro entitled "Millennium." The photograph is of two enormous wings that appear to have been carved from ice. An ocean surrounds the wings with the shoreline shown close to the bottom of the photograph. The print includes the words of Ralph Waldo Emerson: "What lies behind us and what lies before us are tiny matters to what lies within us."

I share Emerson's words and a description of Caponigro's photograph as a peace blessing to everyone who reads this book. We are now living in a new millennium that begins with the number "2." Plato regarded numbers as the essence of harmony and harmony as the basis of the cosmos and of man. The number 2 is the number of cooperation and balance and is symbolic of the two parts that make up each of us— the masculine and feminine. It conveys a message of dual forces existing in equilibrium. It is the connection between mortal and immortal. It is the expression of the universal law: "As above, so below." Whether the dual forces are in and out, up and down, male and female, or you and me—this millennium is an opportunity for the dualities to exist in a state of balance—to exist in peace.

When I inspire others through consultation, I always ask their birth date. I ask for the month, the day, and the year in which they were born. Being one whom the angels have tutored, I have come to learn of the messages from God that are tucked away in the qualities and essences of numbers. As a result of this, God has gifted me with what I call an "Evolved Numerology." Each of us began as a God-thought. I do not in any way pretend to know the fullness of that thought. What I share through Evolved Numerology is a glimmer or glimpse of the God-thought of you. When the Divine created you, placed within you was a masculine energy or essence and a feminine essence. These energies mirror to you vibrationally that you are a walking, talking, breathing "Holy of Holies." The masculine essence of you conveys to you the vibration of Abba, Father—the Will/Power of the Divine. It is Spirit/Sky/Heaven. It is the giving essence of you; what you do with your gifts, your life.

The feminine is the "receiving" part of you. It is the vibration of Matrona, Mother, and the Love/Grace of the Divine. It is Soul/Earth/Gaia. It is what you have come to accept and love about yourself. This acceptance becomes the kindling fire that burns forever beneath the passion and expression of you. You need to honor both of these energies. In honoring these energies equally you create sacred space within yourself that allows for the birthing of the Christ Consciousness within you. When Jesus inspired us with His teaching, "All this and more you shall do," the "more" He spoke of is the birthing of the Christ Consciousness that you have within you.

When people share their birth dates with me, I give them back an understanding of the blessing of the Will of God/Spirit upon their life through the month in which they were born. The year is the blessing of the Love of God/Soul upon their life. The birth date is a blessing of the birthing potential that is within them waiting to come forth in expression on the earth.

Additionally, I convey the archangels that are around the individual and I give both the masculine and feminine expression of the God Ideal. Even though the angels are genderless, we are beings of duality and the divine blesses us with energies that are masculine and feminine. For example, a "1" vibration holds the divine message of God's Will. The angelic masculine messenger of Divine Will is Archangel Michael. The feminine is Faith. If you would like to determine for yourself your Evolved Numerology, follow these simple steps:

Write down the number of the month you were born, i.e., December = 12, August = 8, May = 5. This number gives a message of God's Will for your life. It is your divine spirit number. It is the masculine essence of you. You will have a number that is from 1 to 12. Write down the number of the year you were born. Reduce this number to one digit, i.e., 1951 = 1+ 9 = 10, + 5 = 15, + 1 = 16. Reducing 16 to one digit = 7. This number gives you a message of God's Love for your life. It is your divine Soul number. It is the number of the feminine essence of you. Of course, there are a couple of exceptions to keep in mind. If in reducing any numbers you achieve an 11, 22, or 33 as the total of the numbers, you do not reduce the number any further, because these numbers carry a master vibration. So, if your birth year is 1984, then 1 + 9 + 8 + 4 = 22. You keep the 22, and that is the vibration of your divine soul number.

Write down your birthday number—the day of the month you were born. If it is 1 through 12, keep it intact as it is. If it is 22, keep it. If it is 13 through 31 (excluding 22), add the two numbers together to determine a one digit number. For example, a birthday of 31 is 3+ 1= 4; your Christ Consciousness inspiration number is 4.

I've outlined below inspirational messages for numbers 1 through 12, as well as the master vibration message for 22. These messages are meant to support you in embracing your divine identity as God's holy gift and encourage you to love your masculine and feminine energies and make sacred space for the birthing of the "more" of you—the Christ Consciousness of you.

I consider the essences or vibrations of the numbers as God Light in our lives, so I have outlined them as God Light One, etc.

---

**God Light One—***Faithfulness, leadership empowerment through faith—Archangel Michael as Guardian. Affirmation: I Am God's Faithfulness.*

God Light Two—*Wisdom, illumination, and understanding. Archangel Jophiel as Guardian. Affirmation: I Am God's Wisdom.*

God Light Three—*Love, adoration, communication, and artistic expression. Archangel Chamuel as Guardian. Affirmation: I Am God's Expression of Love.*

God Light Four—*Hope, purity, connectedness to source. Archangel Gabriel as Guardian. Affirmation: I Am Connected to God.*

God Light Five—*Inner child/innocence energy. Archangel Raphael and Divine Mother as Guardians. Affirmation: I Am a Child of God.*

God Light Six—*Ministration, service, and stewardship. Archangel Uriel as Guardian. Affirmation: I Am Ready, Willing, and Able to Serve God.*

God Light Seven—*Relationships, forgiveness of others, compassion. Archangel Zadkiel as Guardian. Affirmation: I Am Relating God's Forgiving Love to Others and Myself.*

God Light Eight—*Clarity, perception, discernment. Archangel Aquariel as Guardian. Affirmation: I Am Seeing Life Through God's Eyes.*

God Light Nine—*Harmony, higher vision, and enlightenment. Archangel Anthriel as Guardian. Affirmation: I Am in Harmony with All Creation.*

God Light Ten—*Peacefulness, balance, the courage to be the fullness of the divine gifts you are. Archangel Valeoel as Guardian. Affirmation: I Am an Instrument of God's Peace.*

God Light Eleven—*Victory, fulfillment, joy, hopes, wishes, dreams. Archangel Perpetiel as Guardian. Affirmation: I Am God's Joy.*

God Light Twelve—*Transformation, rebirth, and oneness. Archangel Omniel as Guardian. Affirmation: I Am Transformed by God.*

God Light Twenty-two—*Master Architect, creator of divine designs that are the bridge between heaven and earth. Archangels Gabriel, Michael, Uriel, Raphael serve as Guardians covering all four directions of your service. Affirmation: I Am God's Divine Design. I Am God's Bridge Between Heaven and Earth.*

---

It is important that we nurture and nourish our souls and spirits as the God-thoughts we are. I encourage you to surround yourself with energies that inspire you as a "great thinker." Think of yourself as a one who began as a "great thought" and continue that energy by thinking great thoughts of love, service, healing, and kindness. I am constantly reading newspapers, magazines, books, and scanning the Internet to learn all people's "great thoughts." I share what I find in my monthly tape subscription series. Once a month, with the inspiration of the angels, I produce a ninety-minute tape that goes out to those who subscribe to the tape series. The angels are constantly reminding us to think uplifting thoughts.

One of the angelic assignments we have been given is to each find a scientist, political leader, spiritual leader, and artist that we each believe in. It may be a scientist who is researching a subject that we find fascinating and want to know more about, too. The political leader may be our president or a local councilwoman. The spiritual leader may be a priest. The artist may be someone whose music, art, or words have touched our souls. It is a blessing upon science, government, religion, and arts. We have been asked to pray for these people every day in our prayers. We have been asked to call upon the angels to be ever near these precious souls who are dedicating their energies to new discoveries in the laboratories, wise leadership in the city halls, inspirational messages in the pulpits, and divine artistry in the studios. In blessing them we bless ourselves. We are focusing upon what is good in our society, and we are praying for the goodness and greatness of God to be expressed through these individuals and through ourselves. Peace on earth is achieved in focusing on the goodness inside of each of us and the goodness in others.

The peace on earth we yearn for begins with peace inside ourselves. We are ourselves comprised of dual forces that can set in motion the energies of peace on the planet by embracing the reality of peace within ourselves. How do we claim peace on earth within ourselves? First we have to *believe* peace is possible and believe that we are able to create for ourselves a reality of peace and maintain that reality daily. In the words of Eleanor Roosevelt: "It isn't enough to talk about peace. One must believe in it. And it isn't enough to believe in it. One must work at it."

Once we have made peace our clear intention, we can support our focus by seeking out those who have achieved for themselves a reality of peace. We can research the message of peace in the Bible. The word peace is derived from the Hebrew translation of shalom, which appears in the Bible over 250 times. The word shalom is the root for the town name of Salem, a town name found repeatedly throughout America. People long to live in "Shalom"—to live in *peace*.

We can support ourselves with this vision by reading the writings of the Dalai Lama, Mother Teresa, Peace Troubadour James Twyman, and Peace Pilgrim—just to name a few modern-day authors who have written about peace. We can support the Peace Pole Project by sponsoring the purchase of a Peace Pole. A Peace Pole is a handcrafted monument that displays the message and prayer: *May peace prevail on earth* on each of its four or six sides, usually in different languages. There are more than 100,000 Peace Poles in 160 countries all over the world dedicated as monuments to peace. They serve as constant reminders to us to visualize and pray for world peace.

In celebration of the eighth annual Be an Angel Day—August 22, 2000—I participated in the dedication of a Peace Pole on Main Street in Reisterstown, Maryland, on the property of Joshua's Lighthouse Angels. On April 28, 2002, I led the dedication ceremony of the Peace Pole on Illuminata—the property of Sharon and John Shreve in Clifton, Virginia.

It is important to support our quest for peace through prayer. My Web site is part of an Internet community called "Angel Haven." Angel Haven offers prayer support for all those who ask for it. All of us at Angel Haven welcome the opportunity to be of service to God through supporting you in prayer. We can include in our daily prayers our request for peace to be experienced in our own lives personally and globally as well. Those who have known of my service with the angels, know that for over twenty years I have made myself available for prayer support. In my travels I have shared the message of "Raphael's Guest Book"—my prayer book in which I record the names of everyone who has written me, called me, e-mailed, or talked to me personally about their prayer needs. Raphael is God's Messenger of healing, and mentioning all names I have been given, I have gone to God in prayer on their behalf every morning and evening for 21 days. The angels inspired me with the number "21"—as it is the sacred number of creation—7 times the number of the Trinity blessing—"3." The angels have shared that there is a holy manifestation energy about the vibration of 21. For example, if you want to rid yourself of an unhealthy habit, it will take your vigilant focus for a minimum of 21 days continuously to be successful in your endeavor. For this reason, I have maintained a prayer vigil for 21 days for all who have asked.

Additionally one can participate in meditations in which the global focus is world peace. Such an event is World Healing Day. I am an avid supporter of this one-hour meditation that has taken place every year since 1986 on December 31 at twelve noon Greenwich time. The World Healing Meditation was written by John Randolph Price and first appeared in his book, *The Planetary Commission*. Since 1986, millions of people have turned this into a global event. During this one-hour service, people around the world gather in spirit and visualize world peace and simultaneously send out their love and light in meditation, prayer, song, or whatever expression of worship is meaningful to them. I included the entire World Healing Meditation script in *Commune with the Angels*.

Visualize peace. I encourage people to visualize our government creating a Department of Peace. We would have a cabinet member known as the Secretary of Peace. We need to reflect to the world and to ourselves, as a united fifty states, the importance of peace. We allocate monies for war readiness. What are we allocating for peace readiness?

Not only do I hold the vision of a Department of Peace, I would like additionally to recommend that Gregory Smith be nominated as the first Secretary of Peace. Greg is thirteen years old. He is a college senior majoring in mathematics with minors in history and biology at Randolph-Macon College, where he is the youngest student in the history of the college. He will graduate with honors on May 31, 2003. In short he is child genius.

Gregory is the founder of International Youth Advocates and the youth spokesperson for World Centers of Compassion for Children. He travels globally speaking about the needs of the world's children. As an advocate for peace, he has organized humanitarian aid projects for East Timor orphans and the youth in San Paulo, Brazil, and he is helping Rwanda build their first public library. Gregory is working with Christian Children's Fund as Youth Ambassador to build Peace Schools in Kenya and other regions of conflict. He talks with American youth groups about the importance of education as they prepare for their future and how community involvement can create a safe environment.

In all his public appearances, Greg appeals to governmental leaders and audiences to value their children as their country's greatest resource. He teaches about ending the cycle of violence and has pledged his life in the pursuit of peace. I have personally heard the powerful message of this boy wonder on two occasions and was thrilled to learn that he had been nominated for the 2002 Nobel Peace Prize. His is a message of hope for a brighter, more peaceful tomorrow.

Attune to peace vibrationally through art, music, literature, and dance. Bring peace to your soul through your senses. Carve images of peace, paint pictures of peace, sing songs of peace, write words of peace, and dance with peace. Mirror to the world your commitment to peace. Have your checks imprinted with a message of peace. Have a stamp with which you imprint your cards and letters in a sign of peace. I offer to you a free "Be a Peacemaker" bumper sticker. All I ask is that you send a self-addressed stamped envelope to: EarthAngel4Peace, Angel Heights, P.O. Box 95, Upperco, MD 21155.

There are numerical sequences that oftentimes capture our attention and when we notice these numbers, whether on a clock or appearing on a total for our grocery bill, we pause to reflect upon the numbers. Many people are struck with curiosity when 11:11 appears. I am in total support of Nick Bunick's divine inspirations around the sequence of 444. Nick is also a member of the Angel Haven Internet community, and

I encourage you to treat yourself to exploring his Web site.

I have been inspired by the angels to create a practical peace exercise around the "444" numerical appearances. Whenever the clock indicates the time is 4:44—either 4:44 a.m. or 4:44 p.m.—pause and take a relaxing breath of peacefulness into your body and release a breath of peacefulness from your body. Let your thought be: *It's Peace Time; Time for Peace in All Seasons, Peace in All Directions, Peace in All Dimensions.*

As I have shared previously, I produce a monthly inspirational tape series available to subscribers. I invited the group members to each write a line or verse about peace and all of the lines were woven together to create *a peace sonnet.* Fifteen members of my subscription group joined me on a trip to France in October 1999. We visited the Eisenhower Memorial in Caen and heard from Spirit the voices of those who died in World War II. They spoke to us through the message of the Memorial: "Rise up in defense of peace." I believe we lift ourselves up or "rise up" whenever we make choices that support that which is beautiful, good, poetic, artistic, inspirational, and God-inspired in our lives.

Our group went to Omaha Beach where we joined together in prayer for peace and then read aloud our Peace Sonnet. We wanted our individual verses to be a unified verse for all peace.

In November 2000 the same Peace Sonnet was read in Gallipoli, Turkey, where a half million soldiers died in World War I and where thirty cemeteries now exist.

At the ANZAC Memorial there is a poem written by Kemal Ataturk in 1934:

---

*"Those heroes that shed their blood and lost their lives . . . You are now lying in the soil of a friendly country, therefore rest in peace. There is no difference between Johnnies and the Mehmets to us where they lie side by side, here in this country of ours. You, the mothers, who sent your sons from faraway countries, wipe away your tears. Your sons are now lying in our bosom and are in peace. After having lost their lives on this land, they have become our sons as well."*

---

When I visited Bosnia, I remember seeing playgrounds converted into cemeteries to accommodate the casualties of war. Let us hold in our hearts the belief that now truly is the time for *peace*.

During my recent Angel Tour 2000 to Turkey, our tour bus stopped at a remote village. We visited a village outside Konya, where tour buses do not go. There are no museums, no tourist sights. This village is not on the list of places not to be missed in Turkey. However, this stop was the highlight of our tour for every single member of our bus trip. Our tour guide encouraged us to go into the village and meet the people. He believes that peace on earth will be achieved by the people of the earth getting to know each other, one-on-one.

With my friends I walked up the dusty roads and gave a big smile, friendly "Hello!" and warm hug to anyone I met. Not only did we receive smiles, greetings, and hugs in return, but also these precious people gave us bread hot from the oven, apples from their trees, and goat cheese. They opened their doors and their hearts to us. What they had, they wanted to share graciously. They saw us as a blessing from God. We represented an opportunity for them to give to God by giving to these strangers God had sent to their village. This response reminded me of the Bible verse from Hebrews which conveys the message that the strangers you attend to may easily be angels in disguise.

Think for a moment how you would respond if a tour bus pulled up into your community and a group of people got off and came to your home. A group of strangers not speaking your language. People from a foreign country walking with big smiles on their faces through the streets of your community. Would you invite them into your home? I wonder if we would be as giving as these people. I hope we would.

We went to the local school and found the children spic and span in their school uniforms. One of their courses was English and they delighted in asking us, "What is your name?" and then would demonstrate their English to us by saying, "My name is—." My husband's name is Chuck. Whenever the children asked his name and he told them, the children would erupt in laughter. We later learned that in Turkish, "Chuck" is the term to give someone a "High-Five."

The things this village did not have were obvious to us who have so much. However, it was also obvious that we have so much more than we need. Whatever this village may have lacked in technology paled in comparison to the spontaneous generosity that came from every household. I knew in Turkey I would be blessed with many precious experiences; however, none was sweeter than the kindnesses of the people of Meram, the name of Mary—originated from the word "mer." I couldn't help thinking that the people of Meram were messengers of divine love: "Mer Am"—Divine Love I Am. I came to realize that we were not the angels in disguise; the people of Meram were.

M. Scott Peck's words, "Focus your energy and being on what you are for rather than what you are against," are dear to my heart. I am for *peace* and have focused my energy on being an Earth Angel 4 Peace, and so I offer this peace blessing to you:

May the spring, summer, fall, and winter of your life be blessed with God's peace. May the direction of your sacred walk in life, whether it be to the north, south, east, or west, be blessed with God's peace; and may all the dimensions of your existence—physical, mental, emotional, and spiritual—be blessed with God's peace.

Now is the time to determine for ourselves the peace energy we will experience at the moment of our transition. As a spiritual consultant, I ask all of my clients one question:

When it is the divine time for you to close your eyes to earth, and open them to heaven—how to do you want to be remembered? How do you want your epitaph to read: Remember me, as a woman/man who: _____(fill in the blank). There is no right or wrong answer. One of the greatest gifts given to us by God is our free will. With that free will we make choices. One of the choices you are making with every heartbeat of your life and every breath you take is how *you* want to be remembered. If you want to be remembered as someone who loved, are you filling your today with moments when you are loving and letting yourself be loved? If you want to be remembered as someone who cared, are you taking opportunities given to you today by God to show you care?

I believe that when we do close our eyes to earth and open them to heaven, the "judgment" will be that which we make upon ourselves. There is no harsher critic of our life than we are. We will perhaps sit in front of a motion picture and review our life. We will see people we recognize—family and friends we know—and we will observe how the big and little things we did for them impacted their lives. We will then begin to see a parade of strangers that we do not recognize. We will wonder why we are being shown these people. We will come to recognize that as a result of a book we had purchased and then lent to a friend who lent it to a friend, the book found its way to a particular person shown on the screen. The book changed that person's life. A book we have purchased with our money/energy and have freely released to go forth into the community, without concern that it might not make its way back to our own personal library. Without harboring hurt that it hasn't been returned to us.

A stranger we complimented, perhaps noticing how beautiful she looked in a lovely dress, might be revealed to us as a widow who hasn't heard a compliment since her sweet husband had died some years prior. Our kind compliment was a gesture that warmed a sad and lonely heart.

And then after we have stood witness to all the ways that our choices to share our energies and resources, to smile and to be kind, have had an incredible rippling effect of love everlasting on the planet, we will sit and watch a blank tape. The film will be rolling but there will be nothing on the screen of our life. The blank screen will have captured our lost opportunities. We will come to realize all the moments—hours, days, weeks, and years—that we had wasted; time we could have spent being a blessing to others and, in doing so, becoming a blessing to ourselves. How do you want to be remembered? Your epitaph is not something written in stone after you die. That's the illusion. The truth is that with every choice you make every day of your life you are conveying the message:

Remember me as a woman/man who_____ (fill in the blank)

I dedicate my lectures and seminars to a little Irish boy named Sean McLaughlin. In 1998, Sean wrote a peace poem with five of his little classmates. The poem was entitled, "The Bridge." Not only was Sean a messenger of peace through writing, but he was also chosen to read the poem to the President of Ireland. So he became a "voice of peace" on the planet. Through the words of the poem the children expressed their heartfelt desire for there to be peace among all people. Here is the children of Ireland's poem:

### The Bridge

*"Orange and green it doesn't matter, united now don't shatter our dream. Scatter the seeds of peace over our land, so we can travel hand in hand across the bridge of hope."*

---

Three months after coauthoring this poem, Sean, along with twenty-seven other children, was killed by terrorists. I have been asked by the angels to carry forth Sean's inspirational light on the planet and share it with as many people as possible. In May 2001 I led a group of "earth angels" to Ireland in fulfillment of an angelic assignment to embody "The Bridge" energy.

And so to honor the children of the planet, I believe achieving peace can be easy as learning our ABC's. Here are my ABC's of Peace:

---

*Actualize peace in all your activities.*
*Be a peacemaker.*
*Create peaceful moments.*
*Declare peace.*
*Embody peace.*
*Foster peace.*
*Get in touch with peace.*
*Heal with peace.*
*Indulge in peace.*
*Join a peace organization.*
*Keep the peace.*
*Let peace begin with you.*
*Make peace.*
*Nurture peace.*
*Open your heart to peace.*
*Promote peace.*
*Quest for peace.*
*Rise up in defense of peace.*

*Support peace daily.*
*Take the peaceful path.*
*Understand the power of peace.*
*Visualize peace.*
*Welcome peace into your home.*
*X-pect peace.*
*Yearn for peace.*
*Zap all your problems with peaceful energy.*

There is a beautiful Jewish tradition of placing a small stone on gravesites. I remember the very emotional scene at the end of Steven Spielberg's movie *Schindler's List*, where the concentration camp survivors who had survived because of Schindler's efforts, place small stones on his gravesite. In Genesis 28, the Bible tells us of Jacob taking a stone as a pillow and laying down and going to sleep. During his sleep Jacob dreams of a ladder that leads from heaven to earth. On that ladder were angels of God ascending and descending. During the dream God spoke to Jacob saying, "Behold, I am with you . . . " When Jacob awoke, he knew that God was with him and the place he had slept was a "gate of heaven." He anointed the stone with oil and the stone became the foundation stone for the city of "Bethel." In Hebrew, "Bethel" means "House of God." In this story we see a stone acting as the symbol of a foundation for the presence of God in our lives. The stone is not being worshipped; rather the vision God gave to Jacob while sleeping on the stone is being honored.

In reading Jacob's story, and contemplating the beauty of the Jewish tradition of placing a small stone on a grave, I was inspired by the angels to do something combining the two energies. The stones are called "Peace Pebbles." When someone dies who I have known, or their death has been made known to me by a newspaper article, I create a small pebble with their name on it. I write their name on one side of the pebble. On the other side I write one word that this person represents to me. For example, for Joshua Dansicker I have a Peace Pebble that says *Joshua* on one side and *Friendships* on the other. Through Joshua I met his mother, Mary; father, Arnie; and brother, Skeets. They have become the dearest friends to me. For Sean McClaughlin, I have *Sean* on one side of a Peace Pebble, and on the other, the word *Bridges*. I keep the stones in a special box that I call my "Bethel Box."

I encourage you to create your own Peace Pebbles. When you need a message of hope, just reach for a pebble. It will remind me that love is eternal. By thinking of the individual whose pebble you select, you will be blessing them with your thoughts of them and they will be blessing you with the spirit of their life—which never ends! The Peace Pebble is a stone that honors the presence of God in the life of the individual whose name is on the stone.

I always love feeling the touch of God's invisible hand in our lives. Following Joshua's death, Mary Dansicker was inspired to open Joshua's Lighthouse Angels at 311 Main Street in Reisterstown, Maryland. In 2001 the store next door became available—309 Main Street. Mary was "inspired" to open a shop called "Girlfriends" on the first floor, and I opened "The Light at the Top of the Stairs." I will tell you more about "The Light" later in the book. Mary has been inspired by God to make sacred space for friends to go shopping together, a place for girlfriends to come and have a cup of tea together and catch up on each other's lives. What Mary has never known, until perhaps she reads it here, is that I have had a Peace Pebble for Joshua for four years that reads: Friendships.

Give yourself a few moments to reflect upon the good friends you have had throughout your life. Don't fret over whether or not they are still friends in your life. Think back to your early school days. Honor with sweet memories your early childhood friends. Think of the friends that were in your neighborhood. Send them God's blessings wherever they are. Think about friends in college; friends you make at your workplace; friends in your church, your community organizations. A friend of mine, Chris Buffington, created a sweet bumper sticker: "I Have Friends in High Places." Think about your friends in "high places," and maybe you'll want to create a Peace Pebble in honor of them. One of the greatest gifts God gives to us is a friend. Think about the friends in your life now. Maybe you'll be inspired to call them or send them a card to thank them for being a gift from God to you.

In the book *The Fourteen Holy Helpers*, Fr. Bonaventure Hammer, O.F.M., writes of a group of fourteen saints revered in early times because of the aid they gave to the faithful. They are Saints: Acacius, Barbara, Blaise, Catherine of Alexandria, Christopher, Cyriacus, Dionysius of Paris, Erasmus, Eustace, George, Margarat, Pantaleon, Vitus, and Giles. In my own life I feel blessed by being surrounded by "Holy Helpers." God has been wonderful to me in gifting me precious friends.

My husband, Charles, is not only the greatest love of my life, he is also my best friend. Even though we have only been married three years, we know each other so well that we finish each other's sentences and speak out loud each other's thoughts. He is the best supporter of my angelic service, and truly ours is a marriage made in heaven. It's so much fun being married to Chuck.

Mary Dansicker, whom I have honored in my chapter about Joshua and whose friendship I absolutely treasure, Celeste McDonald, and I make up a girlfriend threesome. Some years ago the angels shared that I would be meeting someone special who would gift me a medal of Our Lady of Knock. I led a women's retreat at Leaf Lake Lodge in West Virginia, which Celeste McDonald attended. One evening she and I were getting to know each other as we chatted casually. We quickly came to realize that we shared a calling from the Blessed Mother. During that conversation Celeste reached into her purse. She opened my hand and said, "I'm being inspired to give this to you." I looked into my hand and saw a medal of Our Lady of Knock. It was very special to Celeste, as she had received it from Christine Gallagher, founder of Mary's House of Prayer in Ireland. Celeste has traveled with me on angel tours to Bosnia, France, Turkey, Ireland, and Scotland.

Mary Dansicker's husband, Arnie, has been another Holy Helper in my life. When I was on my own, Arnie was my Automotive Angel. He was aware of the tremendous amount of traveling I was doing and my limited finances. One day he came up to me and said, "Your car needs new tires. Mary and I are buying them for you, and I don't want to hear anything about it." When he returned the car with the new tires mounted, I discovered that he had also installed a car cassette player so I could listen to cassette tapes on my long-distance angelic adventures. He looked out for me and my car, and I am eternally grateful for his many kindnesses.

Many storeowners throughout the country have been God's blessings to me by inviting me to offer workshops and private consultations. The arrangement is that the store receives a percentage of all that I earn. I am so grateful for the efforts and energies that the storeowners have made on my behalf and am always so thrilled when I am able to act as a blessing to them, as they are to me.

One storeowner I would like to recognize is Barbara Barrowcliff, owner of Jonas' Attic in Easton, Maryland. Barbara is a gifted psychic who has been a part of numerous government psychic projects. When I was operating on a wing and a prayer and being called to fulfill my angel assignments, Barbie would not take any share of the money that I made while at Jonas' Attic. There were times in my life when my back was to the wall financially and Barbie would help me. Barbie is a wonderful friend and still is hosting my quarterly appearances at her store— Jonas' Attic.

One of the friends that I have known the longest and who has been a lifesaver is Ann Bell. Ann Bell is a Reiki Master, masseuse, herbalist, teacher, and healer. She and I attended the Baltimore School of Massage together. Shortly after my ex-husband announced that he wanted a divorce, I was in massage class with Ann. She took one look at me and said, "What happened to you!" I shared the atom bomb that had dropped. Ann took me under her healing wing, and I give thanks for her steadfast commitment to my well-being. She has always been there for me.

In 1997, the angels said two words to me, "Park it." The Creator's Star assignment was fulfilled, and it was time for me to unpack the suitcase and join the nine-to-five world. I was being inspired to do this so I could be in "one place"—in order to make the connection God was setting up with Charles Feldman. I had no idea what type of work for which I could apply. My resume reads "Serves God with angels."

I shared my dilemma with Ann Bell. Ann was masseuse and Reiki healer to Greg Mullaney, co-owner of Gardiner's Furniture. Ann spoke to Greg about me, and I was given an interview and a job with Gardiner's. I thank Ann for the introduction and Greg for believing in me. I worked at Gardiner's until my marriage to Charles, at which time I moved temporarily to Gaithersburg, Maryland, to live at Charles's home. Ann and I have led many spiritual retreats and spiritual development classes together and it is always pure joy teaming up with Ann.

A friend who has inspired me with her creative talents and her inner and outer beauty is Rosemary Ellen Guiley. Rosemary is a prolific author of forty–plus books. Rosemary and I met when I attended a presentation she gave on crop circles at Spiritual Frontiers. She was part of a spiritual study group and through the meetings she and I became good friends. She has lived out of a suitcase as much as I have. Every few months we call each other on the phone or make contact by e–mail and plan time to treat ourselves to lunch and time to catch up on our lives.

Early in our friendship I received an angelic inspiration for Rosemary that she would be meeting her husband–to–be at a local meeting. Sure enough, she attended one of the monthly lectures hosted by the Baltimore Chapter of A.R.E. At that meeting she met Thomas Wright and it was love at first sight for both of them. On May 5, 1995, they were married beneath the two–hundred–year–old tulip poplar tree on Angel Heights, and I was the officiating pastor. Rosemary's father had died years earlier; however, he truly did make his happiness and blessing for Rosemary and Tom known to all of us. At the conclusion of their beautiful wedding ceremony a double rainbow appeared in the sky above them.

Rosemary always has a new book project in the works. I remember that at one luncheon she shared that she was working on *I Bring You Glad Tidings* and asked if I knew of an angelic–related Christmas story. I said to her, "Do I have a contact for you for an incredible angel Christmas story!" I encourage you to gift yourself a copy of Rosemary's *Glad Tidings* and read the wonderful stories including, "The Miracle of the Light and the Life."

My friends are angel sisters to me. And my sister Joyce is an angel to me. I have been so blessed by her friendship and the many kindnesses she has offered me in my life. When I began work as a member of the sales staff of Gardiner's Furniture, my sister helped enrich my clothing wardrobe with clothes appropriate for sales work. My sister is blessed with "fashion genes." I am the youngest child of a family of six children. My mother and father were blessed with Virginia, Charles Robert, Rosemary, James, Joyce, and I should have been the third son. Surprise! I love surprises, don't you? In my lectures I have shared that there are three little words God has whispered to each and every one of us: Surprise! Surprise! Surprise!

My mother and father had been the best parents a child could ask for and I treasure their love and friendship. When *Commune with the Angels* was published in 1992, the local community paper did a front-page feature entitled, "Angelic Visions." I knew the paper's story was coming out the next day and would be the talk of my parents' church, come Sunday morning. My parents have known of my love of the angels and my service with the angels; they just didn't know I talked to them and saw them.

Out of respect to my parents, I first went to the pastor of their church and told him of the story and my service. I said to him, "I am not asking for your blessing. I have God's blessing. I'm just here to give you a heads-up on tomorrow's news." Rev. Gribble said to me, "Even though you haven't asked for it, I want to give my blessing to you, Jayne. The Bible tells us of communion with the saints and the angels. God Bless you and your work for God."

I then drove to my parents' home, where I informed my parents of the story and the fact that their youngest child not only believed in angels, but had been seeing and talking to the angels for thirty years. I remember it got quiet in my parents' kitchen and my Dad pushed his chair back from the kitchen table and said, "Well, let me tell you about the time God sent an angel to help your mother and me out of a problem."

I later shared with Ann Bell my total amazement at the occurrence at my parents' home. She laughed and said, "Why? Angels are part of your genes."

Every summer I attend the Southeastern Conference held at Guilford College in Greensboro, Maryland. As I mentioned earlier, this is one of the most joyous conferences held annually on the planet. It is a weeklong family reunion. The conference began as a vision held by five people, and to this day these same people make it happen every summer. In 2002, the Southeastern Conference celebrated its tenth year. In 1999, the conference was held the week prior to my wedding to Charles. The conference members joined in my celebration by hosting a bridal shower for me.

I think it's important in our lives that we make time to go on retreats and attend conferences. It is important to make time for creating new friendships and having reunions with old friends. Southeastern Conference has a Guardian Angel Program. When you arrive and sign in, you place your name in a pool of other conference attendees. You each pull a name from the pool. You are that person's Guardian Angel for the week and leave little gifts for them at their dorm door. This is one conference that I have found is a week of "pure heart energy." It is a heart-blessing experience.

Years ago I attended a one-day workshop in a private home that introduced me to the inspirational life service of Sister Paula Matthew, csj. Sister Paula can truly be called a modern "Renaissance woman." She is the creator of "Original Vision," a seminar conducted round the world, and an author of numerous books. With over twenty years of astrological study, she offers unique spiritual solar return workshops at the Spiritual Center in Windsor, New York, every summer, which I attended for many years; and now the relationship has evolved so that I co-teach solar return weekends with an angelic touch. Additionally we have teamed up together to offer one-hour taped Solar Return Readings for clients from around the world. There is a divine moment every year when the earth/sun come together exactly the same as the divine moment when you were born. It is truly a sacred experience. This divine moment is known in astrology as your solar return.

In our readings we offer insights for the upcoming year: trends, themes, and messages about what's in store for the individual. I share angelic inspirations and astrological interpretation from a celestial consciousness. Sister Paula gives areas of spiritual growth for the year, major themes of development, lessons to be learned, and gifts given for your new birthday year.

Paula is a professional sculptor who specializes in hard woods. In addition to her commission pieces found in private and public collections throughout the U.S., the "Gallery of the Soul" located at the Spiritual Center houses a private collection of her work. These highly symbolic and thought-provoking pieces are used as the basis for individual and group retreats offered at the Spiritual Center.

The Spiritual Center is a community of Sisters of St. Joseph that includes Sister Liz, Sister Susan, Sister Lois, and Sister Paula. Each one of these precious women I consider a God blessing to my life, and a good friend.

Years ago in my days of conducting angel workshops in private homes, I was doing a number of workshops in the community of Columbia, Maryland. Time after time the name "Lucky Sweeny" would be mentioned to me. People would ask if I knew Lucky Sweeny. I didn't know her, but I loved her name. My path would finally cross with Lucky's, and I instantly loved the woman who came with the name. She and I become long-time friends. She was an incredible friend at the time of Walt's death.

Lucky introduced me to Life Coaching, as she herself is a life coach who now resides in Santa Barbara, California. Additionally she has been an astrologer for thirty-plus years. Lucky has been a pioneer in pursuing quantum spiritual leaps of consciousness. I remember she attended an evolutionary conference and she called me and left a message, "Jayne, I now know what I will be doing in 26,000 years." Lucky has been a great inspiration to me; I now tell people, "If you are not living on the edge, you are taking up too much space." Once a week Lucky and I have a standing appointment for one hour on the telephone to "coach" each other.

I want to honor my "friends in high places," good friends who have gone home ahead of me. One of those people is Charlie Cole, owner of the Charlie Horse. Charlie came to me some years ago and shared with me that he had a vision for a healing center in Hampstead, Maryland. He had leased a building where he had an office and the Charlie Horse, a store offering horse-motif giftware.

Charlie asked if I would offer workshops on a weekly basis at his location. I was on the road almost constantly at that stage of my life and initially couldn't envision it being possible. I went home and prayed to God for inspiration. The message came forth loud and clear. God wanted me to be willing to serve those in my own backyard, as I was willing to serve in other people's communities. Charity does begin at home.

I met with Charlie and said I would develop a weekly spiritual development class to be held at his store. I would promote the schedule so people would know when I was in town teaching and when I would be out of town teaching. I remember the first class held at the Charlie

Horse. It consisted of two people—Charlie and me. Charlie and I agreed that if the vision was to be birthed, we had to be willing to hold the sacred space. Week by week attendance grew. We grew to classes of thirty-plus people. The class schedule at the Charlie Horse went on for several years. Charlie had an ice cream stand that he operated in front of the Charlie Horse. Many of our classes would end with Charlie announcing, "Ice cream for everyone!" I think God must have been pleased with Charlie's vision and generosity as He called him home to set up classes in heaven and have ice cream socials with the angels. After Charlie's death, the property was sold and my classes moved to Joshua's Lighthouse Angels.

I give special thanks for Walt for his friendship, love, and support. I know he still watches over me. In some way I know that Walt helped Chuck and me find each other.

And I would be remiss not to honor my editor, Kathleen. I needed to find an editor for this project and the angels pointed Kat's name in the advertisements for editors in *Writer's Digest*. She is such a blessing in my life. Kat shared that just before I contacted her, she had prayer for an edit that would be spiritual. She also asked the angels if she could help them and asked her guardian angel to work with her. At the same time she was making this prayer request, I was asking my angel team to guide me to the person that God wanted on board for editing *Driving Under the Influence of Angels.* God is so wonderful! While working on this chapter, I shared with Chuck all the precious people I was honoring and asked if there was anyone he could think of that I should include. He immediately said, "Benny." I wholeheartedly agreed with him. Benny, my nine-year-old Jack Russell terrier has been the Rock of Gibraltar in my life. His unconditional love has been a life preserver to me when I felt like I was drowning in a sea of emotion in times of loss and grief. When I traveled, my Dad was the guardian of Benny and referred to him as his grand-dog. Now our household is doubly blessed as we have Riot, a five-year-old female Jack Russell; however, Benny has earned a special place in my heart for having been there when no one else was. If you've ever seen the bumper sticker "Jack Russells Rule," I want to assure you that it is true statement at my house.

I honor these friends because they are all God's blessings to my life.

They have been my own "Holy Helpers." I encourage you to take time in your life to reflect upon the people and animals in your life who have been your own personal helpers.

I remember listening to Robert Schuller's *Hour of Power* one Sunday morning. Dr. Schuller emphasized that even though he loved those who supported his television ministry it is equally important to have a local church that you attend and support. Dr. Schuller explained that we all need someone's hand to hold ours as we walk across a cemetery. We need the touch of a friend—a pat on the back conveying things will get better, a hug expressing "you're not alone, I'm here." God's love is so huge. Sometimes I think of God as a great sun with a million rays that go out in all directions. There's no place that the light of God doesn't touch. One of the ways our wonderful creator sends us daily dosages of "love beams" is in the joy of friendships. Be a love beam today in someone's life. Give thanks for your friends and be a good friend.

Additionally, be a good friend to yourself. As I shared earlier in this chapter, we are walking, talking, breathing houses of God. We are, in a physical expression, each "Bethels"—houses of God. There's popularity in having garden steppingstones with messages on them. Once again, the stone is symbolic of a word, i.e., the *happiness*, *peace*, or *joy* that is important to our lives. Perhaps this is a way of mirroring the "foundation" essence of our soul. When we see the stone with the word *peace*, we are reminded to build our day with choices that create an energy structure of peace around our lives. If you find yourself having a challenging day, just take a few minutes and quietly whisper your name with the letters "el" after your name. "El" in Hebrew means "of God," i.e., "Beth-el" means "House" and "of God"—put them together and you have "House of God." Put your name together with "el" and you have the divine message of truth—you are God's. If your name is Kathleen, simply add "el" and whisper. I am Kathleen-el; I am Kathleen-el; I am Kathleen-el. I guarantee that as you say your name with "el" after it, you will feel a shifting of energy around you and within you. You will feel the comforting energy of God's profound peace enveloping you like the wings of an angel. It is God's energy reminding you that you were created by God and are loved by God. Be an angel friend to yourself. Accept now God's love for you with every beat of your heart, with every breath you take.

# CHAPTER 17

# The Light at the
# Top of the Stairs

*I*n spring, 2000, in my meditations I repeatedly heard the same angelic assignment message: "It is time to bring forth a place where
people can worship God." Whenever I heard this divine message, I
would cringe, thinking I was being called to establish a church.

I heard the words, "place where people can worship God," and I
thought: "church."

In an attempt to fulfill the angelic assignment, I approached the United
Metaphysical Churches of America to determine if it was possible for
me to be sanctioned as one of their churches, if I were to establish a
church in Maryland. Rev. Reed Brown, one of the leaders of the United
Metaphysical Churches, indicated that I could do this and prepared the
necessary paperwork to begin the process. He mailed the application. I
never received it. He mailed the application a second time. Again, it
never showed up in my mailbox. A third time I requested the paperwork and even though the secretary mailed it to me, I did not receive it.
It was clear to me that my interpretation of what the angelic assignment
meant was incorrect, because the angels were intercepting the mail.

During the summer of 2000, I was teaching a week–long class at the Southeastern Conference in Greensboro, N.C. One morning I asked my students to pray for me. I was in the midst of a spiritual crisis. I knew that God was calling me to bring forth a place where people could worship God; however, I had not yet been able to understand exactly how God wanted me to do it. I felt totally wrapped around the axle with this assignment.

One young lady in my class said to me, "You're not in a crisis situation. You are in a 'Christ Is' situation. Christ is working through you. Christ will reveal what you need to know when you need to know it. Be at peace." I felt an incredible peace wash over me. I knew that I had become the student and Jesus was the teacher, communicating to me through this young woman.

Also in the summer of 2000, my husband, Chuck, retired from forty–two years of service as an engineer. I wanted to honor his divine service with a special gift. Chuck told me that he always wanted to see the Panama Canal. This was a lifelong dream. I decided I was going to make that dream come true. I didn't quite know how.

One night in my dreams, Josh Dansicker came to me and told me simply I would be going to Key West. Key West was of importance in the life of Josh as he and a buddy had traveled to Key West. Josh had asked his parents if he could go beforehand. They said no because it was a long drive for two college students. Being good parents, the Dansickers were concerned for the boys' safety. Key West wasn't brought up again until several years later. When attending Joshua Dansicker's funeral, the college friend's parents remarked to Mary and Arnie how wonderful it was that her son and Josh had gone off together to Key West and had had such a fun time there. Until then Mary and Arnie didn't know about Josh's secret Key West adventure; however, now knowing that his life was to last only twenty–one years on earth, they were so happy he and his friend had taken this vacation. And so Key West symbolizes a "youthful adventure" for all of us with whom Mary shared the story.

Shortly after the night of Josh appearing in a dream, I felt inspired to look at Ebay, the Internet auction site, to see if there was a cruise for two to visit the Panama Canal. There was! I scanned the ports of call and the last port listed was Key West. I jumped into the bidding. The cruise company indicated the amount they needed to break even; I posted my bid for that amount. I wanted this trip to be a blessing to us and a blessing to the people offering it for sale. Interestingly enough, no one else wanted to pay the break–even amount. People wanted it for less, and so I won the cruise for two. The break–even price was an incredible bargain.

I shared the news with Chuck and he was thrilled. We looked forward with excitement to our Panama Canal cruise, which was booked for January 2001. One month prior to our departure the cruise company contacted us. We were informed that Carnival had overbooked for this cruise and was willing to make us an offer to buy back our room because we had bought the cruise at such a low price. The offer was that we would receive all our money back and would receive a free seven-day Carnival cruise for two. The cruises we could choose from would not include the Panama Canal; however, wonderful destinations in the Caribbean were offered. Carnival was also going to upgrade us to a suite with a balcony. My husband could hardly contain himself with excitement over our good fortune. We accepted the offer and were booked on a nonsmoking ship called Paradise.

While on the Paradise cruise in January 2001, I saw a painting that was going to be auctioned by Park West Gallery at their Auction at Sea. The moment I laid eyes on the painting it commanded my attention. I knew I had to find out about the artist. The style reminded me of Marc Chagall and yet I knew it wasn't Chagall who was the painter. The artist's energy spoke to me. "Get to know me and you will get to know yourself." I was intrigued and so I attended my first art auction at sea on Monday, January 15, 2001.

At the auction I was introduced to the talent of Zamy Steynovitz, the artist who had created the painting I had seen, entitled "Artist's Palette." Up until that time I knew nothing about this gifted artist.

Born in Poland in 1951, Zamy studied at the Art School of Tel Aviv and at the Royal Academy of London. His images are reflections of his Jewish and East European heritage. Zamy was one of Israel's most popular artists and had studios in both New York City and Tel Aviv. Widely exhibited, he was honored by heads of state throughout the world. Official bodies have presented his works to President Jimmy Carter, Prime Minister Begin, Pope John Paul II, and the Dalai Lama. Zamy was commissioned to paint the official portrait of peace for the proposals between Israel and Egypt in 1977. He was the number one student of Marc Chagall, which didn't surprise me.

Even though Zamy died of cancer on September 1, 2000, his spirit continues to bless the planet through his paintings of joyousness, peace, sanctity of family, and love. His works of art are rich with color and with intrinsic love. When I saw his art, I felt as if I was witnessing the glorious work of a brother. Though I never had the blessed opportunity to meet Zamy in person, I "knew" Zamy through his art.

I ended up buying a number of Zamy's paintings. My husband will tell you that the free cruise ended up costing us money because of the art I brought home!

When I returned home to Angel Heights, I knew I had to contact Zamy's family in Israel. I knew that Zamy had reached out to me as a fellow peacemaker and had entrusted me with the mission to bring peace to his family. I was to contact them and let them know I had "heard" from him and to extend comfort to them. "Blessed are those that mourn for they shall be comforted."

Through the kindness of an art dealer, I was able to obtain the address of Zamy's family and I wrote them immediately. I received a letter back from Zamy's brother. He shared with me what a blessing my letter was for him and Zamy's mother. He also shared that the day I first saw and bought Zamy's painting, January 15, 2001, would have been Zamy's fiftieth birthday. Additionally, he sent me via e-mail a drawing of an angel that Zamy had drawn at the age of fourteen. He confirmed what I already knew. Zamy loved the angels and the angels loved Zamy!

When I wrote to Zamy's family, I shared that there are very special people among us who are on God assignments. The assignments don't necessarily last as long as we would like them to. We would love for Zamy to still be with us here on earth, because we miss him. However, even though Zamy's life was short in the number of human years, in God-years his life is an eternal blessing. While here on earth, Zamy was truly an Ambassador of Peace and he continues to serve as an Ambassador of Peace in heaven.

I know God had a special studio waiting for Zamy on September 1, 2000, and Zamy now continues to shower us from heaven with his angelic energies of peace.

One exercise the angels have given to me is to encourage people to create a First Will and Testament for Heaven. Many people prepare a Last Will and Testament for their belongings here on earth, such as who will receive the set of pearls after they have died. We can also write a First Will and Testament for Heaven. The words could begin, "I, (fill in your name), being of sound physical body and mind, do look forward to the day when I close my eyes to earth and open them to heaven to continue to serve God with my body and mind of light." Then proceed to make known your requests. With whom do you wish to have reunions? I know for myself I want to meet Jesus. Think about all the precious family members and friends you want to see again. Include them in your First Will and Testament. By doing so it is testimony that the circle is never broken. Then think about how you want your service to continue in heaven. How do you want to go on glorifying God? Your service doesn't end when your life ends here. Love is eternal! At lectures I have joked that someone who teaches about "near-death experiences" here on earth will teach "near-birth experiences" in heaven. I know the joys we experience here on earth in some way continue to be expressed in heaven. The angels have pointed out to me that we humans have no problem calling up a travel agent, booking a room with a view in Hawaii, and fully expecting—sight unseen—that the room with the view will be waiting for us. Do the same with your First Will and Testament. Plan now to have a room with a view waiting for you—a view of all that you hold sacred in your heart. Think upon the words of this oft-quoted poem: "Do not stand at my grave and weep. I am not there. I do not sleep. Do not stand at my grave and cry. I am not there. I did not die."

While I was on the Paradise, buying Zamy's art, I received an e-mail from Mary Dansicker that the landlord had agreed to rent 309 Main Street in Reisterstown, Maryland, to us. This is the building that is connected to Joshua's Lighthouse Angels, which is located at 311 Main Street.

Mary wanted to open a shop on the first floor called "Girlfriends." Mary shared with me that I had been instrumental in her opening

Joshua's Lighthouse Angels. I had been one of numerous friends who had encouraged her to open her store. Mary said it was her turn to encourage me and tell me that it was time for me to open a place of my own, to rent the second floor of 309 Main Street in Reisterstown. Chuck and I agreed that "309" would be the place where we would fulfill the angelic assignment of having a place where people could worship God, yet we weren't clear on what it would look like.

One evening while still on the Paradise, I was meditating in a lounge chair on one of the decks. The ocean surrounded the ship in all directions. During this meditation I felt compartments in my mind open up. I remember years ago seeing a children's toy called a Transformer. You can rearrange the parts to transform the toy into different shapes. That's what my mind seemed to be doing. The words: "a place where people could worship God" no longer brought forth the thought of a church. Instead, I saw before me in my mind's eye a healing arts center.

I heard the words: Spread the message. Inspire your heart with art! In a holy instant I recognized the golden thread that has been woven through my life by God. I have been gathering together art that is for sharing, healing, and inspiring hearts. Now God was showing me where He wanted the vision to unfold into reality. It was "above" where the painting of the vision of Mary in Egypt was hanging. As I mentioned, the painting had been placed on the wall of Joshua's Lighthouse Angels and had been holding sacred space for another of God's plans that was in the works. I realized that the angel art I had been buying now had a home. The wooden statue of Archangel Michael that I purchased in Mexico; the powerful folk art painting of Michael with flaming sword purchased in Russia; Michael and the Sacred Geometry Blessing purchased in Egypt, all the art I had been inspired to buy was now being gathered together by God.

God gave the name to me (and how divine it is!): *The Light at the Top of the Stairs.* I was told that the healing center is not about buying, but rather about being. There is nothing for sale at the center. The Light at the Top of the Stairs is a sacred space where people can come and commune with God through art.

On Memorial Day Weekend, 2001, The Light at the Top of the Stairs officially opened. Because Mary Dansicker has the store beneath and next to "The Light," she kindly turns on the lights, fountains, and music for the center. People come to "The Light" to pray, meditate, journal, and sit in peace with art energy surrounding them and blessing them.

As you walk up the steps to the second floor of 309 Main Street in Reisterstown, there are angels and heavenly messages created by Sandra Magsamen to the right and left of you.

At the "Top of the Stairs" there is a peace room and a heart room. The heart room contains a big Peter Max heart poster entitled "Valentine," which he so graciously dedicated to the center. Peter Max is a divine artisan who spreads "MAX–imum" joy through his art. Additionally in the heart room there is another wonderful Max painting entitled, "Angel with Heart." She is the guardian of the healing arts center. The heart room also contains numerous paintings by Zamy Steynovitz, P. Buckley Moss, Ted DeGrazia, and others.

The peace room features a Max poster entitled "Peace 2000," as well as more of Zamy's work, and Dali angels, too. There's a wonderful flowing fountain and kneeler donated by the sisters of the Spiritual Center.

As I mentioned in an earlier chapter, "Food will sustain us as humans; art inspires us to be divine!" God has sent so many angels to uplift us; some have wings of light and some have paintbrushes in hand.

Once "The Light" was up and running I was inspired by the angels to establish Inspire Your Heart with Art Day. When I inquired what would be the date of this annual celebration, I was told to make that choice myself. I chose my birthday, January 31. I chose this day because for as long as I can remember I have celebrated my birthday in an "art-full" way. One year I went to the movies to see the re-release of Disney's *Fantasia*; one year I went to see *The Lion King* on Broadway; this year I went to see *Mamma Mia*. I believe that on your birthday it is important to set into motion the energies you want to be a part of your life for the year ahead. My desire is to surround myself with art and artists, poetry and poets, music and musicians, books and writers, and so on.

In promoting The Light at the Top of the Stairs, I sent out a mailing in which I stated that it's a place to inspire your heart with art. It's a place to nurture your soul with peace. It's a place to *BE*.

I then shared Elizabeth Landeweer's poem "Harmony":

---

*"What poet but Almighty God*
*Could breathe this world to birth*
*Could sing green verse into sod,*
*And rhyme the roots of earth?*
*What poet but Immortal Faith*
*Could make a man like me,*
*Could live in him and give him breath,*
*And say unto him: "BE!"*

---

One woman, who came to the center shortly after we opened, stated that she had been in a counseling session seeking help to deal with feeling overwhelmed by life. She felt she was being crushed under all the demands placed on her by life, family, work, etc. Her therapist encouraged her to find a place for herself where she could go and just *BE*. She went home after the session, opened her mail, and read the flyer for The Light at the Top of the Stairs. She said to me, "You knew I was going to need this place. You opened this center just for me." I replied, "No, I didn't. God did."

In celebrating the inauguration of Inspire Your Heart with Art on January 31, 2002, I wrote the following ABCs:

---

Awaken the inner artist. Live your life as a work of art.
Believe in your creative power and express it daily.
Commission a budding artist—a Michaelangelo in the making.
Draw—Dance—Drum to the feelings within yourself.
Explore your local art museums and galleries.
Fill your home with comforting art and music.
Get in touch with your creative spirit through movement and
    dance.
Heal your body and soul with art therapy.
Immerse yourself in a good book.
Journey inward with journaling.

Keep *art programs in schools.*

Listen *to music. Sing. Chant. Tone.*

Make *a studio, a sacred space in your home.*

Nurture *your soul by attending a concert.*

Open *up an art book.*

Photograph *your pets.*

Quest *to make time daily to make art.*

Release *the inner critic.*

See *yourself as an artist in all that you create; this includes din-ner!*

Tell *the story of you.*

Uplift *your spirit with art that inspires your soul.*

Visualize *and manifest through mandalas.*

X-press *yourself. Write the first word. Draw the first line. Make the first sound.*

You *are God's work of art. Treat yourself like the treasure you are.*

Zero *in on sculpture, painting, music, dance, poetry, and the-ater that inspires your heart.*

---

Some years ago I read a quote by Jose Arguelles in which he applied to the letters A–R–T the words—A Radical Transformation. Many com-posers, artists, and authors have been inspired by and felt the presence of angels while in the midst of creating music, art, and books. Why does this occur? Because the angels are messengers who deliver God's gifts to us. One such gift is God's healing. God wills our healing, and one of the infinite ways that healing occurs is through art. When we open our-selves to our creative, artistic energies, we open the doorway to "a radi-cal transformation." Art supports you. Support art and you are supporting yourself.

Marianne Williamson, in her book *A Return to Love*, wrote these in-spiring words:

❧

*"Our deepest fear is not that we are inadequate.*
*Our deepest fear is that we are powerful beyond measure.*
*It is our light not our darkness, that most frightens us.*
*We ask ourselves, who am I to be brilliant, gorgeous,*
  *talented and fabulous?*
*Actually who are you not to be?*
*You are a child of God.*
*Your playing small doesn't serve the world.*
*There is nothing enlightened about shrinking so that other people*
  *won't feel insecure around you.*
*We are born to manifest the glory of God that is within us.*
*It's not just in some of us; it's in everyone.*
*And as we let our own light shine, we unconsciously*
  *give other people permission to do the same.*
*As we are liberated from our own fear,*
  *our presence automatically liberates others."*

Ephesians in the Bible teaches that we are children of God. The words inspire us to be God-like as the children of God that we are. We are inspired to imitate God as children of His light. Just as God blesses our lives with all His creations, we can glorify God by creating with our artistic light. We can imitate God by saying, "Let there be light" through our music, paintings, dance, poetry, and writing.

A friend of mine, Hannelore Hahn, is the founder and executive director of the International Women's Writing Guild, an organization to which I belong. The Guild was founded in 1976 "and is a network for the personal and professional empowerment of women through writing and is open to all women. As such, it has established a remarkable record of achievement in the publishing world, as well as in circles where lifelong learning and personal transformation are valued for their own sake."

Part of the Guild's mission statement is to nurture and support "holistic thinking by recognizing the logic of the heart—the ability to per-

ceive the subtle interconnections between people, events, and emotions—alongside conventional logic."

On July 31, 2001, Hannelore was in New York City just as the sun was
beginning to set. She was walking by the World Trade Center and noticed the hundreds of fingerprints on WTC's revolving doors. Hannelore
had her camera with her and took a photograph of the revolving door
that would cease to exist on September 11.

When the photograph was developed, Hannelore realized it was one
of those moments where she held the camera while God did the photographing. In the picture the setting sun shines its light upon the revolving doors. Everything is a luminescent gold. Hundreds of handprints
and fingerprints shine brilliantly in the light. A woman is seen going
into the building in the photograph. An almost "ghostly" image of a
man is seen through the glass of the revolving door. Hannelore was
inspired to call this photograph "Fingerprints." She created a card in
remembrance of September 11 with the Fingerprints photograph on the
front and the following words inside: "Each life is unique. Each life is
sacred."

In February 2000, I ordered matinee theater tickets to see *The Producers*
in New York City on Wednesday, September 19, 2001. I had placed the
order for that date because Chuck and I like taking the train up to New
York City for a day-trip to see a Wednesday matinee of a Broadway
show. *The Producers* was such a hot ticket that it took one and a half years
for tickets that were close to the stage to become available. Little did I
know that God was writing a divine appointment with Archangel
Michael into my life date book.

When we take a New York City day-trip, we get on board at Penn
Station in Baltimore at 6:17 a.m. We arrive at Penn Station in New York
City just before 9 a.m. On every trip we make to New York, we always
walk to the Church of St. John the Baptist located at 210 West 31st Street,
which is adjacent to the train station. The friary and church courtyard
have been dedicated to St. Padre Pio, whose wonderful service to God
with the angels I praised in *Commune with the Angels*. The Blessed Padre
Pio Prayer Garden has been a place of quiet meditation and prayer in
the heart of New York City for over twenty-five years. The flyer produced by the Capuchin Friars of St. John the Baptist Church, encourag-

ing the public to honor a loved one in the beautiful Padre Pio Prayer Garden, reads: *Be an Angel*. Chuck and I find such joy in giving ourselves the gift of quiet time in Padre's garden, where a beautiful marble statue depicts the saint with his hand raised in benediction, welcoming all visitors. It is truly a place of peace.

On September 19, 2001, we hailed a cab in front of St. John the Baptist and asked to be taken as close as possible to Ground Hero (as perhaps it should truly be called). The cab took us to Greenwich Street. We walked past hundreds of posters with photographs of missing loved ones. We walked past street shrines with flowers, candles, drawings, and flags. We walked to the police barricade. We stood in silence as we watched rescue workers removing the rubble that was once the World Trade Center. There was no way to verbalize what our sight was witnessing, what our minds were attempting to comprehend. I stood numb from trying to cope with standing at the site of our nation's worst disaster. I was experiencing grief for the tremendous loss that occurred on September 11; anger at those who caused this loss; and an incredible patriotism in seeing the policemen, firemen, and rescue workers working so tirelessly.

While in this state of mixed emotions, I felt a familiar presence come over me. The presence of Archangel Michael. It was the same energy I experienced while watching the Mt. St. Helens volcanic eruption video. Even though there was an incredible devastation in front of me, I was at peace for I knew without a shadow of a doubt who was in control. God was. The presence of Michael came to me because in my life I have been asked to share messages I receive from Michael. The messages given to me are God-messages of hope. God shares them with me not because I am more special than anyone else; rather, because I am willing to share the messages I receive.

In a vision, I saw Michael's name before me: M–I–C–H–A–E–L. Messages were given to me quickly woven into the letters in Michael's name. When I returned home, and composed the messages in written form, I was inspired by the angels to add biblical and inspirational verses in support of the messages given. I personally have found a profound peace when I read the following as a daily prayer.

*"Almighty God, give us grace that we may cast away the works of darkness and put upon us the armour of light." (Book of Common Prayer)*

M—*Move forward fearlessly. Move forward with God. Be not afraid for God is your protector. "Fear nothing, for I am with you; be not afraid for I am your God." (Isa. 41:10)*

I—*Intuitive with Light Sight is your identity. See all things with Light Sight. You are here to shine. God is your creator. God has created you as a God-star to shine. "The stars shone at their appointed stations and rejoiced; He called them and they answered, 'We are here!' Joyfully they shone for their Maker." (Baruch 3:34)*

C—*Courageously live your life. Do not be shaken by the deeds of man. God is your deliverer. "He is my rock and deliverance, my haven; I shall not be shaken." (Psalm 62:6, Tanakh)*

H—*Help where the need has been divinely defined. God is the guide of our heart. Let God call us to service. "He renews life within me, and for His name's sake guides me in the right path." (Ps. 23:3)*

A—*America—a country whose foundation is built upon God's Grace. God's grace is shed on thee. "By God's grace I am what I am, nor has His grace been given to me in vain." (1 Cor. 15:10)*

E—*Energize all you do with God's light. Light bridges need to be built now. God's first words at creation were, "Let there be light." Create now with light.*

*"If only we knew how to look at life as God sees it, we should realize that nothing is secular in the world, but that everything contributes to the building of the kingdom of God." (Michel Quoist, Prayers of Life)*

*"What is service? The rent we pay for our room on earth." (Toc H)*

L—*Let the Great Work begin. "There must be no limit to your goodness, as your heavenly father's goodness knows no bounds." (Matt. 5:48)*

Immediately after receiving the basic components of Michael's message while standing at the barricade at Ground Hero, I felt my consciousness rapidly brought back to the street where I stood. I looked in front of me and there, passing by, was a white van with the words: *Arch Angel Mechanical Contractor.* I immediately drew my camera up to eye level and snapped a picture. I knew God was revealing to all of us that we are called to be mechanical contractors and build God's kingdom here on earth with light.

On September 29, 2001, Michaelmas Day, I led a workshop devoted to service with Archangel Michael. Michael called upon the attendees to be light connections for God. As Michael had shared at Ground Hero, "Light bridges need to be built NOW."

I was asked to give each of the class members pages of names of those who perished on September 11. We were asked to pray, from September 29 to November 1, 2001 (All Saints/All Souls Day), for these individuals and to visualize a laser beam of light and love from our hearts to the person on the list. We were asked to bless them with God's light and love. Then we were asked to visualize the light going from this individual (in heaven) back to all their loved ones, friends, and family members here on earth. God wants us to build a light bridge that will serve as a bridge for healing and for communication. A bridge of love everlasting.

In my work I often teach teleclasses using phone bridges. At a designated time, students call a telephone number and we are linked together through a bridge. The class can have members from all corners of the earth.

Through our light bridge building, God was calling us to create a bridge that would assist those in heaven in making connections with their loved ones on earth. We were being asked to be divine architects of bridges of light between heaven and earth.

I was sharing this inspiration with a HA HA member whose husband had died a few years earlier. She confided that following her husband's death her entire focus was on finding out, "Where is he now?" and "Is he all right?" Our service was to become a blessing for those mourning the loss of their loved ones.

Shortly after the attack on America on September 11, President Bush spoke to the nation. During that speech he was inspired to hold out before the television camera the shield of a policeman who had given his life in service. As I watched this telecast, I again felt the enveloping presence of Michael. Archangel Michael is the patron saint of the brotherhood of policemen. Just as policemen are our protectors, Michael serves as God's messenger of God's unequalled protection.

On November 1, 2001—All Saints Day—I was called by the angels to return to New York City. The angelic assignment was given to Celeste McDonald and myself. We were called to serve as prayer partners alongside the angels and saints.

Upon our arrival in New York City, we first went to the Church of St. John the Baptist and prayed in the Padre Pio Garden. We went to Ground Hero and prayed with the priests and pastors who had placed themselves there in service. We were guided to the site where President George Washington took his oath of office. We prayed for President Bush at this site. We prayed for America and all Americans. We went to Trinity Church and though the church was not yet reopened, we prayed outside its gates. Trinity Church is one of the oldest churches in the United States, receiving its charter and land grant from King William III of England on May 6, 1697. At St. Paul's Chapel, where following his inauguration as the first president of the United States, George Washington knelt in prayer to give thanks to God, we too knelt in prayer. We went to St. John the Divine Cathedral and prayed throughout the church and were guided to the alcove dedicated to firemen who have died in the line of duty.

Prior to our November 1 trip, many of the members of the HA HA Group contacted me asking how they could honor the firemen of New York City. I asked in prayer what would be a way to fulfill their hearts' desires. I was told that God would guide me to a New York City fire department that we could "adopt," and we could serve as a blessing to the members of this department. Honoring one fire department in New York City would be a way to convey our heartfelt thanks to all members of the New York City Fire Department, New York Police Department, rescue workers, and relief workers.

As our prayer partners service drew to a close, Celeste and I still hadn't been guided to the fire department we were to adopt. Before going to the train station for our ride home, Celeste wanted to show me the Church of St. Francis of Assisi located near Penn Station. We first entered the church through the basement. In the lower level the ceiling is covered with paintings of hundreds of saints. It was the perfect place to visit on All Saints Day. All the saints were truly watching over us from above.

As we walked into the upper sanctuary of the church we saw a large photo of Father Mychal Judge. Father Judge was a chaplain for the New York City Fire Department and resided at a friary next to the Church of St. Francis of Assisi on New York's 31st Street. He died on September 11, 2001, administering last rites to a firefighter who was mortally injured, when falling debris from the collapsing towers killed both men. Father Judge was the first to die in the line of duty on September 11. "He was where the action was, he was praying, talking to God, helping someone," said Reverend Michael Duffy at Judge's funeral. "Can you honestly think of a better way to die?" At the time of his funeral, three hundred firemen were still buried there. It would have been impossible for him to minister to all of them in this life. In the next life he'll greet them with that big Irish smile and say, "Welcome. Let me take you to our Father." I read a quote given to the *Washington Post* by Harry Ryttenberg, a friend of Father Mike. He said, "Father Mike's face was 'a map of Ireland.'"

One of the first pictures that Mary Dansicker shared with me of her son Joshua captured a moment when his eyes were closed with the beautiful bright sun beaming down on his handsome face. When I saw the photograph, I felt Josh was saying, "Shine it on me, God!" Josh didn't want to miss one ray or one sunbeam of light. His life was and *is* full of light.

When I saw Father Judge's photograph for the first time, I had that same feeling. His handsome face beamed with light and life. God's light shined through Father Judge and warmed the lives of all who knew him.

We joined with our heavenly prayer partners inside the Church of St. Francis of Assisi. By kneeling before God we continued the energy—the energy of prayer we had woven throughout the city of New York.

In my lectures and at my Web page, I offered prayer support. I have always believed it is a privilege to be asked to serve through prayer. I believe God calls all of us to be prayer partners in fulfillment of a heavenly duty and earthly necessity. Prayer can move mountains and accomplish miracles. When we join with the angels and saints in prayer to God, there is power in the union. When thousands of us pause to kneel humbly before God once or twice every day, so many untold blessings can occur. I have witnessed the sick healed through prayer. I have seen sorrows transformed into joys through prayer.

As we left the church through a side door, going down the steps to the street, to our surprise, directly in front of us we saw a fire department—Engine 1/Hook and Ladder 24—in the shadow of Madison Square Garden. The wide fire station doors were open, revealing a picture of Father Judge, who was the unit's chaplain. This fire station lost four members, including their captain, in the rubble of the World Trade Center. We stood before a memorial outside the firehouse. Additionally there was a large poster on display depicting the Firefighters' Angel. Celeste and I both felt chills come over us. The poster was produced by ArtAid.

At the Web site www.artaid.org you will find the inspirational story of how and why ArtAid came into being. "ArtAid initially sought to sponsor the creation and distribution of a beautiful memorial image to promote healing and elevate the spirits of those most affected by the World Trade Center tragedy, specifically the families of the victims from the FDNY."

ArtAid's initial project was to print and distribute an FDNY Angel Memorial to the New York City fire departments with the intent of offering comfort to the company members and families in their grief and loss. "Upon arriving at a firehouse to present a set of the prints to the station 'chief' for the families of the fallen firefighters, it became obvious that everyone else there wanted one too (or several copies)."

As of January 1, 2002, ArtAid had distributed for free to the entire FDNY over 13,000 copies of the Firefighters Angel with the names of the fallen firefighters.

Additionally ArtAid has produced and distributed NYPD Guardian Angel posters and Healing Angels of the Emergency Medical Services posters. They are responsible for the creation of a Ground Zero Memorial, the first installation of its kind to memorialize the names of all the victims of the terrorist attack on the World Trade Center.

At The Light at the Top of the Stairs we display the series of Angel Memorials in tribute to those affected by September 11. ArtAid truly inspires hearts with their angel art!

I believe that Father Judge and the angels guided us to the doorstep of the fire department we were to honor. Throughout the year the HA HA group sends yummies and food gifts to Engine 1/Hook and Ladder 24 with a big thank you for being our heroes. The prayers and gifts we shower upon Engine 1/Hook and Ladder 24 is our way of honoring the entire New York City Fire Department, New York City Police Department, rescue workers, and relief workers.

Betsy Keyser, a HA HA member, shared with me a prayer written by Father Judge that appeared in *Parade* magazine. I found it especially inspiring because it truly describes how God guided us to Engine 1/ Hook and Ladder 24:

---

*Lord, take me where you want me to go.*
*Let me meet who you want me to meet.*
*Tell me what you want me to say,*
*And keep me out of your way.*

---

In January 2002 Chuck and I returned to New York City to visit Max Protetch's Gallery at West 22nd Street. Max Protetch hosted a show entitled "A New World Trade Center, Design Proposals" co-curated by Max, Aaron Betsky, the staffs of *Architectural Record* and *Architecture* magazines, and other architecture professionals.

At the gallery Chuck and I spent several hours studying sketches, renderings, and multimedia projects through which architects shared their visions and ideas for the possibilities of the World Trade Center site.

One of the architectural designs, which was suggested as a temporary installation, came into reality from mid-March to mid-April, 2002. It was two beacons of light that rose from the site of the World Trade Center. In the proposal the beacons were to be white light. The lights were symbolic of strength, hope, and resiliency. They represented the reclaiming of the skyline and of New York City's identity. The final color selection for the lights was blue. Chuck and I drove to New York City on the Saturday evening of March 16, 2002. As we drove into New York City, we saw the two huge blue beams of light beaconing us to their place of origin.

As we usually take the train to New York City, we were concerned with driving and being able to maneuver our car through the streets to the location of the blue lights. When we came out of the Holland Tunnel, I leaned out of the car's window and once again the lights made their presence known. We followed the lights. I had commented to Chuck, "If we find Greenwich Street, we're there!" After only a few turns, keeping our focus on the direction of the lights, we saw before us a street sign that read: Greenwich Street.

Traffic was bumper to bumper as we drove closer to the lights. Chuck commented that the experience might be simply a drive-by because there appeared to be no available parking space. However, the parking angels wouldn't hear of it. Just as we were one block away from the lights, a car pulled out and left the space open for us. We giggled with delight over heaven's parking blessing. We parked our car and walked to the lights.

As we stood at the location of the two beams, we looked up into the sky and saw that the two lights that had guided us into the city became one large blue light. Many of us who serve with Archangel Michael have seen his powerful blue light in our meditations. Without a doubt, this is the largest beam of Michael's energy I have ever seen. It felt so comforting to be standing there near to Ground Hero and knowing that the Blue Sword of Archangel Michael—God's holy messenger and champion—was beaming above us. Once again, I remembered Michael's words: Move forward fearlessly with God!

I feel it is vitally important that we acknowledge the importance of art and architecture in our lives. Chuck and I enjoy watching programs such as "Wonders of the World," and are inspired by engineering and architectural feats of the past and present. I know there will be much discussion and debate before a final decision is made over what will be built at the World Trade Center site. The property was and will continue to be divinely blessed by God's light; a light I stood witness to on March 16.

The property has been blessed by those who worked round the clock, seven days a week to clear away the debris and who every day held the hope in their hearts that they would retrieve bodies to give families some closure. The property has been blessed by the millions of world-wide prayers focused upon those who died there.

On Sunday, September 23, 2001, at Yankee Stadium the "Prayer for America" Memorial Service was held. The service was watched by millions of people around the world. Speaker after speaker spoke about angels. Oprah Winfrey ended the service with the words: "We have gained an angel."

Additionally, I feel we have gained an angel's point of view. We see how important our service is to each other and to the planet. We see how we are messengers of hope in each other's lives. We see that we are the ones God has sent to deliver strength and inspiration in the darkest hours.

Perhaps at times we look around at what's happening on the earth, and everywhere we look we see something that desperately needs God's intervention. Wars that never end. Famine that never ceases to exist. And in our frustration we call out to God and ask, "Why don't you do something, God!"

Perhaps in those frustrating moments we hear a divine response come back to us to reassure us that God is aware of the problems and help is at hand. We hear from the heavens: "I did. I sent you."

# ANGELIC RESOURCE GUIDE

Within the pages of *Driving Under the Influence of Angels* I have mentioned the names of people and organizations that have been blessings in my life. I have listed here contact information for them in alphabetical order.


**AmericanSingles**
 www.AmericanSingles.com
**Angel Haven**
 www.angelhaven.com
**ArtAid**
 511 Avenue of Americas
 New York, NY 10011
 www.artaid.org
**Association for Research and Enlightenment, Inc.**
 215 67th Street
 Virginia Beach, VA 23451
 1-800-333-4499
 www.edgarcayce.org
**Ann Bell**
 3306 Milford Mill Road
 Baltimore, MD 21207
 410-922-8137
 dbell13589@comcast.net
**Sean Bradley**
**Angel Garden Designs**
 4 Crombouke Fold
 Worsley, Manchester
 M28 1ZE
 United Kingdom
 Tel: 0161-799-7356
 E-mail: enquiry@angelgardens4u.com
**Rev. Reed Brown**
**Arlington Metaphysical Chapel**
 5618 Wilson Blvd.
 Arlington, VA 22205-1303
 Tel: 703-276-8738
**Fay Byrd**
 Tel: 410-661-0295

E-mail: Faysangelharp@aol.com
Web site: www.faysangelharp.com

**Chalice of Repose**
312 East Pine Street
Missoula, MT 59802
Tel: 406-329-2810
Fax: 406-329-5614
www.saintpatrick.org/chalice/

**Carol A. Cox**
**Inner Vision**
950 Jackson Street
Pottstown, PA 19464
Tel: 610-970-1970
Fax: 775-640-3947
E-mail: innervision2000@hotmail.com
Web site: www.innervision2000.com

**Dorothy Daniel**
25 Sheldon Ave.
Depew, NY 14043-3508
Tel: 716-684-1412

**Barbie Edwards**
**The Harp Lady**
Westminster, CO 80030
Tel: 303-427-8880

**Favorite Poem Project**
Boston University
236 Bay State Road
Boston, MA 02215
Attn: Maggie Dietz
www.favoritepoem.org

**Jayne Howard Feldman**
**Angel Heights**
P.O. Box 95
Upperco, MD 21155
Tel: 866-peace2u (732-2328)
Fax: 410-429-5425
E-mail: earthangel4peace@aol.com
Web site: www.earthangel4peace.com

**Green Hope Farm Flower Essences**
P.O. Box 125
Meriden, NH 03770
Tel: 603-469-3662
Fax: 603-469-3790
E-mail: green.hope.farm@valley.net
Web site: www.greenhopeessences.com

**Rosemary Ellen Guiley**
1290 Bay Dale Drive
Suite 311
Arnold, MD 21012
REGuiley@aol.com

**Hannelore Hahn, Director**
International Women's Writing Guide
P.O. Box 810
Gracie Station
New York, NY 10028
Tel: 212-737-7536
E-mail: dirhahn@aol.com

**Harp Therapy Journal**
9 East 3rd Street
Bethlehem, PA 19015
Heart Forest
123 W. Armour Blvd.
Kansas City, MO 64111
www.creativeprocess.net

**Jonas' Attic**
Barbara Barrowcliff
14 North Washington Street
Easton, MD 21601
Tel: 410-820-8266
E-mail: jonattic@dmv.com

**Joshua's Lighthouse Angels**
Mary Dansicker, Owner
311 Main Street
Reisterstown, MD 21136
Tel: 410-517-0200
Fax: 410-517-3107
E-mail: liteshop@aol.com

**Light at the Top of the Stairs**
Jayne Howard Feldman, curator
309 Main Street/2nd Floor
Reisterstown, MD 21136
Tel: 866-732-2328 (866-peace2u)
E-mail: earthangel4peace@aol.com

**Michele Livingston**
Tel: 717-737-3888
E-mail:Michele@maryvisons.com
www.maryvisions.com

**James Mullaney**
P. O. Box 1146
Exton, PA 19341
arcturussj@aol.com

**New York Restoration Project**
31 West 56th Street
New York, NY 10019
Tel: 212-333-2552
www.nyrp.org

**The Random Acts of Kindness Foundation**
1801 Broadway Street, Suite 250
Denver, Colorado 80202
www.actsofkindness.org

**Rachael Salley**
1118 Cactus Cut Road
Middleburg, FL 32068
904-282-9612

**Alan Seale**
P.O. Box 134
Cathedral Station
New York, NY 10025
Tel: 212-749-1817
www.mystic21.com

**Gregory R. Smith**
www.gregoryrsmith.com

**Southeastern Conference**
c/o Anne Atwell
2017 Orange Factory Road
Bahama, NC 27502
E-mail: aatwell@earthlink.net

**The Spiritual Center**
712 New York Route 79
Windsor, NY 13865
Tel: 607-655-2264
**Lucky Sweeny**
3905 State Street #7133
Santa Barbara, CA 93105
Tel: 805-884-1531
E-mail: coachlucky@aol.com
**Vietnam Veterans of America Foundation**
1725 Eye Street NW, Fourth Floor
Washington, DC 20006-2412
Tel: 202-483-9222
Fax: 202-483-9312
www.vvaf.org

# A.R.E. PRESS